Microsoft®

Exploring PowerPoint® 2002

Microsoft®

PowerPoint® 2002
Exploring

Robert T. Grauer

University of Miami

Maryann Barber

University of Miami

PRENTICE HALL   *Upper Saddle River, New Jersey 07458*

Senior Acquisitions Editor: David Alexander
VP/Publisher: Natalie Anderson
Managing Editor: Melissa Whitaker
Assistant Editor: Kerri Limpert
Editorial Assistant: Maryann Broadnax
Technical Editor: Cecil Yarbrough
Media Project Manager: Cathleen Profitko
Marketing Assistant: Jason Smith
Production Manager: Gail Steier deAcevedo
Project Manager: Lynne Breitfeller
Production Editor: Greg Hubit
Associate Director, Manufacturing: Vincent Scelta
Manufacturing Buyer: Lynne Breitfeller
Design Manager: Pat Smythe
Interior Design: Jill Yutkowitz
Cover Design: Blair Brown
Cover Illustration: Marjorie Dressler
Composition: GTS
Printer/Binder: Banta Menasha

10 9 8 7 6 5 4
ISBN 0-13-092431-8

To Marion —
my wife, my lover, and my best friend

Robert Grauer

To Frank —
for giving me the encouragement, love, and the space

Maryann Barber

APPROVED COURSEWARE

What does this logo mean?

It means this courseware has been approved by the Microsoft® Office User Specialist Program to be among the finest available for learning **PowerPoint® 2002**. It also means that upon completion of this courseware, you may be prepared to become a Microsoft Office User Specialist.

What is a Microsoft Office User Specialist?

A Microsoft Office User Specialist is an individual who has certified his or her skills in one or more of the Microsoft Office desktop applications of Microsoft Word, Microsoft Excel, Microsoft PowerPoint®, Microsoft Outlook® or Microsoft Access, or in Microsoft Project. The Microsoft Office User Specialist Program typically offers certification exams at the "Core" and "Expert" skill levels.[*] The Microsoft Office User Specialist Program is the only Microsoft approved program in the world for certifying proficiency in Microsoft Office desktop applications and Microsoft Project. This certification can be a valuable asset in any job search or career advancement.

More Information:

To learn more about becoming a Microsoft Office User Specialist, visit www.mous.net

To purchase a Microsoft Office User Specialist certification exam, visit www.DesktopIQ.com

To learn about other Microsoft Office User Specialist approved courseware from Prentice Hall, visit http://www.prenhall.com/phit/mous_frame.html

---

[*]The availability of Microsoft Office User Specialist certification exams varies by application, application version and language. Visit www.mous.net for exam availability.

Microsoft, the Microsoft Office User Specialist Logo, PowerPoint and Outlook are either registered trademarks or trademarks of Microsoft Corporation in the United States and/or other countries.

CONTENTS

2

GAINING PROFICIENCY: SLIDE SHOW TOOLS, THE WEB, AND SLIDE MASTERS 65

ESSENTIALS OF MICROSOFT® WINDOWS®

INDEX

PREFACE

Continuing a tradition of excellence, Prentice Hall is proud to announce the latest update in Microsoft Office texts: the new Exploring Microsoft Office XP series by Robert T. Grauer and Maryann Barber.

The hands-on approach and conceptual framework of this comprehensive series helps students master all aspects of the Microsoft Office XP software, while providing the background necessary to transfer and use these skills in their personal and professional lives.

WHAT'S NEW IN THE EXPLORING OFFICE SERIES FOR XP

The entire Exploring Office series has been revised to include the new features found in the Office XP Suite, which contains Word 2002, Excel 2002, Access 2002, PowerPoint 2002, Publisher 2000, FrontPage 2002, and Outlook 2002.

In addition, this revision includes fully revised end-of-chapter material that provides an extensive review of concepts and techniques discussed in the chapter. Many of these exercises feature the World Wide Web and application integration.

Building on the success of the Web site provided for previous editions of this series, Exploring Office XP will introduce the MyPHLIP Companion Web site, a site customized for each instructor that includes on-line, interactive study guides, data file downloads, current news feeds, additional case studies and exercises, and other helpful information. Start out at www.prenhall.com/grauer to explore these resources!

Organization of the Exploring Office Series for XP

The new Exploring Microsoft Office XP series includes four combined Office XP texts from which to choose:

- *Volume I* is MOUS certified in each of the major applications in the Office suite (Word, Excel, Access, and PowerPoint). Three additional modules (Essential Computer Concepts, Essentials of Windows, and Essentials of the Internet) are also included.

- *Volume II* picks up where Volume I left off, covering the advanced topics for the individual applications. A VBA primer has been added.

- The *Brief Microsoft Office XP* edition provides less coverage of the individual applications than Volume I (a total of 8 chapters as opposed to 14). The supplementary modules (Windows, Internet, and Concepts) are not included.

- A new volume, *Getting Started with Office XP*, contains the first chapter from each application (Word, Excel, Access, and PowerPoint), plus three additional modules: Essentials of Windows, Essentials of the Internet, and Essential Computer Concepts.

Individual texts for Word 2002, Excel 2002, Access 2002, and PowerPoint 2002 provide complete coverage of the application and are MOUS certified. For shorter courses, we have created brief versions of the Exploring texts that give students a four-chapter introduction to each application. Each of these volumes is MOUS certified at the Core level.

To complete the full coverage of this series, custom modules on Microsoft Outlook 2002, Microsoft FrontPage 2002, Microsoft Publisher 2002, and a generic introduction to Microsoft Windows are also available.

APPROVED COURSEWARE

This book has been approved by Microsoft to be used in preparation for Microsoft Office User Specialist exams.

The Microsoft Office User Specialist (MOUS) program is globally recognized as the standard for demonstrating desktop skills with the Microsoft Office suite of business productivity applications (Microsoft Word, Microsoft Excel, Microsoft PowerPoint, Microsoft Access, and Microsoft Outlook). With a MOUS certification, thousands of people have demonstrated increased productivity and have proved their ability to utilize the advanced functionality of these Microsoft applications.

By encouraging individuals to develop advanced skills with Microsoft's leading business desktop software, the MOUS program helps fill the demand for qualified, knowledgeable people in the modern workplace. At the same time, MOUS helps satisfy an organization's need for a qualitative assessment of employee skills.

Customize the Exploring Office Series with Prentice Hall's Right PHit Binding Program

The Exploring Office XP series is part of the Right PHit Custom Binding Program, enabling instructors to create their own texts by selecting modules from Office XP Volume I, Volume II, Outlook, FrontPage, and Publisher to suit the needs of a specific course. An instructor could, for example, create a custom text consisting of the core modules in Word and Excel, coupled with the brief modules for Access and PowerPoint, and a brief introduction to computer concepts.

Instructors can also take advantage of Prentice Hall's Value Pack program to shrinkwrap multiple texts together at substantial savings to the student. A value pack is ideal in courses that require complete coverage of multiple applications.

The **Instructor's CD** that accompanies the Exploring Office series contains:

- Student data disks
- Solutions to all exercises and problems
- PowerPoint lectures
- Instructor's manuals in Word format enable the instructor to annotate portions of the instructor manual for distribution to the class
- A Windows-based test manager and the associated test bank in Word format

Prentice Hall's New MyPHLIP Companion Web site at www.prenhall.com/grauer offers current events, exercises, and downloadable supplements. This site also includes an on-line study guide containing true/false, multiple-choice, and essay questions.

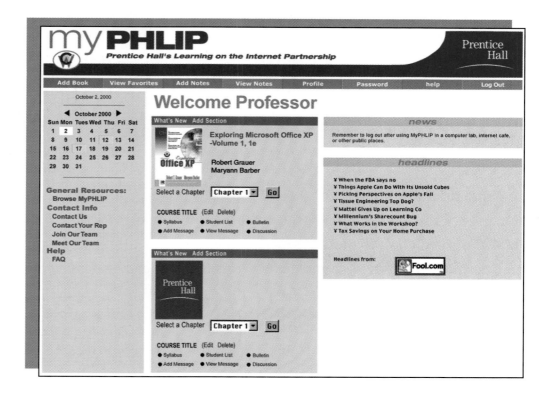

WebCT www.prenhall.com/webct

GOLD LEVEL CUSTOMER SUPPORT available exclusively to adopters of Prentice Hall courses is provided free-of-charge upon adoption and provides you with priority assistance, training discounts, and dedicated technical support.

Blackboard www.prenhall.com/blackboard

Prentice Hall's abundant on-line content, combined with Blackboard's popular tools and interface, result in robust Web-based courses that are easy to implement, manage, and use—taking your courses to new heights in student interaction and learning.

CourseCompass www.coursecompass.com

CourseCompass is a dynamic, interactive on-line course management tool powered by Blackboard. This exciting product allows you to teach with marketing-leading Pearson Education content in an easy-to-use customizable format.

Exploring Microsoft Office XP assumes no prior knowledge of the operating system. A 64-page section introduces the reader to the Essentials of Windows and provides an overview of the operating system. Students are shown the necessary file-management operations to use Microsoft Office successfully.

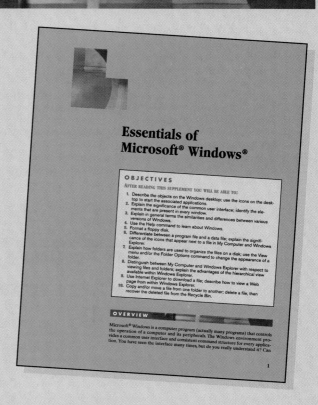

In-depth tutorials throughout all the Office XP applications enhance the conceptual introduction to each task and guide the student at the computer. Every step in every exercise has a full-color screen shot to illustrate the specific commands. Boxed tips provide alternative techniques and shortcuts and/or anticipate errors that students may make.

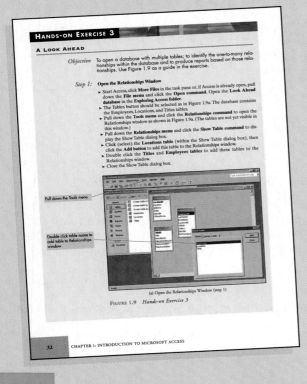

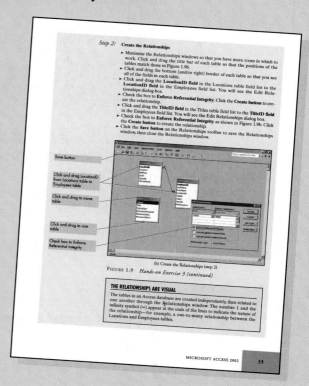

The authors have created an entirely new set of end-of-chapter exercises for every chapter in all of the applications. These new exercises have been written to provide the utmost in flexibility, variety, and difficulty.

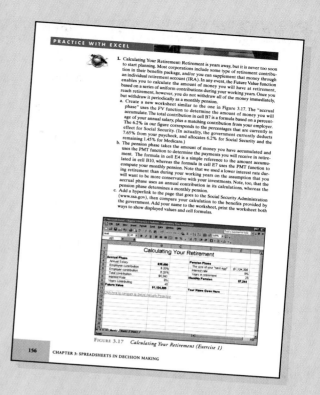

 Web-based Practice exercises and On Your Own exercises are marked by an icon in the margin and allow further exploration and practice via the World Wide Web.

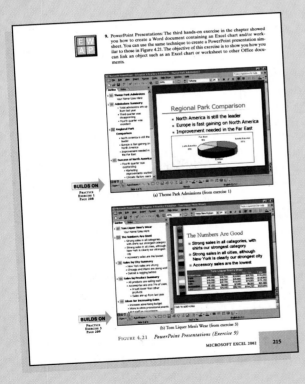

 Integration Exercises are marked by an icon in the margin. These exercises take advantage of the Microsoft Office Suite's power to use multiple applications in one document, spreadsheet, or presentation.

BUILDS ON ➡ **Builds On Exercises** require students to use selected application files as the starting point in later exercises, thereby introducing new information to students only as needed.

The end-of-chapter material includes multiple-choice questions for self-evaluation plus additional "on your own" exercises to encourage the reader to further explore the application.

ACKNOWLEDGMENTS

We want to thank the many individuals who have helped to bring this project to fruition. David Alexander, senior editor at Prentice Hall, has provided new leadership in extending the series to Office XP. Cathi Profitko did an absolutely incredible job on our Web site. Melissa Whitaker coordinated the myriad details of production and the certification process. Greg Christofferson was instrumental in the acquisition of supporting software. Lynne Breitfeller was the project manager and manufacturing buyer. Greg Hubit has been masterful as the external production editor for every book in the series. Cecil Yarbrough did an outstanding job in checking the manuscript for technical accuracy. Chuck Cox did his usual fine work as copyeditor. Kerri Limpert was the supplements editor. Cindy Stevens, Tom McKenzie, and Michael Olmstead wrote the instructor manuals. Patricia Smythe developed the innovative and attractive design. We also want to acknowledge our reviewers who, through their comments and constructive criticism, greatly improved the series.

Lynne Band, Middlesex Community College
Don Belle, Central Piedmont Community College
Stuart P. Brian, Holy Family College
Carl M. Briggs, Indiana University School of Business
Kimberly Chambers, Scottsdale Community College
Alok Charturvedi, Purdue University
Jerry Chin, Southwest Missouri State University
Dean Combellick, Scottsdale Community College
Cody Copeland, Johnson County Community College
Larry S. Corman, Fort Lewis College
Janis Cox, Tri-County Technical College
Martin Crossland, Southwest Missouri State University
Paul E. Daurelle, Western Piedmont Community College
Carolyn DiLeo, Westchester Community College
Judy Dolan, Palomar College
David Douglas, University of Arkansas
Carlotta Eaton, Radford University
Judith M. Fitspatrick, Gulf Coast Community College
James Franck, College of St. Scholastica
Raymond Frost, Central Connecticut State University
Midge Gerber, Southwestern Oklahoma State University
James Gips, Boston College
Vernon Griffin, Austin Community College
Ranette Halverson, Midwestern State University
Michael Hassett, Fort Hays State University
Mike Hearn, Community College of Philadelphia
Wanda D. Heller, Seminole Community College
Bonnie Homan, San Francisco State University
Ernie Ivey, Polk Community College
Mike Kelly, Community College of Rhode Island
Jane King, Everett Community College

Rose M. Laird, Northern Virginia Community College
John Lesson, University of Central Florida
David B. Meinert, Southwest Missouri State University
Alan Moltz, Naugatuck Valley Technical Community College
Kim Montney, Kellogg Community College
Bill Morse, DeVry Institute of Technology
Kevin Pauli, University of Nebraska
Mary McKenry Percival, University of Miami
Delores Pusins, Hillsborough Community College
Gale E. Rand, College Misericordia
Judith Rice, Santa Fe Community College
David Rinehard, Lansing Community College
Marilyn Salas, Scottsdale Community College
John Shepherd, Duquesne University
Barbara Sherman, Buffalo State College
Robert Spear, Prince George's Community College
Michael Stewardson, San Jacinto College—North
Helen Stoloff, Hudson Valley Community College
Margaret Thomas, Ohio University
Mike Thomas, Indiana University School of Business
Suzanne Tomlinson, Iowa State University
Karen Tracey, Central Connecticut State University
Antonio Vargas, El Paso Community College
Sally Visci, Lorain County Community College
David Weiner, University of San Francisco
Connie Wells, Georgia State University
Wallace John Whistance-Smith, Ryerson Polytechnic University
Jack Zeller, Kirkwood Community College

A final word of thanks to the unnamed students at the University of Miami, who make it all worthwhile. Most of all, thanks to you, our readers, for choosing this book. Please feel free to contact us with any comments and suggestions.

Robert T. Grauer
rgrauer@miami.edu
www.bus.miami.edu/~rgrauer
www.prenhall.com/grauer

Maryann Barber
mbarber@miami.edu
www.bus.miami.edu/~mbarber

CHAPTER 1

Introduction to Microsoft® PowerPoint®: Presentations Made Easy

OBJECTIVES

AFTER READING THIS CHAPTER YOU WILL BE ABLE TO:

1. Start PowerPoint; open, modify, and view an existing presentation; describe the different ways to print a presentation.
2. List the different views in PowerPoint; describe the unique features of each view.
3. Use the outline to create and edit the text of a presentation; expand and collapse slides within an outline.
4. Add a new slide to a presentation; explain how to change the layout of the objects on an existing slide.
5. Use the Microsoft Media Gallery to add and/or change the clip art on a slide; use the Drawing toolbar to modify existing clip art.
6. Apply a design template to a new presentation; change the template in an existing presentation.
7. Add transition effects to the slides in a presentation; apply custom animation effects to the objects on a slide.
8. Insert user comments into a presentation.
9. Use Microsoft WordArt to insert a WordArt object into a presentation.
10. Distinguish between linking and embedding; link or embed Excel charts and Word tables into a presentation.

OVERVIEW

This chapter introduces you to PowerPoint, one of the four major applications in Microsoft Office (Microsoft Word, Microsoft Excel, and Microsoft Access are the other three). PowerPoint enables you to create a professional presentation without relying on others, then it lets you deliver that presentation in a variety of ways. You can show the presentation on the computer, on the World Wide Web, or via 35mm slides or overhead transparencies.

1

PowerPoint is easy to learn because it is a Windows application and follows the conventions associated with the common user interface. Thus, if you already know one Windows application, it is that much easier to learn PowerPoint because you can apply what you know. It's even easier if you use Word, Excel, or Access since there are over 100 commands that are common to Microsoft Office.

The chapter begins by showing you an existing PowerPoint presentation so that you can better appreciate what PowerPoint is all about. We discuss the various views within PowerPoint and the advantages of each. We describe how to modify an existing presentation and how to view a presentation on the computer. You are then ready to create your own presentation, a process that requires you to focus on the content and the message you want to deliver. We show you how to enter the text of the presentation, how to add and/or change the format of a slide, and how to apply a design template. We also explain how to animate the presentation to create additional interest. The last portion of the chapter describes how to enhance a presentation through the inclusion of other objects such as a Word table or an Excel chart.

As always, learning is best accomplished by doing, so we include four hands-on exercises that enable you to apply these concepts at the computer. One final point before we begin, is that while PowerPoint can help you create attractive presentations, the content and delivery are still up to you.

A POWERPOINT PRESENTATION

A PowerPoint presentation consists of a series of slides such as those in Figure 1.1. The various slides contain different elements (such as text, clip art, and WordArt), yet the presentation has a consistent look with respect to its overall design and color scheme. You might think that creating this type of presentation is difficult, but it isn't. It is remarkably easy, and that is the beauty of PowerPoint. In essence, PowerPoint allows you to concentrate on the content of a presentation without worrying about its appearance. You supply the text and supporting elements and leave the formatting to PowerPoint.

In addition to helping you create the presentation, PowerPoint provides a variety of ways to deliver it. You can show the presentation on a computer using animated transition effects as you move from one slide to the next. You can include sound and/or video in the presentation, provided your system has a sound card and speakers. You can also automate the presentation and distribute it on a disk for display at a convention booth or kiosk. If you cannot show the presentation on a computer, you can convert it to 35mm slides or overhead transparencies.

PowerPoint also gives you the ability to print the presentation in various ways to distribute to your audience. You can print one slide per page, or you can print miniature versions of each slide and choose among two, three, four, six, or even nine slides per page. You can prepare speaker notes for yourself consisting of a picture of each slide together with notes about the slide. You can also print the text of the presentation in outline form. Giving the audience a copy of the presentation (in any format) enables them to follow it more closely, and to take it home when the session is over.

POLISH YOUR DELIVERY

The speaker is still the most important part of any presentation, and a poor delivery will kill even the best presentation. Look at the audience as you speak to open communication and gain credibility. Don't read from a prepared script. Speak slowly and clearly and try to vary your delivery. Pause to emphasize key points, and be sure the person in the last row can hear you.

Introduction to PowerPoint

Robert Grauer and Maryann Barber

(a) Title Slide

The Essence of PowerPoint

- **You focus on content**
  - Enter your thoughts in an outline or directly on the individual slides
- **PowerPoint takes care of the design**
  - Professionally designed templates
  - Preformatted slide layouts

(b) Bullet Slide

Add Objects for Interest

- Clip art, WordArt, and organization charts
- Charts from Microsoft Excel
- Photographs from the Web
- Animation and sound

(c) Clip Art

Flexibility in Output

- Computer presentations
- Overhead transparencies
- Presentation on the Web
- 35mm slides
- Audience handouts
- Speaker notes

(d) Clip Art

Easy To Learn

- **It follows the same conventions as every Windows application**
- **It uses the same menus and command structure as other Office applications**
- **Keyboard shortcuts also apply such as Ctrl+B for boldface**
- **Help is only a mouse click away**

(e) Animated Text

(f) WordArt

FIGURE 1.1 *A PowerPoint Presentation*

The desktop in Figure 1.2 should look somewhat familiar even if you have never used PowerPoint, because PowerPoint shares the common user interface of every Windows application. You should recognize, therefore, the two open windows in Figure 1.2—the application window for PowerPoint and the document window for the current presentation.

The PowerPoint window contains the Minimize, Maximize (or Restore) and Close buttons. The document window, however, contains only a Close button for the current presentation, allowing you to close the presentation, but keep PowerPoint open. The title bar indicates the application (Microsoft PowerPoint) as well as the name of the presentation on which you are working (Introduction to PowerPoint). The *menu bar* appears immediately below the title bar and provides access to the pull-down menus within the application. The presentation appears within the document window and shows the outline of the entire presentation, a graphical image of one slide (the title slide in this example), and speaker notes for the selected slide.

The Standard and Formatting toolbars are displayed below the menu bar and are similar to those in Word and Excel. Hence, you may recognize several buttons from those applications. The *Standard toolbar* contains buttons for the most basic commands in PowerPoint such as opening, saving, and printing a presentation. The *Formatting toolbar*, under the Standard toolbar, provides access to formatting operations such as boldface, italics, and underlining.

The vertical *scroll bar* is seen at the right of the document window and indicates that the presentation contains additional slides that are not visible. This is consistent with the *status bar* at the bottom of the window that indicates you are working on slide 1 of 6. The *Drawing toolbar* appears above the status bar and contains additional tools for working on the slide. The view buttons above the Drawing toolbar are used to switch between the different views of a presentation. PowerPoint views are discussed in the next section.

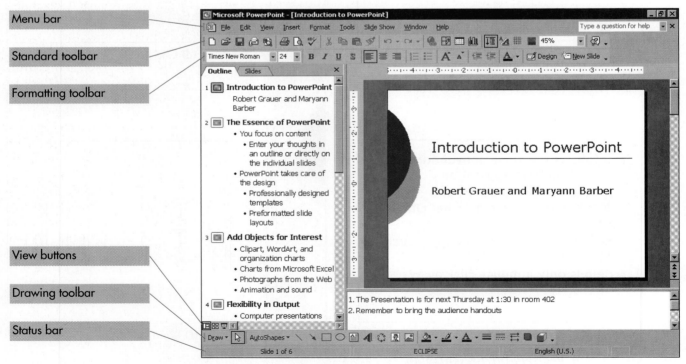

FIGURE 1.2 *Introduction to PowerPoint*

PowerPoint Views

PowerPoint offers multiple views in which to create, modify, and/or deliver a presentation. Each view represents a different way of looking at the presentation and each view has unique capabilities. (There is some redundancy among the views in that certain tasks can be accomplished from multiple views.) The View menu and/or the View buttons at the bottom of the presentation enable you to switch from one view to another.

The *Normal view* in Figure 1.3a divides the screen into three panes containing an outline of the presentation, an enlarged view of one slide, and the associated speaker notes (if any) for the selected slide. The *outline* provides the fastest way to enter or edit text for the presentation. You type directly into the outline and can move easily from one slide to the next. The outline can also be used to move and copy text from one slide to another and/or to rearrange the order of the slides within a presentation. The outline is limited, however, in that it does not show graphic elements that may be present on individual slides. Thus, you may want to switch to the Normal view in Figure 1.3b that contains *thumbnail images* (slide miniatures) rather than the outline. This view also lets you change the order of the slides by clicking and dragging a slide to a new position. The Outline and Slides tabs in the left pane let you switch back and forth between the two variations of the Normal view.

The Normal view also provides access to the individual slides and/or speaker notes, each of which appears in its own pane. The size of the individual panes in the Normal view can be changed by dragging the border that separates one pane from another. The Normal view is all that you will ever need, but many individuals like to close the left pane completely to see just an individual slide as shown in Figure 1.3c. The individual slide, whether it is in the Normal view or displayed in a window by itself, is where you change text or formatting, add graphical elements or apply various animation effects.

You can also elect to work in the Notes Page and/or Slide Sorter view. The *Notes Page view* in Figure 1.3d is redundant in that speaker notes can be entered from the Normal view. It is convenient, however, to print audience handouts of this view, since each page will contain a picture of the slide plus the associated speaker notes. The notes do not appear when the presentation is shown, but are intended for use by the speaker to help him or her remember the key points about each slide.

The *Slide Sorter view* in Figure 1.3e offers yet another view in which to reorder the slides within a presentation. It also provides a convenient way to delete one or more slides and/or to set transition effects for multiple slides simultaneously. Anything that you do in one view is automatically reflected in the other view. If, for example, you change the order of the slides in the Slide Sorter view, the changes will be automatically reflected in the outline or thumbnail images within the Normal view.

The *Slide Show view* in Figure 1.3f is used to deliver the completed presentation to an audience, one slide at a time, as an electronic presentation on the computer. The show may be presented manually where the speaker clicks the mouse to move from one slide to the next. The presentation can also be shown automatically, where each slide stays on the screen for a predetermined amount of time, after which the next slide appears automatically. Either way, the slide show may contain various transition effects from one slide to the next.

THE TASK PANE

All views in PowerPoint 2002 provide access to a *task pane*, which facilitates the execution of subsequent commands. The task pane serves many functions. It can be used to open an existing presentation, apply clip art to a slide, change the layout of the elements on a slide, apply transition and animation effects, or change the template of the entire presentation.

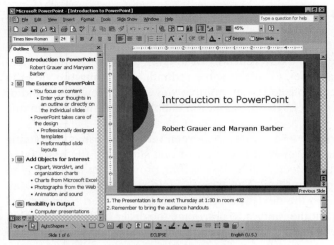

(a) Normal View with Outline

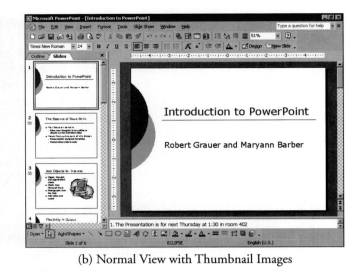

(b) Normal View with Thumbnail Images

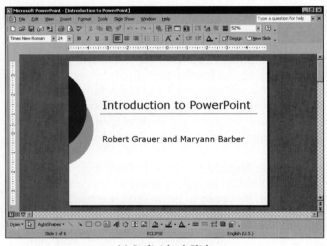

(c) Individual Slide

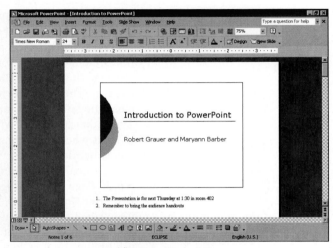

(d) Notes Pages View

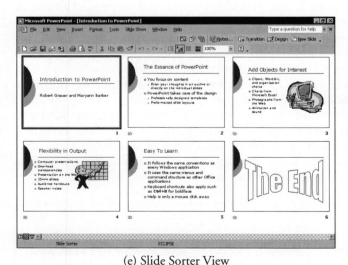

(e) Slide Sorter View

(f) Slide Show View

FIGURE 1.3   *Multiple Views*

The File Menu

The *File menu* is a critically important menu in virtually every Windows application. It contains the Save and Open commands to save a presentation on disk, then subsequently retrieve (open) that presentation at a later time. The File menu also contains the *Print command* to print a presentation, the *Close command* to close the current presentation but continue working in the application, and the *Exit command* to quit the application altogether.

The *Save command* copies the presentation that you are working on (i.e., the presentation that is currently in memory) to disk. The command functions differently the first time it is executed for a new presentation, in that it displays the Save As dialog box as shown in Figure 1.4a. The dialog box requires you to specify the name of the presentation, the drive (and an optional folder) in which the presentation is to be stored, and its file type. All subsequent executions of the command save the presentation under the assigned name, replacing the previously saved version with the new version.

The *file name* (e.g., My First Presentation) can contain up to 255 characters including spaces, commas, and/or periods. (Periods are discouraged, however, since they are too easily confused with DOS extensions.) The Save In list box is used to select the drive (which is not visible in Figure 1.4a) and the folder (e.g., Exploring PowerPoint) in which the file will be saved. The *Places bar* provides shortcuts to frequently used folders without having to search through the Save In list box. Click the Desktop icon, for example, and the file is saved on the Windows desktop. The *file type* defaults to a PowerPoint 2002 presentation. You can, however, choose a different format, such as an RTF (Rich Text Format) outline that can be imported into Microsoft Word. You can also save any PowerPoint presentation as a Web page (or HTML document).

The *Open command* is the opposite of the Save command as it brings a copy of an existing presentation into memory, enabling you to work with that presentation. The Open command displays the Open dialog box in which you specify the file name, the drive (and optionally the folder) that contains the file, and the file type. PowerPoint will then list all files of that type on the designated drive (and folder), enabling you to open the file you want. The Save and Open commands work in conjunction with one another. The Save As dialog box in Figure 1.4a, for example, saves the file My First Presentation in the Exploring PowerPoint folder. The Open dialog box in Figure 1.4b loads that file into memory so that you can work with the file, after which you can save the revised file for use at a later time.

The toolbars in the Save As and Open dialog boxes have several buttons in common that facilitate the execution of either command. The Views button lets you display the files in different views. The Details view (in Figure 1.4a) shows the file size as well as the date and time that the file was last modified. The Preview view (in Figure 1.4b) shows the first slide in a presentation, without having to open the presentation. The List view displays only the file names, and thus lets you see more files at one time. The Properties view shows information about the presentation, including the date of creation and number of revisions.

SORT BY NAME, DATE, OR FILE SIZE

The files in the Save As and Open dialog boxes can be displayed in ascending or descending sequence by name, date modified, or size. Change to the Details view, then click the heading of the desired column; for example, click the Modified column to list the files according to the date they were last changed. Click the column heading a second time to reverse the sequence—that is, to switch from ascending to descending, and vice versa.

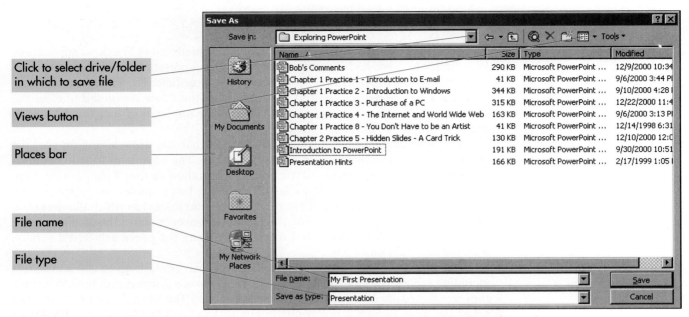

Click to select drive/folder in which to save file

Views button

Places bar

File name

File type

(a) Save As Dialog Box (Details View)

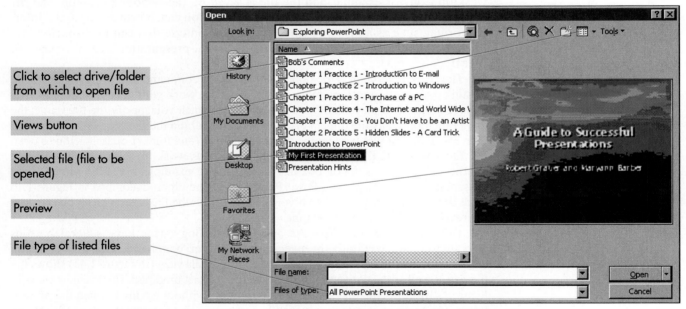

Click to select drive/folder from which to open file

Views button

Selected file (file to be opened)

Preview

File type of listed files

(b) Open Dialog Box (Preview View)

FIGURE 1.4   *The Save and Open Commands*

INTRODUCTION TO POWERPOINT

Objective To start PowerPoint, open an existing presentation, and modify the text on an existing slide; to show an existing presentation and print handouts of its slides. Use Figure 1.5 as a guide in the exercise.

Step 1: **Welcome to Windows**

➤ Turn on the computer and all of its peripherals. The floppy drive should be empty prior to starting your machine. This ensures that the system starts by reading from the hard disk, which contains the Windows files, as opposed to a floppy disk, which does not.

➤ Your system will take a minute or so to get started, after which you should see the desktop in Figure 1.5a. Do not be concerned if the appearance of your desktop is different from ours.

➤ You may also see a Welcome to Windows dialog box with commands to take a tour of the operating system. If so, click the appropriate button(s) or close the dialog box.

➤ You should be familiar with basic file management and should be very comfortable moving and copying files from one folder to another. If not, you may want to review the material in the Essentials of Microsoft Windows section of this text.

(a) Welcome to Windows (step 1)

FIGURE 1.5 *Hands-on Exercise 1*

Step 2:   **Download the Data Disk**

➤ We have created a series of practice files (also called a "data disk") for you to use throughout the text. Your instructor will make these files available to you in a variety of ways:
  • The files may be on a network drive, in which case you use Windows Explorer to copy the files from the network to a floppy disk.
  • There may be an actual "data disk" that you are to check out from the lab in order to use the Copy Disk command to duplicate the disk.
➤ You can also download the files from our Web site, provided you have an Internet connection. Start Internet Explorer, then go to the Exploring Windows home page at **www.prenhall.com/grauer**.
  • Click the book for **Office XP**, which takes you to the Office XP home page. Click the **Student Resources tab** (at the top of the window) to go to the Student Resources page as shown in Figure 1.5b.
  • Click the link to **Student Data Disk** (in the left frame), then scroll down the page until you can select PowerPoint 2002. Click the link to download the student data disk.
  • You will see the File Download dialog box asking what you want to do. The option button to save this program to disk is selected. Click **OK**. The Save As dialog box appears.
  • Click the down arrow in the Save In list box to enter the drive and folder where you want to save the file. It's best to save the file to the Windows desktop or to a temporary folder on drive C..
  • Double click the file after it has been downloaded to your PC, then follow the onscreen instructions.
➤ Check with your instructor for additional information.

Click link to Student Resources

Enter address

Click link to Student Data disk

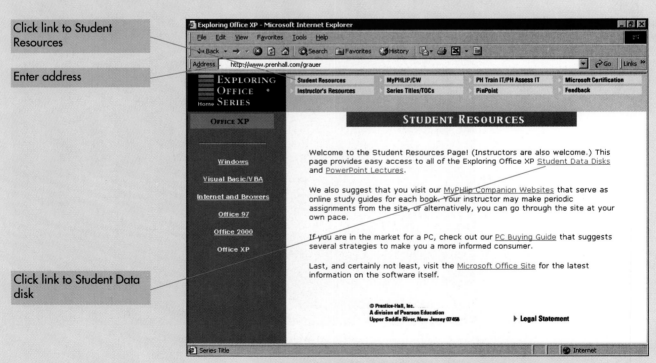

(b) Download the Data Disk (step 2)

FIGURE 1.5   *Hands-on Exercise 1 (continued)*

Step 3: **Start PowerPoint**

➤ Click the **Start button** to display the Start menu. Slide the mouse pointer over the various menu options and notice that each time you point to a menu item, its submenu (if any) is displayed.

➤ Point to (or click) the **Programs menu**, then click **Microsoft PowerPoint 2002** to start the program and display a screen similar to Figure 1.5c. Right click the Office Assistant if it appears, then click the command to hide it. We return to the Assistant in step seven.

➤ If you see the task pane, click the link to **More Presentations**, which in turn will display the Open dialog box. If you do not see the task pane, pull down the **File menu** and click the **Open command** or click the **Open button** on the Standard toolbar.

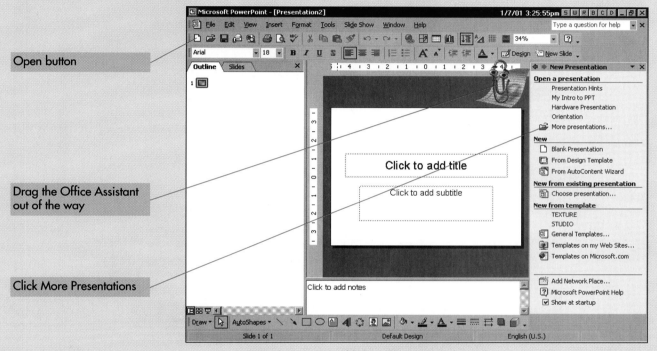

Open button

Drag the Office Assistant out of the way

Click More Presentations

(c) Start PowerPoint (step 3)

FIGURE 1.5   *Hands-on Exercise 1 (continued)*

ABOUT THE ASSISTANT

The Assistant is very powerful and hence you want to experiment with various ways to use it. To ask a question, click the Assistant's icon to toggle its balloon on or off. To change the way in which the Assistant works, click the Options button within this balloon and experiment with the various check boxes to see their effects. If you find the Assistant distracting, click and drag the character out of the way or hide it altogether by pulling down the Help menu and clicking the Hide the Office Assistant command. Pull down the Help menu and click the Show the Office Assistant command to return to the Assistant.

Step 4: **Open a Presentation**

➤ You should see an Open dialog box similar to the one in Figure 1.5d. Click the **drop-down arrow** on the Look In list box. Click the appropriate drive, drive C or drive A, depending on the location of your data.

➤ Double click the **Exploring PowerPoint folder** within the Look In box to make it the active folder. This is the folder from which you will retrieve and into which you will save the presentation.

➤ Click the **Views button** repeatedly to cycle through the different views. We selected the Preview view in Figure 1.5d.

➤ Double click **Introduction to PowerPoint** to open the presentation and begin the exercise.

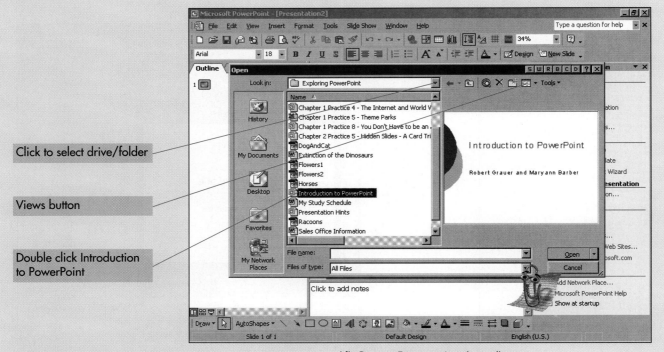

Click to select drive/folder

Views button

Double click Introduction to PowerPoint

(d) Open a Presentation (step 4)

FIGURE 1.5 *Hands-on Exercise 1 (continued)*

SEPARATE THE TOOLBARS

You may see the Standard and Formatting toolbars displayed on one row to save space within the application window. If so, we suggest you separate the toolbars, so that you see all of the buttons on each. The easiest way to do this is to click the down arrow at the end of any toolbar, then click the option to show the buttons on two rows. You can click the down arrow a second time to show the buttons on one row if you want to return to the other configuration.

Step 5: **The Save As Command**

➤ If necessary, click the **Maximize button** in the application window so that PowerPoint takes the entire desktop.

➤ Click the **Maximize button** in the document window (if necessary) so that the document window is as large as possible.

➤ Pull down the **File menu**. Click **Save As** to display the dialog box shown in Figure 1.5e. Enter **Finished Introduction** as the name of the new presentation. Click the **Save button**.

➤ There are now two identical copies of the file on disk, "Introduction to PowerPoint", which is the original presentation that we supplied, and "Finished Introduction", which you just created. The title bar shows the latter name, as it is the presentation currently in memory.

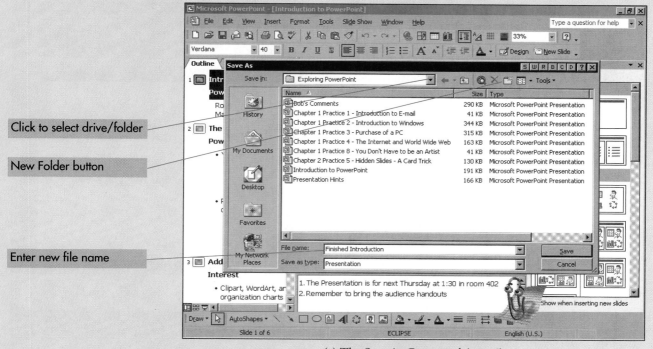

Click to select drive/folder

New Folder button

Enter new file name

(e) The Save As Command (step 5)

FIGURE 1.5 *Hands-on Exercise 1 (continued)*

CREATE A NEW FOLDER

All Office documents are stored in the My Documents folder by default. It's helpful, however, to create additional folders, especially if you work with a large number of different documents. You can create one folder for school and another for work, and/or you can create different folders for different applications. To create a folder, pull down the File menu, click the Save As command, then click the Create New Folder button to display the New Folder dialog box. Enter the name of the folder, then click OK to create the folder. Once the folder has been created, use the Look In box to change to that folder the next time you open or save a presentation. See practice exercise 11 at the end of the chapter.

Step 6: **Modify a Slide**

➤ Press and hold the left mouse button as you drag the mouse over the presenters' names, **Robert Grauer and Maryann Barber.** You can select the text in either the outline or the slide pane.

➤ Release the mouse. The names should be highlighted (selected) as shown in Figure 1.5f. The selected text is affected by the next command.

➤ Type your name, which automatically replaces the selected text in both the outline and the slide pane. Press **enter.**

➤ Type your class on the next line and note that the entry is made in both the slide and the outline pane.

➤ Pull down the **File menu** and click **Save** (or click the **Save button** on the Standard toolbar).

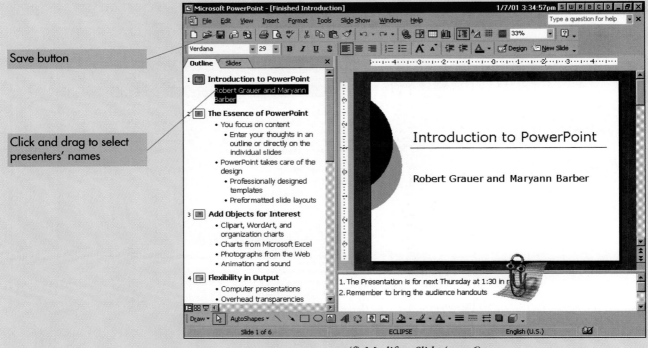

Save button

Click and drag to select presenters' names

(f) Modify a Slide (step 6)

FIGURE 1.5 *Hands-on Exercise 1 (continued)*

THE AUTOMATIC SPELL CHECK

A red wavy line under a word indicates that the word is misspelled, or in the case of a proper name, that the word is spelled correctly, but that it is not in the dictionary. In either event, point to the underlined word and click the right mouse button to display a shortcut menu. Select the appropriate spelling from the list of suggestions or add the word to the supplementary dictionary. To enable (disable) the automatic spell check, pull down the Tools menu, click the Options command, click the Spelling and Style tab, then check (clear) the option to check spelling as you type.

Step 7:   **The Office Assistant**

> ➤ You can display the Assistant in one of three ways—press the **F1 key**, click the **Microsoft PowerPoint Help button** on the Standard toolbar, or pull down the **Help menu** and click the **Show the Office Assistant command**.
> ➤ If necessary, click the **Office Assistant** to display a balloon, then enter your question, for example, **How do I check spelling?** Click the **Search button** within the balloon.
> ➤ The Assistant will return a list of topics that it considers potential answers to your question. Click the second topic, **Show or hide spelling errors**, to display the Help window in Figure 1.5g.
> ➤ Click other topics to display additional information about spelling. You can print the contents by clicking the **Print button** in the Help window.
> ➤ Close the Help window.

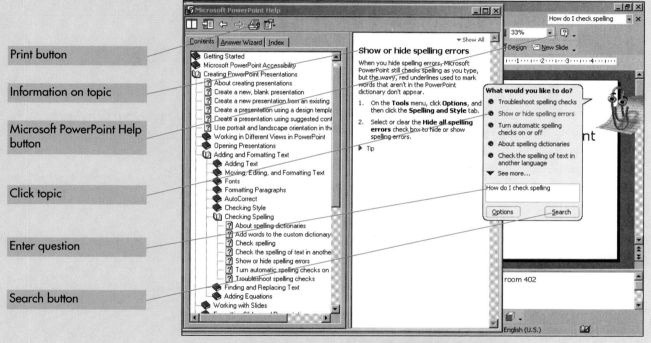

Print button

Information on topic

Microsoft PowerPoint Help button

Click topic

Enter question

Search button

(g) The Office Assistant (step 7)

FIGURE 1.5   *Hands-on Exercise 1 (continued)*

CHOOSE YOUR OWN ASSISTANT

You can choose your own personal assistant from one of several available candidates. If necessary, press the F1 key to display the Assistant, click the Options button to display the Office Assistant dialog box, then click the Gallery tab, where you choose your character. (The Office XP CD is required in order to select some of the other characters.) Some assistants are more animated (distracting) than others. The Office logo is the most passive, while Rocky is quite animated. Experiment with the various check boxes on the Options tab to see the effects on the Assistant.

Step 8: **Show the Presentation**

➤ Click the **Slide Show button** above the status bar, or pull down the **View menu** and click **Slide Show**. The presentation will begin with the first slide as shown in Figure 1.5h. You should see your name on the slide because of the modification you made in the previous step.

➤ Click the mouse to move to the second slide, which comes into the presentation from the right side of your monitor. (This is one of several transition effects used to add interest to a presentation.)

➤ Click the mouse to go to the next (third) slide, which illustrates an animation effect. This requires you to click the mouse to display each succeeding bullet.

➤ Continue to view the show until you come to the end of the presentation. (You can press the **Esc key** at any time to cancel the show and return to the PowerPoint window.) Note the transition effects and the use of sound (provided you have speakers on your system) to enhance the presentation.

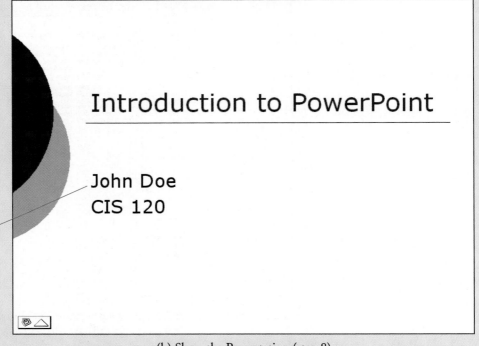

Introduction to PowerPoint

John Doe
CIS 120

Your name and class are displayed

(h) Show the Presentation (step 8)

FIGURE 1.5   *Hands-on Exercise 1 (continued)*

TIP OF THE DAY

You can set the Office Assistant to greet you with a "tip of the day" each time you start PowerPoint. Click the Microsoft PowerPoint Help button (or press the F1 key) to display the Assistant, then click the Options button to display the Office Assistant dialog box. Click the Options tab, check the Show the Tip of the Day at Startup box, then click OK. The next time you start PowerPoint, you will be greeted by the Assistant, who will offer you the tip of the day.

Step 9: **Print the Presentation**

➤ Pull down the **File menu**. Click **Print** to display the Print dialog box in Figure 1.5i. (Clicking the Print button on the Standard toolbar does not display the Print dialog box.)

➤ Click the **down arrow** in the **Print What** drop-down list box, click **Handouts**, and specify 6 slides per page as shown in Figure 1.5i.

➤ Check the box to **Frame Slides**. Check that the **All option button** is selected under Print range. Click the **OK command button** to print the handouts for the presentation.

➤ Pull down the **File menu**. Click **Close** to close the presentation but remain in PowerPoint. Click **Yes** when asked whether to save the changes.

➤ Pull down the **File menu**. Click **Exit** to exit PowerPoint if you do not want to continue with the next exercise at this time.

Click All option button

Click to select 6 slides per page

Click to select Handouts

Check Frame slides

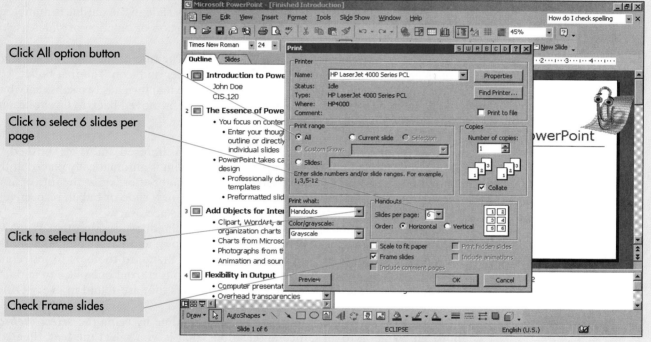

(i) Print the Presentation (step 9)

FIGURE 1.5 *Hands-on Exercise 1 (continued)*

SHOW THE KEYBOARD SHORTCUT IN A SCREENTIP

You can expand the ScreenTip associated with any toolbar button to include the equivalent keyboard shortcut. Pull down the View menu, click Toolbars, then click Customize to display the Customize dialog box. Click the Options tab and check the box to show the shortcut keys in the ScreenTips. Close the dialog box, then point to any toolbar button, and you should see the name of the button as well as the equivalent keyboard shortcut. There is no need to memorize the shortcuts, but they are useful.

You are ready to create your own presentation, a process that requires you to develop its content and apply the formatting through the use of a template or design specification. You can do the steps in either order, but we suggest you start with the content. Both steps are iterative in nature and you are likely to go back and forth many times before you are finished.

You will also find yourself switching from one view to another as you develop the presentation. It doesn't matter which view you use, as long as you can accomplish what you set out to do. You can, for example, enter text one slide at a time in the Slide Normal view. You can also use the outline as shown in Figure 1.6, to view the text of many slides at the same time and thus gain a better sense of the overall presentation.

Each slide in the outline contains a title, followed by bulleted items, which are indented one to five levels, corresponding to the importance of the item. The main points appear on level one. Subsidiary items are indented below the main point to which they apply. Any item can be *promoted* to a higher level or *demoted* to a lower level, either before or after the text is entered. Each slide in the outline is numbered and the numbers adjust automatically for the insertion or deletion of slides as you edit the presentation.

Consider, for example, slide 4 in Figure 1.6a. The title of the slide, *Develop the Content*, appears immediately after the slide number and icon. The first bullet, *Use the outline*, is indented one level under the title, and it in turn has two subsidiary bullets. The next main bullet, *Review the flow of ideas*, is moved back to level one, and it, too, has two subsidiary bullets.

The outline is (to us) the ideal way to create and edit the presentation. The *insertion point* marks the place where new text is entered and is established by clicking anywhere in the outline. (The insertion point is automatically placed at the title of the first slide in a new presentation.) Press enter after typing the title or after entering the text of a bulleted item, which starts a new slide or bullet, respectively. The new item may then be promoted or demoted as necessary.

Editing is accomplished through the same techniques used in other Windows applications. For example, you can use the Cut, Copy, and Paste commands in the Edit menu (or the corresponding buttons on the Standard toolbar) to move and copy selected text or you can simply drag and drop text from one place to another. You can also use the Find and Replace commands that are found in every Office application.

Note, too, that you can format text in the outline by using the *select-then-do* approach common to all Office applications; that is, you select the text, then you execute the appropriate command or click the appropriate button. The selected text remains highlighted and is affected by all subsequent commands until you click elsewhere in the outline.

Figure 1.6b displays a collapsed view of the outline, which displays only the title of each slide. The advantage to this view is that you see more slides on the screen at the same time, making it easier to move slides within the presentation. The slides are expanded or collapsed using tools on the *Outlining toolbar*.

CRYSTALLIZE YOUR MESSAGE

Every presentation exists to deliver a message, whether it's to sell a product, present an idea, or provide instruction. Decide on the message you want to deliver, then write the text for the presentation. Edit the text to be sure it is consistent with your objective. Then, and only then, should you think about formatting, but always keep the message foremost in your mind.

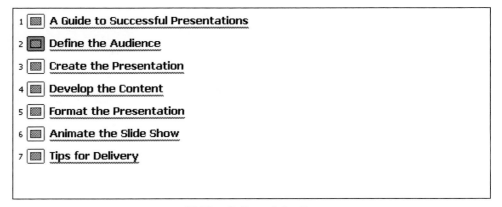

1 ▦ **A Guide to Successful Presentations**
    Robert Grauer and Maryann Barber

2 ▦ **Define the Audience**
- Who is in the audience
  - Managers
  - Coworkers
  - Clients
- What are their expectations

3 ▦ **Create the Presentation**
- Develop the content
- Format the presentation
- Animate the slide show

4 ▦ **Develop the Content**
- Use the outline
  - Demote items (Tab)
  - Promote items (Shift+Tab)
- Review the flow of ideas
  - Cut, copy, and paste text
  - Drag and drop

5 ▦ **Format the Presentation**
- Choose a design template
- Customize the template
  - Change the color scheme
  - Change the background shading
- Modify the slide masters

6 ▦ **Animate the Slide Show**
- Transitions
- Animations
- Hidden slides

7 ▦ **Tips for Delivery**
- Rehearse timings
- Arrive early
- Maintain eye contact
- Know your audience

(a) The Expanded Outline

1 ▦ **A Guide to Successful Presentations**

2 ▦ **Define the Audience**

3 ▦ **Create the Presentation**

4 ▦ **Develop the Content**

5 ▦ **Format the Presentation**

6 ▦ **Animate the Slide Show**

7 ▦ **Tips for Delivery**

(b) The Collapsed Outline

FIGURE 1.6 *The Presentation Outline*

Slide Layouts

New slides are typically created as text slides, consisting of a slide title and a single column of bullets. The layout of a text (or any other) slide can be changed, however, to include clip art or other objects, and/or to display a double column of bullets. The new elements can be added manually by using the various tools on the Drawing toolbar or by letting PowerPoint change the layout for you.

PowerPoint provides a set of predefined *slide layouts* that determine the nature and position of the objects on a slide. The layouts are displayed by default within the task pane whenever the Insert menu is used to add a slide. Just insert the slide, then select the desired layout from the task pane. You can also change the layout of an existing slide by selecting the slide and choosing a different layout from the task pane. (Use the View menu to toggle the task pane open, then click the down arrow within the task pane to display the slide layouts.)

Figure 1.7 illustrates the creation of a two-column text slide, which in turn has three *placeholders* that determine the position of each object. Once the layout has been selected, you simply click the appropriate placeholder to add the title or text. Thus, you would click on the placeholder for the title and enter the text of the title as indicated. In similar fashion, you click the placeholder for either column of bullets and enter the associated text. Other layouts include clip art, organization charts, and other objects. (You can change the size and/or position of the placeholders by moving and sizing the placeholders just as you would any other object.) It's easy, as you will see in the exercise, which follows shortly.

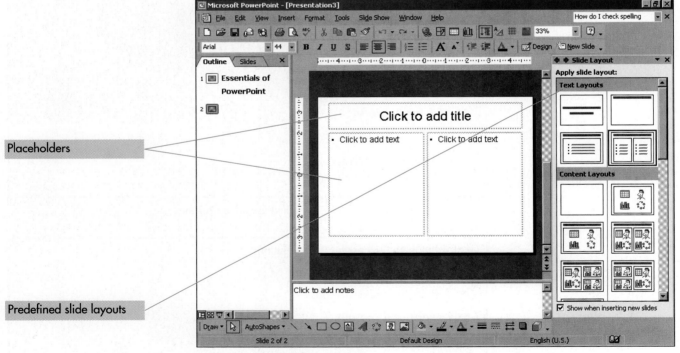

Placeholders

Predefined slide layouts

FIGURE 1.7   *Slide Layouts*

PowerPoint enables you to concentrate on the content of a presentation without concern for its appearance. You focus on what you are going to say, and trust in PowerPoint to format the presentation attractively. The formatting is implemented automatically by selecting one of the many templates that are supplied with PowerPoint.

A *template* is a design specification that controls every element in a presentation. It specifies the color scheme for the slides and the arrangement of the different elements (placeholders) on each slide. It determines the formatting of the text, the fonts that are used, and the size and placement of the bulleted text.

Figure 1.8 displays the title slide of a presentation in four different templates. Just choose the template you like, and PowerPoint formats the entire presentation according to that template. And don't be afraid to change your mind. You can use the Slide Design command at any time to select a different template and change the look of your presentation.

(a) Cliff

(b) Fireworks

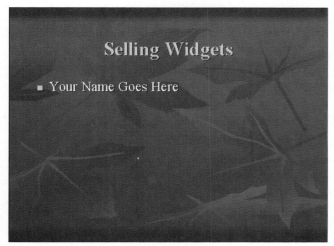

(c) Maple

(d) Ocean

FIGURE 1.8   *Templates*

CREATING A PRESENTATION

Objective To create a new presentation; to apply a design template to a presentation. Use Figure 1.9 as a guide.

Step 1: **Create a New Presentation**

➤ Click the **Start button**, click **Programs**, then click **Microsoft PowerPoint** to start PowerPoint. PowerPoint opens with a new blank presentation.
➤ If necessary, pull down the **View menu** and switch to the **Normal view** and click the **Outline tab** as shown in Figure 1.9a.
➤ Hide the Office Assistant if it appears. (You can display the Assistant at any time by clicking its button on the Standard toolbar. You can also get help without the Assistant by using the Ask a Question.) Close the task pane.

Click Outline tab

Click to close task pane

Normal View button

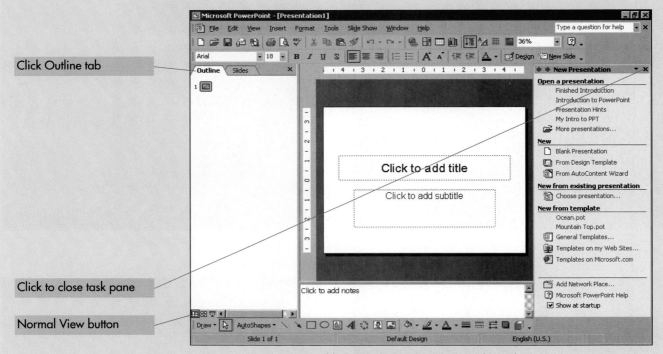

(a) Create a New Presentation (step 1)

FIGURE 1.9 *Hands-on Exercise 2*

ASK A QUESTION

Click in the "Ask a Question" list box that appears at the right of the document window, enter the text of a question such as "What are Speaker Notes?", press enter, and PowerPoint returns a list of potential help topics. Click any topic that appears promising to open the Help window with detailed information. You can ask multiple questions during a PowerPoint session, then click the down arrow in the list box to return to an earlier question, which will return you to the help topics.

Step 2: **Create the Title Slide**

➤ Click anywhere in the box containing **Click to add title**, then type the title, **A Guide to Successful Presentations** as shown in Figure 1.9b. The title will automatically wrap to a second line.

➤ Click anywhere in the box containing **Click to add subtitle** and enter your name. Click outside the subtitle placeholder when you have entered your name on the slide.

➤ The outline now contains the title of the presentation as well as your name. You can use the outline to change either element.

➤ Click in the Notes pane and enter a speaker's note that pertains to the title slide—for example, the date and time that the presentation is scheduled. The notes are for the speaker, but not for the audience.

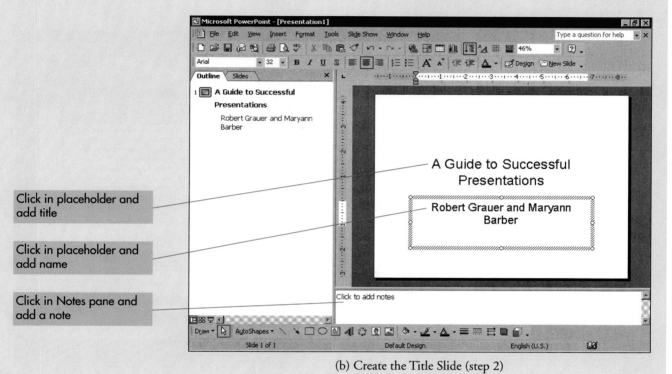

Click in placeholder and add title

Click in placeholder and add name

Click in Notes pane and add a note

(b) Create the Title Slide (step 2)

FIGURE 1.9   *Hands-on Exercise 2 (continued)*

CONTENT, CONTENT, AND CONTENT

It is much more important to focus on the content of the presentation than to worry about how it will look. Start with the AutoContent Wizard (described later in the chapter) or with a blank presentation in the Outline. Save the formatting for last. Otherwise you will spend too much time changing templates and too little time developing the text.

Step 3:   **Save the Presentation**

➤ Pull down the **File menu** and click **Save** (or click the **Save button** on the Standard toolbar). You should see the Save As dialog box in Figure 1.9c. If necessary, click the **down arrow** on the **Views button** and click **Details**.

➤ To save the file:
- Click the **drop-down arrow** on the Save In list box.
- Click the appropriate drive, drive C or drive A, depending on whether or not you installed the data disk on your hard drive.
- Double click the **Exploring PowerPoint folder** to make it the active folder (the folder in which you will save the document).
- Enter **My First Presentation** as the name of the presentation.

➤ Click **Save** or press the **enter key**. The title bar changes to reflect the name of the presentation.

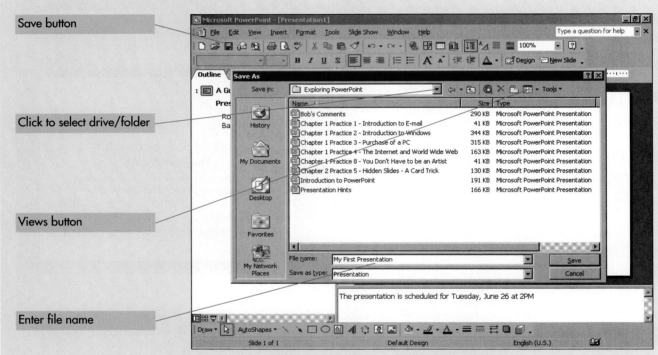

Save button

Click to select drive/folder

Views button

Enter file name

(c) Save the Presentation (step 3)

FIGURE 1.9   *Hands-on Exercise 2 (continued)*

CHANGE THE DEFAULT FOLDER

The default folder is where PowerPoint goes initially to open an existing presentation or to save a new presentation. If you have your own machine, however, you may find it useful to change the default folder. Pull down the Tools menu, click the Options command, then click the Save tab within the Options dialog box. Click in the text box that contains the default file location, enter a new folder, and click OK. The next time you open or save a file, PowerPoint will go automatically to that location.

Step 4: **Enter the Text**

➤ Check that the Outlining toolbar is displayed. If not, pull down the **View menu**, click the **Toolbars command**, then click **Outlining** to show the toolbar.

➤ Click and drag the border between the Outline pane and the Slide pane to enlarge the Outline pane.

➤ Click after your name in the Outline pane. Press **enter** to begin a new item, then press **Shift+Tab** to promote the item and create slide 2. Type **Define the Audience**. Press **enter**.

➤ Press the **Tab key** (or click the **Demote button** on the Outline toolbar) to enter the first bullet. Type **Who is in the audience** and press **enter**.

➤ Press the **Tab key** to enter the second-level bullets. Type **Managers**. Press **enter**. Type **Coworkers**. Press **enter**. Type **Clients**. Press **enter**.

➤ Press **Shift+Tab** (or click the **Promote button** on the Outline toolbar) to return to the first-level bullets. Type **What are their expectations**. Press **enter**.

➤ Press **Shift+Tab** to enter the title of the third slide. Type **Tips for Delivery**. Press **enter**, then press **Tab key** to create the first bullet.

➤ Add the remaining text for this slide and for slide 4 as shown in Figure 1.9d.

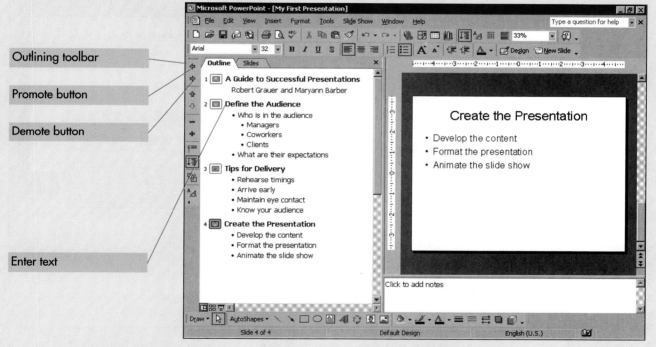

Outlining toolbar

Promote button

Demote button

Enter text

(d) Enter the Text (step 4)

FIGURE 1.9 *Hands-on Exercise 2 (continued)*

JUST KEEP TYPING

The easiest way to enter the text for a presentation is to type continually in the outline. Just type an item, then press enter to move to the next item. You will be automatically positioned at the next item on the same level, where you can type the next entry. Continue to enter text in this manner. Press the Tab key as necessary to demote an item (move it to the next lower level). Press Shift+Tab to promote an item (move it to the next higher level).

Step 5: **The Spell Check**

➤ Enter the text of the remaining slides as shown in Figure 1.9e. Do *not* press enter after entering the last bullet on the last slide or else you will add a blank bullet.

➤ Click the **Spelling button** on the Standard toolbar to check the presentation for spelling:

- The result of the spell check depends on how accurately you entered the text of the presentation. We deliberately misspelled the word *Transitions* in the last slide.
- Continue to check the document for spelling errors. Click **OK** when PowerPoint indicates it has checked the entire presentation.

➤ Click the **Save button** on the Standard toolbar to save the presentation.

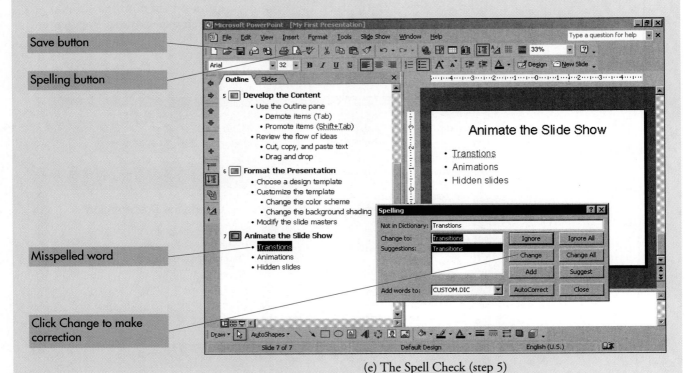

Save button

Spelling button

Misspelled word

Click Change to make correction

(e) The Spell Check (step 5)

FIGURE 1.9 *Hands-on Exercise 2 (continued)*

CREATE YOUR OWN SHORTHAND

Use the AutoCorrect feature, which is common to all Office applications, to expand abbreviations such as "usa" for United States of America. Pull down the Tools menu, click AutoCorrect Options, then type the abbreviation in the Replace text box and the expanded entry in the With text box. Click the Add command button, then click OK to exit the dialog box and return to the document. The next time you type usa in a presentation, it will automatically be expanded to United States of America.

Step 6: **Drag and Drop**

➤ Press **Ctrl+Home** to move to the beginning of the presentation. If you don't see the Outlining toolbar, pull down the **View menu**, click the **Toolbars command**, and check **Outlining** to display the toolbar.

➤ Click the **Collapse All button** on the Outlining toolbar to collapse the outline as shown in Figure 1.9f.

➤ Click the **icon** for **slide 3** (Tips for Delivery) to select the slide. Point to the **slide icon** (the mouse pointer changes to a four-headed arrow), then click and drag to move the slide to the end of the presentation.

➤ All of the slides have been renumbered. The slide titled Tips for Delivery has been moved to the end of the presentation and appears as slide 7. Click the **Expand All button** to display the contents of each slide. Click anywhere in the presentation to deselect the last slide.

Click and drag icon for slide 3 to end of presentation

Collapse All button

Expand All button

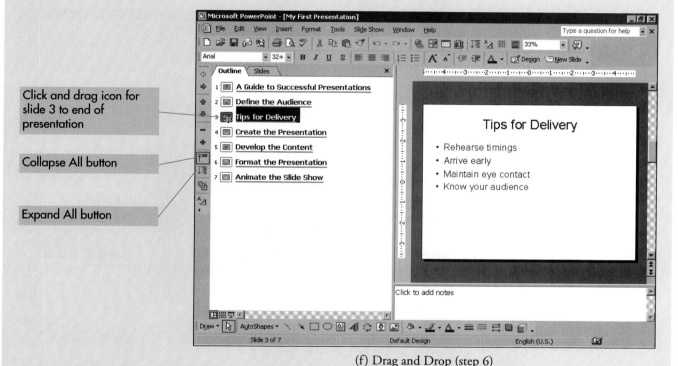

(f) Drag and Drop (step 6)

FIGURE 1.9 *Hands-on Exercise 2 (continued)*

SELECTING SLIDES IN THE OUTLINE

Click the slide icon or the slide number next to the slide title to select the slide. PowerPoint will select the entire slide (including its title, text, and any other objects that are not visible in the outline). Click the first slide, then press and hold the Shift key as you click the ending slide to select a group of sequential slides. Press Ctrl+A to select the entire outline. You can use these techniques to select multiple slides regardless of whether the outline is collapsed or expanded. The selected slides can be copied, moved, expanded, collapsed, or deleted as a unit.

Step 7: **Choose a Design Template**

> ➤ Pull down the **Format menu** and click the **Slide Design command** to open the task pane as shown in Figure 1.9g. (This command will change the contents of the task pane if the task pane is already open.)
> ➤ Click the **down arrow** on the scroll bar within the task pane to scroll through the available designs until you find one that you like. (We chose the Ocean design.) Click the selected design in the task pane to apply this template to your presentation.
> ➤ Select a different design to see how your presentation looks when set in another template.
> ➤ Click the **Undo button** to cancel the last command and return to the previous design. Click the **Redo button** to reverse the undo operation.
> ➤ Spend a few minutes until you have the design you like. Save the presentation.

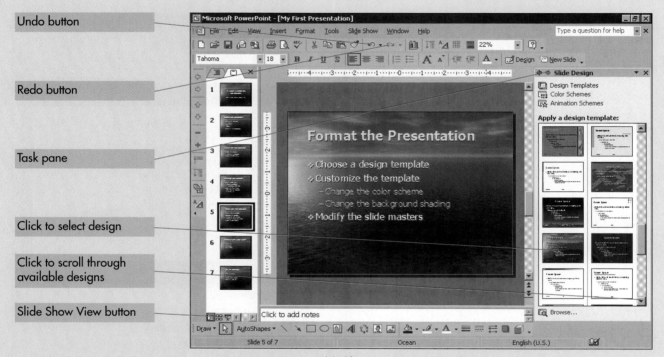

Undo button

Redo button

Task pane

Click to select design

Click to scroll through available designs

Slide Show View button

(g) Choose a Design Template (step 7)

FIGURE 1.9 *Hands-on Exercise 2 (continued)*

THE UNDO AND REDO COMMANDS

Click the drop-down arrow next to the Undo button to display a list of your previous actions, then click the action you want to undo, which also undoes all of the preceding commands. Undoing the fifth command in the list, for example, will also undo the preceding four commands. The Redo command works in reverse and cancels the last Undo command.

Step 8: **View the Presentation**

➤ Press **Ctrl+Home** to move to the beginning of the presentation. Click the **Slide Show button** on the status bar to view the presentation as shown in Figure 1.9h.
  • To move to the next slide: Click the **left mouse button**, type the letter **N**, or press the **PgDn key**.
  • To move to the previous slide: Type the letter **P** or press the **PgUp key**.
➤ Continue to move from one slide to the next until you come to the end of the presentation and are returned to the Normal view.
➤ Save the presentation. Exit PowerPoint if you do not want to continue with the next exercise at this time.

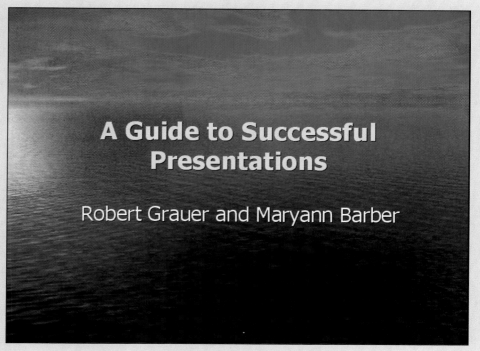

(h) View the Presentation (step 8)

FIGURE 1.9   *Hands-on Exercise 2 (continued)*

ADVICE FROM THE OFFICE ASSISTANT

The Office Assistant indicates it has a suggestion by displaying a lightbulb. Click the lightbulb to display the tip, then click the OK button to close the balloon and continue working. The Assistant will not, however, repeat a tip from an earlier session unless you reset it at the start of a new session. This is especially important in a laboratory situation where you are sharing a computer with many students. To reset the tips, click the Assistant to display the balloon, click the Options button in the balloon, click the Options tab, then click the Reset My Tips button.

You have successfully created a PowerPoint presentation, but the most important step is yet to come—the delivery of the presentation to an audience. This is best accomplished through a computerized slide show (as opposed to using overhead transparencies or 35mm slides). The computer becomes the equivalent of a slide projector and the presentation is called a slide show.

PowerPoint can help you add interest to the slide show in two ways, transitions and animations. *Transitions* apply to the slide as a whole and control the way a slide moves on and off the screen. *Animations* control the appearance of individual elements on a single slide. Transitions and animations are applied from the task pane within the Normal view as shown in Figure 1.10. (Pull down the Slide Show menu and select the Slide Transition or Custom Animation command to open the task pane with the appropriate options.)

The task pane in Figure 1.10a contains a list box with the available *transition effects*. Slides may move on to the screen from the left or right, be uncovered by horizontal or vertical blinds, fade, dissolve, and so on. You select a slide, choose the effect, select a speed and sound, then indicate when you want to advance the slide (either on a mouse click or after a specified number of seconds). Click the Play button at the bottom of the pane to preview the transition, or click the Slide Show button to move directly to a complete show. (Transition effects can also be applied from the Slide Sorter view, where you can apply the same transition to multiple slides by selecting the slides prior to applying the effect.)

Figure 1.10b shows the application of animation effects to a specific slide. You can select a predefined animation scheme for the slide as a whole, or you can animate each object individually. The animation schemes are divided into subtle, moderate, and exciting, and it is fun to experiment with the various effects. *Custom animation* requires you to select an animation effect for each object on the slide, then specify the order in which the objects are to appear. The slide in Figure 1.10b, for example, displays the title, the four bullets in succession, and the clip art in that order. Look closely at the icons in the task pane and you will see that different effects are chosen for the various objects.

Delivering the Presentation

PowerPoint can help you to create attractive presentations, but the content and delivery are still up to you. You have worked hard to gain the opportunity to present your ideas and you want to be well prepared for the session. Practice aloud several times, preferably under the same conditions as the actual presentation. Time your delivery to be sure that you do not exceed your allotted time. Everyone is nervous, but the more you practice, the more confident you will be.

Arrive early. You need time to gather your thoughts as well as to set up the presentation. Start PowerPoint and open your presentation prior to addressing the audience. Be sure that your notes are with you and check that water is available for you during the presentation. Look at the audience to open communication and gain credibility. Speak clearly and vary your delivery. Try to relax. You'll be great!

QUESTIONS AND ANSWERS (Q & A)

Indicate at the beginning of your talk whether you will take questions during the presentation or collectively at the end. Announce the length of time that will be allocated to questions. Rephrase all questions so the audience can hear. If you do receive a hostile question, rephrase it in a neutral way and try to disarm the challenger by paying a compliment. If you don't know the answer, say so.

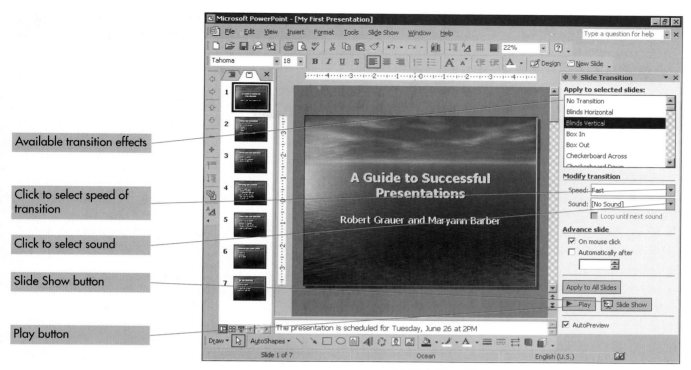

Available transition effects

Click to select speed of transition

Click to select sound

Slide Show button

Play button

(a) Slide Transition

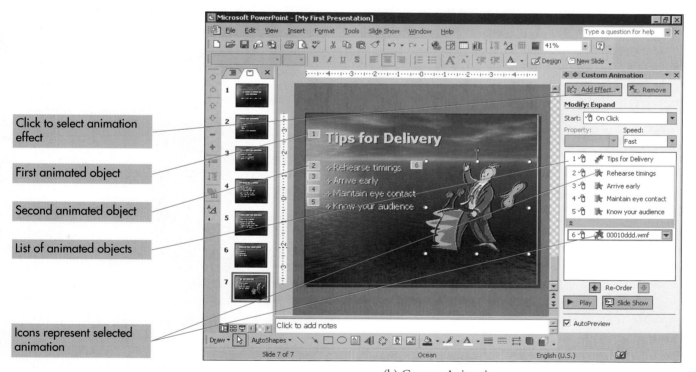

Click to select animation effect

First animated object

Second animated object

List of animated objects

Icons represent selected animation

(b) Custom Animation

FIGURE 1.10   *Transition and Animation Effects*

ANIMATING THE PRESENTATION

Objective   To change the layout of an existing slide; to establish transition and animation effects. Use Figure 1.11 as a guide in the exercise.

Step 1:   **Change the Slide Layout**

> ➤ Start PowerPoint. There are two basic ways to open an existing presentation. You can use the Open command in the File menu, or you can open the presentation from the task pane.
> ➤ Pull down the **View menu** and click the **Task pane command** to display the task pane, then (if necessary) click the **down arrow** in the task pane to select **New from Existing Presentation**.
> ➤ You should see My First Presentation from the previous exercise since the most recently used presentations are listed automatically.
> ➤ Click **My First Presentation**. (Click the link to **More Presentations** if the presentation is not listed, to display the Open dialog box, where you can select the drive and folder to locate your presentation.)
> ➤ Click the **Outline tab**, then scroll in the left pane until you can select the **Tips for Delivery slide**.
> ➤ Click the **down arrow** on the task pane to select **Slide Layout** as shown in Figure 1.11a. Now scroll in the task pane until you can select the **Text & Clip Art layout** as shown in Figure 1.11a. Click the layout to apply it to the current slide.

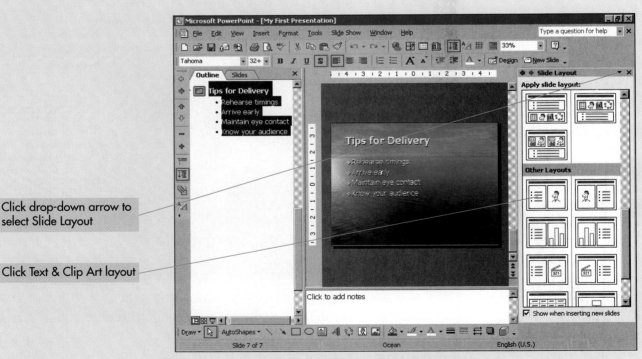

Click drop-down arrow to select Slide Layout

Click Text & Clip Art layout

(a) Change the Slide Layout (step 1)

FIGURE 1.11   *Hands-on Exercise 3*

Step 2:   **Add the Clip Art**

➤ Double click the **placeholder** on the slide to add the clip art. You will see the Select Picture dialog box as shown in Figure 1.11b, although the size, position, and content will be different on your screen.

➤ Click in the **Search** text box and enter the key word **education**, then click the **Search button** to look for clip art that is described by this term.

➤ Select (click) the clip art you want and click **OK**. The clip art should appear on the slide.

➤ The clip art is sized automatically to fit the existing placeholder. You can, however, move and size the clip art just like any other Windows object.

➤ Save the presentation.

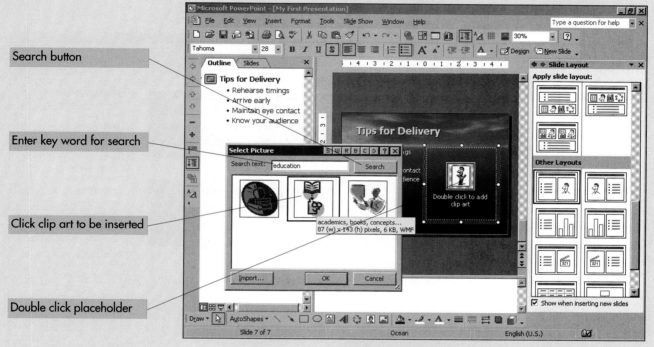

Search button

Enter key word for search

Click clip art to be inserted

Double click placeholder

(b) Add the Clip Art (step 2)

FIGURE 1.11   *Hands-on Exercise 3 (continued)*

SEARCH BY COLLECTION

The Clip Organizer organizes its contents by collections and provides another way to select clip art. Pull down the Insert menu, click (or point to) the Picture command, then click Clip Art to open the task pane, where you can enter a key word to search for clip art. Instead of searching, however, click the link to Clip Organizer at the bottom of the task pane to display the Clip Organizer dialog box. Close the My Collections folder if it is open, then open the Office Collections folder where you can explore the available images by collection.

Step 3:   **Add Transition Effects**

➤ You can apply transitions in either the Normal view (with the thumbnail images) or in the Slide Sorter view. We chose the latter. Thus, click the **Slide Sorter View button** above the status bar to change to this view.
➤ Select (click) the first slide. Click the **Transition button** on the Slide Sorter toolbar to display the transition effects in the task pane.
➤ Click in the list box to select the **Blinds Vertical** transition effect (a preview plays automatically) as shown in Figure 1.11c. A transition icon appears under the slide after the effect has been applied. Change the speed to medium.
➤ Select (click) slide two and apply the **Checkerboard Across** transition effect to this slide. Change the speed to medium.
➤ Apply different transition effects to the other slides in the presentation. Save the presentation.

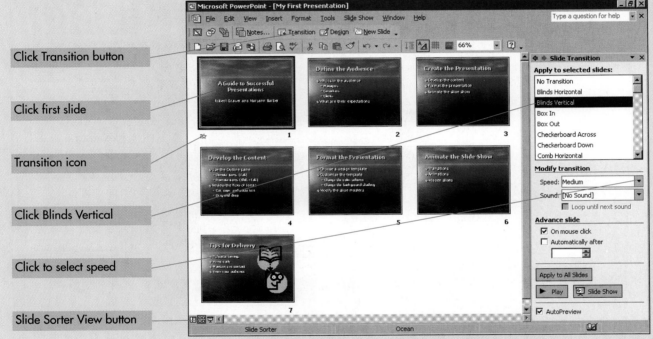

(c) Add Transition Effects (step 3)

FIGURE 1.11   *Hands-on Exercise 3 (continued)*

CHANGE THE MAGNIFICATION

Click the down arrow on the Zoom box to change the display magnification, which in turn controls the size of individual slides. The higher the magnification, the easier it is to read the text of an individual slide, but the fewer slides you see at one time. Conversely, changing to a smaller magnification decreases the size of the individual slides, but enables you to see more of the presentation.

Step 4: **Create a Summary Slide**

➤ Pull down the **Edit menu** and press **Select All** to select every slide in the presentation. (You can also press **Ctrl+A** or press and hold the **Shift key** as you click each slide in succession.)

➤ Click the **Summary Slide button** on the Slide Sorter toolbar to create a summary slide containing a bullet with the title of each selected slide. The new slide appears at the beginning of the presentation as shown in Figure 1.11d.

➤ Click and drag the **summary slide** to the end of the presentation. (As you drag the slide, the mouse pointer changes to include the outline of a miniature slide, and a vertical line appears to indicate the new position of the slide.)

➤ Release the mouse. The summary slide has been moved to the end of the presentation, and the slides are renumbered automatically.

➤ Save the presentation.

Summary Slide button

Click and drag summary slide to end of presentation

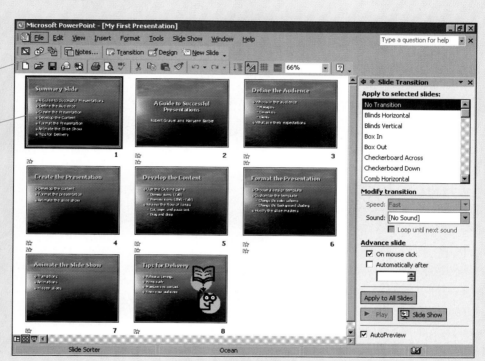

(d) Create a Summary Slide (step 4)

FIGURE 1.11 *Hands-on Exercise 3 (continued)*

SELECTING MULTIPLE SLIDES

You can apply the same transition or animation effect to multiple slides with a single command. Change to the Slide Sorter view, then select the slides by pressing and holding the Shift key as you click the slides. Use the task pane or the Slide Sorter toolbar to choose the desired transition when all the slides have been selected. Click anywhere in the Slide Sorter view to deselect the slides and continue working.

Step 5:   **Create Animation Effects**

➤ Double click the **summary slide** to change to the Normal view. The task pane should still be open. Click the **down arrow** on the task pane to choose **Slide Design—Animation Schemes**.

➤ Scroll in the Open list box to the **Moderate category**, and choose **Spin** as shown in Figure 1.11e. You will automatically see a preview of the effect.

➤ Scroll in the Open list box to the Exciting category and choose a different effect. (We're not sure who rates the effects and why one is deemed to be exciting, while the other is only moderate.) Click the **Undo button** if you prefer the original scheme.

➤ Save the presentation.

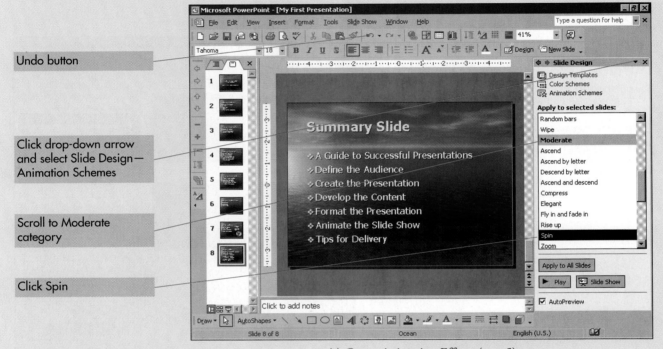

Undo button

Click drop-down arrow and select Slide Design— Animation Schemes

Scroll to Moderate category

Click Spin

(e) Create Animation Effects (step 5)

FIGURE 1.11   *Hands-on Exercise 3 (continued)*

CUSTOMIZE THE ANIMATION

You can modify the effects of a predefined animation scheme for selected slides and/or objects on those slides. Click the down arrow in the task pane and choose Custom Animation. Select the slide, select the object on the slide that is to receive special treatment, click the Add Effect button to display a menu, and choose the effect, which will preview automatically. (Click the Remove button if you do not like the result.) Set a time limit because PowerPoint gives you virtually unlimited flexibility.

Step 6: **Show the Presentation**

> ➤ Press **Ctrl+Home** to return to the first slide, then click the **Slide Show button** above the status bar to view the presentation. You should see the opening slide in Figure 1.11f.
> ➤ Click the **left mouse button** to move to the next slide (or to the next bullet on the current slide when animation is in effect).
> ➤ Click the **right mouse button** to display the Shortcut menu and return to the previous slide (or to the previous bullet on the current slide when an animation is in effect).
> ➤ Continue to view the presentation until you come to the end. Click the **left mouse button** a final time to return to the regular PowerPoint window.
> ➤ Close the presentation. Exit PowerPoint if you do not want to continue with the next exercise at this time.

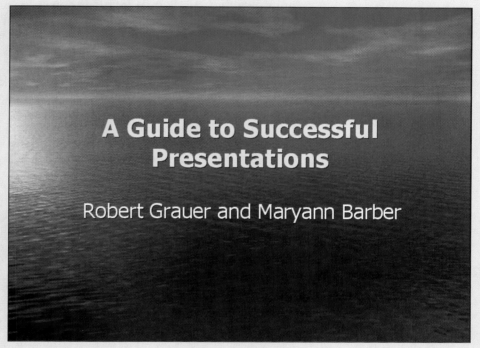

(f) Show the Presentation

FIGURE 1.11   *Hands-on Exercise 3 (continued)*

ANNOTATE A SLIDE

You can annotate a slide just like the sports announcers on television. Click the Slide Show button to begin your presentation, press Ctrl+P to change the mouse pointer to a pen, then click and drag to draw on the slide. The annotation is temporary and lasts only while the slide is on the screen. Use the PgDn and PgUp keys to move forward and back in the presentation when the drawing tool is in effect. Press Ctrl+A at any time to change the mouse pointer back to an arrow.

Thus far we have focused on presentations that consisted largely of text. PowerPoint also enables you to include a variety of visual elements that add impact to a presentation as can be seen in Figure 1.12. (This is the presentation that we will create in the next hands-on exercise.) You can add clip art, sound, or animated clips through the *Microsoft Clip Organizer*, and/or you can obtain the elements from other sources. You can use the supplement applications that are included with Microsoft Office to add organization charts and WordArt. You can also insert objects that were created in other applications, such as a chart from Microsoft Excel or a table from Microsoft Word.

A chart or table is inserted into a presentation through linking or embedding. The essential difference between the two techniques is that embedding places the object into the presentation, whereas linking does not. In other words, an *embedded object* is stored within the presentation. A *linked object*, on the other hand, is stored in its own file, and the presentation is one of many potential documents that are linked to that object. The advantage of linking over embedding is that the presentation is updated automatically if the original object is changed.

Linking is also preferable if the same object is referenced in many documents, so that any change to the object has to be made in only one place (the source document). An Excel chart, for example, may be linked to a Word document and a PowerPoint presentation. You can subsequently change the chart, and both the document and presentation are updated automatically.

You can also add *comments* to any presentation to explain your thoughts to colleagues who may review the presentation prior to delivery. The comments appear on a slide during editing, but not during delivery as you will see in the hands-on exercise that follows shortly.

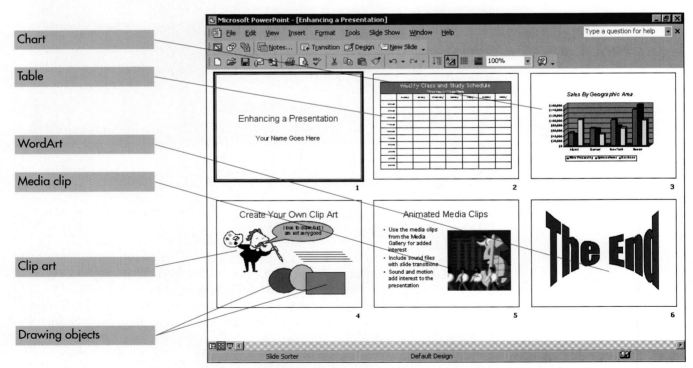

FIGURE 1.12   *Enhancing a Presentation*

Office Art

Everyone likes *clip art*, but relatively few individuals think in terms of enhancing it. It takes a lot of talent to create original clip art, but it takes only a little imagination to create a drawing from existing clip art as shown in Figure 1.13. There is no way that we could have drawn the artist, but it was very easy to copy the artist and create the slide, given the original clip art.

Any piece of clip art is an object that can be copied, moved, and sized like any other Windows object. Thus, we clicked on the original clip art (the artist in the upper left of the slide) to display the sizing handles, clicked the copy and paste buttons to duplicate the object, then moved and sized the copied image to the bottom of the slide. We then copied the smaller artist across the bottom of the slide.

Next we used various tools on the Drawing toolbar to complete the slide. Select the Line tool, for example, then click and drag to create a line. Once the line has been created, you can select it and change its properties (such as thickness, style, or color) by using other tools on the Drawing toolbar. The oval and rectangle tools work the same way. The AutoShapes button on the Drawing toolbar provides access to the balloon and other callouts in which you enter the text.

There are other techniques you can use as well. You can, for example, select multiple objects simultaneously and group them together in order to move and/or size those objects with a single mouse click. Press and hold the Shift key to select multiple objects (e.g., the large artist, the balloon, and the three circles), click the Draw button, then click the Group command. The five objects have been combined into one larger object with a single set of sizing handles.

All it takes is a little imagination and a sense of what you can do. Use different clip art images on the same slide and you get something entirely different. It is fun and it is easy. Just be flexible and willing to experiment. We think you will be pleased with the results.

FIGURE 1.13 *Office Art*

Microsoft WordArt

Microsoft WordArt is an application within Microsoft Office that creates decorative text that can be used to add interest to a document. You can use WordArt in addition to clip art within a document, or in place of clip art if the right image is not available. You can rotate text in any direction, add three-dimensional effects, display the text vertically down the page, slant it, arch it, or even print it upside down. In short, you are limited only by your imagination.

WordArt is intuitive and easy to use. In essence, you choose a style for the text from among the selections in Figure 1.14a. Then you enter the specific text in a subsequent dialog box, after which the result is displayed in Figure 1.14b. The finished WordArt is an object that can be moved and sized within a presentation.

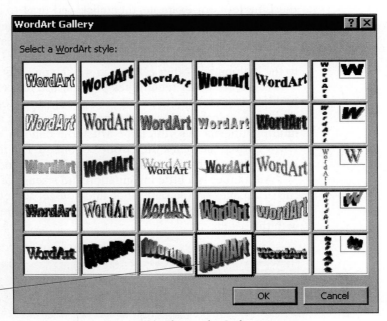

(a) Choose the Style

(b) Completed Entry

FIGURE 1.14   *Microsoft WordArt*

ENHANCING A PRESENTATION

Objective   To include a Word table and Excel chart in a presentation; to modify existing clip art and create a WordArt object. Use Figure 1.15 as a guide.

Step 1:   **Insert a Comment**

> ➤ Start PowerPoint. Click the **New button** on the Standard toolbar to begin a new presentation. Close the task pane. Enter the title of the presentation and your name on the title slide. Save the presentation as **Enhancing a Presentation** in the **Exploring PowerPoint folder**.
> ➤ Click the **Normal View button** above the status bar if you are not in the Normal view. Click the **Slides tab** to display the slides in the left pane.
> ➤ Pull down the **Insert menu** and click the **Comment command** to insert a comment onto the slide as shown in Figure 1.15a.
> ➤ You will see an empty balloon that contains the name of the person who has registered this copy of Office, together with today's date. Enter any text at all as a comment.
> ➤ Click anywhere outside the comment. The balloon closes, and you see a comment marker. Click the marker, and the comment reappears.
> ➤ The Reviewing toolbar appears automatically whenever you are working with comments. The Comments and Changes buttons at the extreme left of the toolbar toggles the comment markers on and off.
> ➤ Click the **New Slide button** on the Formatting toolbar. (This will open the task pane if it is not already open.) Click the **down arrow** in the task pane until you can select a **blank layout**.

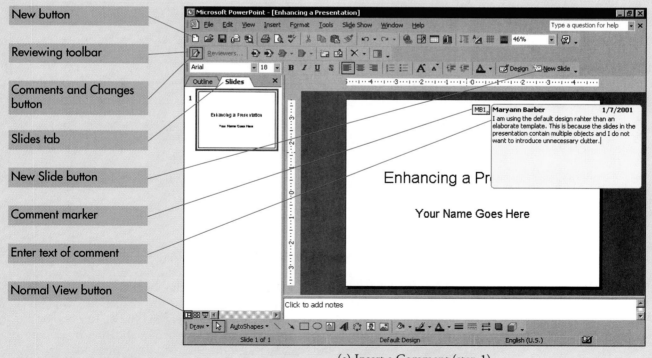

New button

Reviewing toolbar

Comments and Changes button

Slides tab

New Slide button

Comment marker

Enter text of comment

Normal View button

(a) Insert a Comment (step 1)

FIGURE 1.15   *Hands-on Exercise 4*

Step 2: **Copy the Word Table**

➤ Start Word. Open the **My Study Schedule** Word document in the **Exploring PowerPoint folder** as shown in Figure 1.15b. The document consists entirely of a Word table.

➤ Click and drag to select the text **Your Name Goes Here** that appears at the top of the table. Type your first and last name, which automatically replaces the selected text.

➤ You can click in any cell and enter an activity. The text will automatically flow from one line to the next within the cell. Limit the entry to two lines, however, or else the table may not fit on one page (or one slide). Save the document.

➤ Click the tiny square at the upper left of the table to select the entire table. Be sure that every cell is highlighted, or else the table will not be copied successfully. Click the **Copy button** to copy the table to the clipboard.

➤ Exit Word. The copied text remains in the clipboard even though Microsoft Word is no longer open.

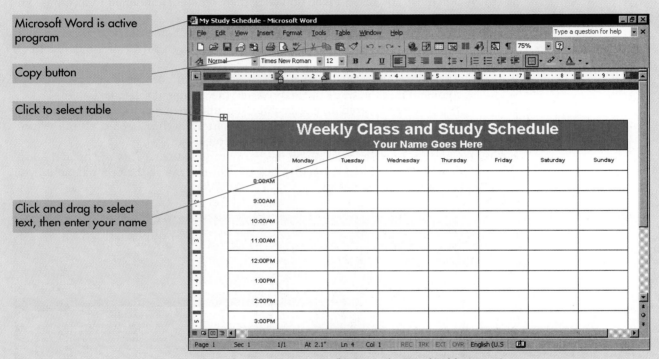

(b) Copy the Word Table (step 2)

FIGURE 1.15 *Hands-on Exercise 4 (continued)*

THE WINDOWS CLIPBOARD

The Windows clipboard is an area of memory that is available to every Windows application. Execution of the copy command in one application places the copied text (or other object) on the clipboard from where it can be accessed by any other application. Microsoft Office has its own clipboard (in addition to the Windows clipboard) that can hold up to 24 objects. You can open the Office clipboard from any Office application by pulling down the Edit menu and selecting the Office Clipboard command.

Step 3:   **Insert the Table**

➤ You should be back in PowerPoint as shown in Figure 1.15c. (If not, click the **PowerPoint button** on the Windows taskbar.)

➤ Click anywhere on the second slide to select this slide. Click the **Paste button** on the Standard toolbar to paste (embed) the Word table onto this slide.

➤ Do not be concerned if the table is slightly larger than the slide. Click anywhere in the table to select the table and display the sizing handles.

➤ Click and drag a corner handle to proportionately shrink the table so that it fits on the slide. Click and drag any hashed border to center the table on the slide.

➤ Pull down the **Insert menu** and click the **Comment command**. Enter the text of the comment shown in the figure, which indicates that the table has been embedded (rather than linked) into the presentation. Click anywhere outside the comment after you have finished.

➤ Click the **Previous Item button** on the Reviewing toolbar to move to the previous comment. Click the **Next Item button** to return to this comment.

➤ Save the presentation.

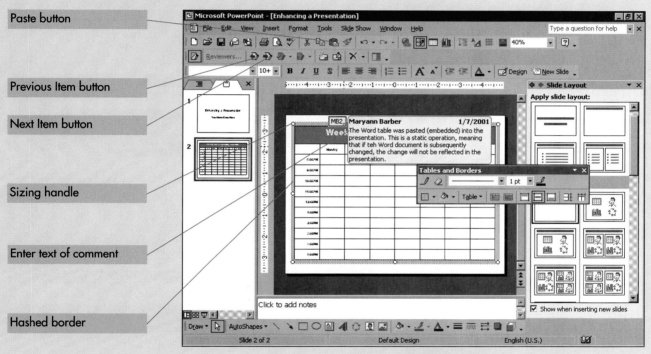

Paste button

Previous Item button

Next Item button

Sizing handle

Enter text of comment

Hashed border

(c) Insert the Table (step 3)

FIGURE 1.15   *Hands-on Exercise 4 (continued)*

SEND SLIDES TO A WORD DOCUMENT

You can embed and/or link Word documents and PowerPoint presentations in either direction; that is, you can insert a Word document into a PowerPoint presentation as was done here, and/or you can send PowerPoint slides to a Word document. Pull down the File menu and click the Send To command, then choose Microsoft Word to display the associated dialog box. You will be given the choice of how to arrange the PowerPoint slides in the resulting Word document. See exercise 10 at the end of the chapter.

Step 4: **Insert the Excel Chart**

➤ Start Excel. Open the **Software Sales** workbook in the **Exploring PowerPoint folder.** The workbook consists of a single sheet that contains data and a chart.

➤ Click anywhere in the chart background to select the entire chart. You should see sizing handles around the white border of the chart. Click the **Copy button** on the Standard toolbar to copy the chart to the clipboard. Do not close the workbook as we will return to it momentarily.

➤ Click the **PowerPoint button** on the Windows taskbar to return to the Power-Point presentation. Click the **New slide button** and use the Slide Layout task pane to insert a blank slide into the presentation. Close the task pane.

➤ Pull down the **Edit menu** and click the **Paste Special command** to display the Paste Special dialog box in Figure 1.15d. Click the **Paste Link Option button**. Click **OK** to insert the chart onto the slide. Do not be concerned about the size or position of the chart at this time.

➤ Save the presentation.

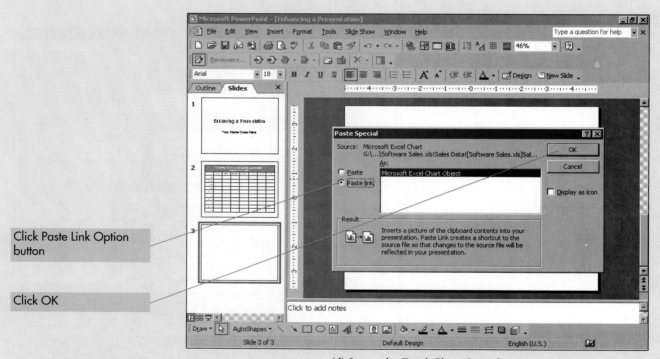

Click Paste Link Option button

Click OK

(d) Insert the Excel Chart (step 4)

FIGURE 1.15 *Hands-on Exercise 4 (continued)*

LINKING VERSUS EMBEDDING

Linking is very different from embedding as it provides a dynamic connection to the source document. A linked object, such as an Excel chart, is tied to its source, so that any changes to the source file are reflected in the PowerPoint presentation. Linking is especially useful when the same object is inserted into multiple documents, as changes to the object are made in only one place (in the source file). A linked object must always be saved in its file.

Step 5: **Update the Chart**

➤ You should see the chart as shown in Figure 1.15e. The sizing handles indicate that the chart is currently selected and can be moved and sized like any other Windows object.

➤ Click and drag a corner handle (the pointer changes to a two-headed arrow) to proportionally increase (decrease) the size of the chart. Point to any border (the pointer changes to a four-headed arrow) to move the chart on the slide.

➤ Note that the database sales for Miami are very low ($12,000). Double click the chart to return to Excel (or click the **Excel button** on the Windows taskbar). Click in cell **B4** and change the database sales for Miami to **$100,000**. Save the workbook. Exit Excel.

➤ Return to PowerPoint. The chart may automatically reflect the change in database sales. If not, right click the chart and select the **Update Link command**.

➤ Pull down the **Insert menu** and click the **Comment command** to insert an appropriate comment indicating that the chart in the presentation is linked to an Excel workbook. Save the presentation.

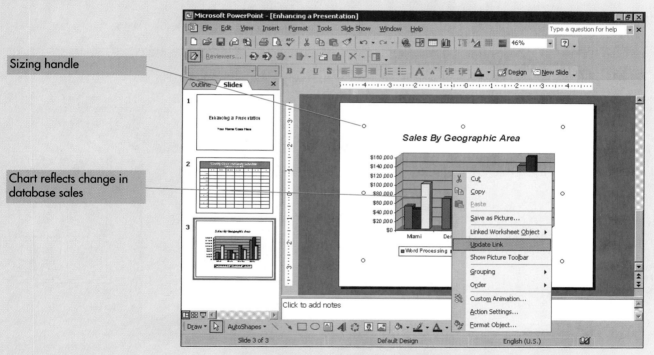

Sizing handle

Chart reflects change in database sales

(e) Update the Chart (step 5)

FIGURE 1.15 *Hands-on Exercise 4 (continued)*

MULTITASKING

Multitasking, the ability to run multiple applications at the same time, is one of the primary advantages of the Windows environment. Switching from one application to another is easy—just click the appropriate button on the Windows taskbar. You can also use the classic Alt+Tab shortcut. Press and hold the Alt key as you click the Tab key repeatedly to display and select icons for the open applications, then release the Tab key when the desired application icon is selected.

Step 6: **Insert the Clip Art**

➤ Click the **New Slide button** and select the **Title Only** layout. Click in the title placeholder and type **Create Your Own Clip Art**.

➤ Pull down the **Insert menu**, click **Picture**, and then click **Clip Art** (or click the **Insert Clip Art button** on the Drawing toolbar). The contents of the task pane change automatically.

➤ Type **Artist** in the Search text box. Be sure the list boxes show you are searching all collections and are looking for all media types. Click the **Search button** to initiate the search.

➤ The system pauses, then starts to return all objects in the Clip Organizer that satisfy the search criteria. The objects are stored on a Web server and hence you need an Internet connection in order to retrieve all of the objects.

➤ Click the **down arrow** in the task pane to scroll through the images until you find the one that you want. Point to the right side of the image, then click the **down arrow** that appears to display a menu. Click **Insert**.

➤ Choose an appropriate clip art image. Click **Insert**, then move and size the clip art so that it is positioned as shown in Figure 1.15f. Close the task pane. Save the presentation.

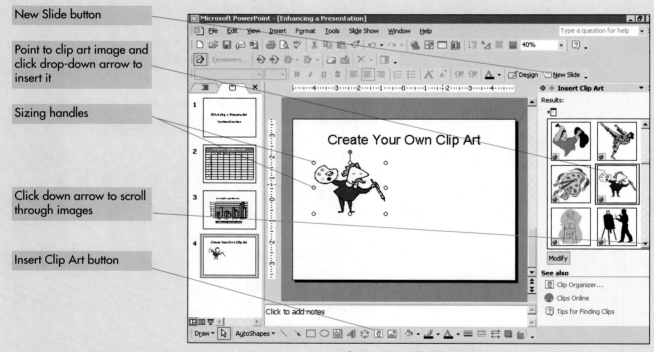

New Slide button

Point to clip art image and click drop-down arrow to insert it

Sizing handles

Click down arrow to scroll through images

Insert Clip Art button

(f) Insert the Clip Art (step 6)

FIGURE 1.15 *Hands-on Exercise 4 (continued)*

THE SHIFT KEY

The Shift key has special significance when used in conjunction with the Line, Rectangle, and Oval tools. Press and hold the Shift key as you drag the line tool horizontally or vertically to create a perfectly straight line in either direction. Press and hold the Shift key as you drag the Rectangle and Oval tool to create a square or circle, respectively.

Step 7: **Use the Drawing Toolbar**

➤ Click the **AutoShapes button** on the Drawing toolbar, click **Callouts**, then click the desired balloon. The mouse pointer changes to a tiny crosshair.
➤ Click and drag on the slide where you want the balloon to go. Release the mouse. The balloon is selected automatically, and the sizing handles are displayed. If necessary, click and drag the balloon to adjust its size or position.
➤ Type the phrase shown in the figure. You can select the text, then change its font, size, or alignment. Click elsewhere on the slide to deselect the balloon.
➤ Click the **Line tool** on the Drawing toolbar, then click and drag to draw a line on the slide. To change the color or thickness, select the line (the sizing handles appear), click the appropriate tool on the Drawing toolbar, then select a new color or thickness.
➤ Select the completed line, click the **Copy button**, then click the **Paste button** several times to copy the line. Use the **Oval** or **Rectangle tools** to draw additional shapes, then use the **Fill Color tool** to change their color.
➤ Move and size the objects as necessary. Save the presentation.

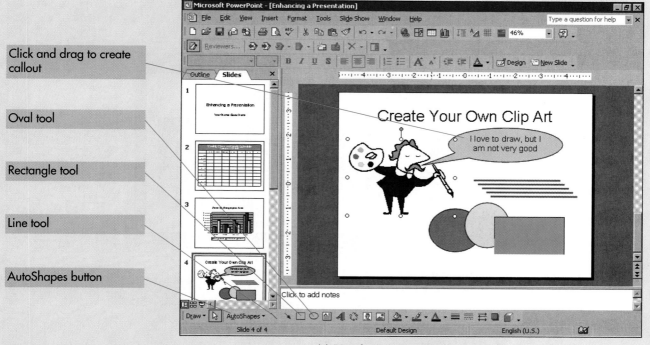

(g) Use the Drawing Toolbar (step 7)

FIGURE 1.15   *Hands-on Exercise 4 (continued)*

AUTOSHAPES

An AutoShape is a predefined shape that is drawn automatically when you select its icon from the AutoShapes toolbar, then click and drag in the slide. (To display the AutoShapes toolbar, click the AutoShape button on the Drawing toolbar.) To place text inside an AutoShape, select the shape and start typing. You can also change the fill color or line thickness by selecting the shape, then clicking the appropriate button on the Drawing toolbar. See exercise 9 at the end of the chapter.

Step 8: **Add a Media Clip**

➤ Click the **New Slide button**. Select the **Title Test & Media Clip** layout. Enter **Animated Media Clips** as the title of the slide. Enter the bulleted text as shown in Figure 1.15h.

➤ Double click the Media placeholder to add the media clip, which in turn displays the Media Clip dialog box. Select the clip that appears in Figure 1.15h and click the **OK button** to insert the clip onto the slide.

➤ Pull down the **Slide Show menu** and click **Slide Transition** to display these options in the task pane. Click the **down arrow** in the Sound list box and select **Cash Register**.

➤ Click the **Play button** to preview the effect. You should see the man passing an object to the sound of a cash register. (You need a sound card and speakers to hear the sound.)

➤ Save the presentation.

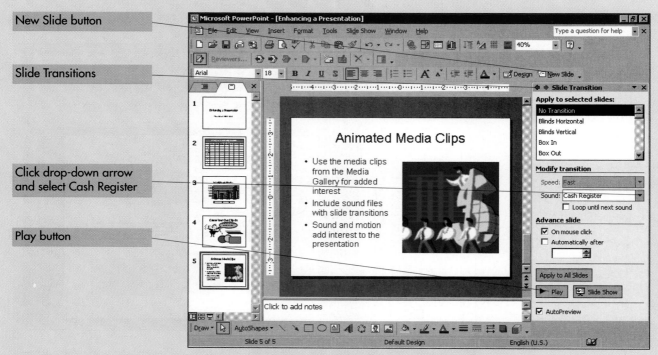

(h) Add a Media Clip (step 8)

FIGURE 1.15   *Hands-on Exercise 4 (continued)*

INSERT SLIDES FROM OTHER PRESENTATIONS

You work hard to develop individual slides and thus you may find it useful to reuse a slide from one presentation to the next. Pull down the Insert menu, click the Slides from Files command to display the Slide Finder dialog box, and click the Browse button to locate the presentation that contains the slides you want. Press and hold the Shift key to select multiple slides from this presentation, then click the Insert button to bring the selected slides into the current presentation.

Step 9:   **Add the WordArt**

> ➤ We're ready to add the sixth and final slide. Click the **New Slide button** and add another blank slide. Close the task pane.
> ➤ Click the **Insert WordArt button** on the Drawing toolbar to display the WordArt Gallery dialog box as shown in Figure 1.15i. Choose any style you like (we took the fourth style from the left in the first row). Click **OK.**
> ➤ You should see the Edit WordArt text box. Enter **The End** as the text for your WordArt object. Click **OK** to close the Edit WordArt text box and insert the WordArt into your presentation.
> ➤ Move and size the WordArt object just as you would any other Windows object. Click and drag a corner sizing handle to increase the size of the WordArt until it takes the entire slide.
> ➤ Point to the middle of the WordArt object (the mouse pointer changes to a four-headed arrow), then click and drag to position the WordArt in the middle of the slide.
> ➤ Save the presentation.

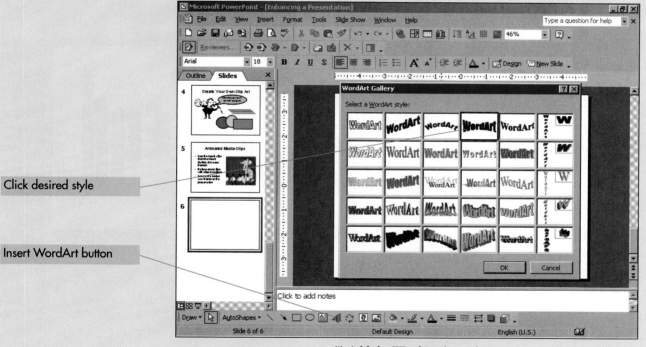

Click desired style

Insert WordArt button

(i) Add the WordArt (step 9)

FIGURE 1.15   *Hands-on Exercise 4 (continued)*

THE WORDART TOOLBAR

The WordArt toolbar is the easiest way to change an existing WordArt object. It is displayed automatically when a WordArt object is selected and is suppressed otherwise. As with any other toolbar, you can point to a button to display a ScreenTip containing the name of the button, which is indicative of its function. You will find buttons to display the text vertically, change the style or shape, and/or edit the text.

Step 10:   **Complete the WordArt**

➤ You should see the WordArt as shown in Figure 1.15j. You can click and drag the yellow diamond to change the slope of the text and/or you can click and drag the green circle to rotate the text.

➤ Click the **down arrow** for the **Fill Color tool** on the Drawing toolbar to display the available fill colors. Select (click) **blue** to change the color of the WordArt object. Experiment with other tools on the Drawing and/or WordArt toolbars to enhance the WordArt image.

➤ Pull down the **Slide Show menu** and click **Slide Transition** to display these options in the task pane. Click the **down arrow** in the Sound list box and select **Applause**. Click the **Play button** to preview the effect. (You will need a sound card and speakers to hear the sound.)

➤ Close the task pane. Save the presentation.

Print Preview button

Green circle

Yellow diamond

Click desired color

Click to display fill colors

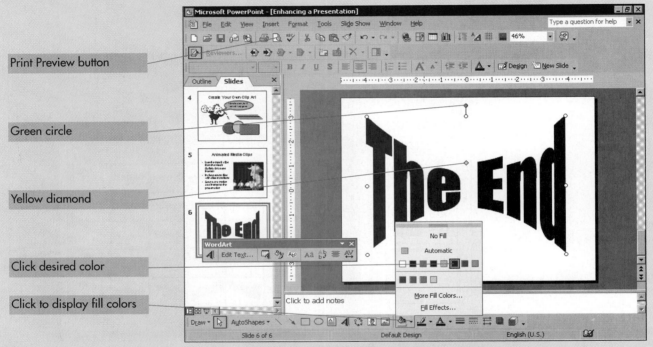

(j) Complete the WordArt (step 10)

FIGURE 1.15   *Hands-on Exercise 4 (continued)*

THE THIRD DIMENSION

You can make your WordArt images even more dramatic by adding 3-D effects. You can tilt the text up or down, right or left, increase or decrease the depth, and change the shading. Pull down the View menu, click Toolbars, click Customize to display the complete list of available toolbars, then check the box to display the 3-D Settings toolbar. Select the WordArt object, then experiment with various tools and special effects. The results are even better if you have a color printer.

Step 11:   **Print the Comments Pages**

➤ Click the **Print Preview button** to preview the presentation. Click the **down arrow** on the Print What list box to select **Handouts (6 per page)**.

➤ Click the **down arrow** on the Options list box and toggle **Include Comments Pages** on, as shown in Figure 1.15k.

➤ The status bar indicates that you are on the first of two pages. Page 1 contains the six handouts. Page 2 contains the comments you entered earlier. Press the **PgDn key** to move to the second page, then scroll to the top of the page to see the comments.

➤ Click the **Print button** to display the Print dialog box, which contains the same information as the Print Preview screen; that is, you are printing audience handouts and will include comments. Click **OK** to print the presentation. Close the Print Preview window.

➤ Press **Ctrl+Home** to move to the first slide in the presentation, then click the **Slide Show button** to view the presentation.

➤ Save the presentation a final time. Exit PowerPoint. Well done!

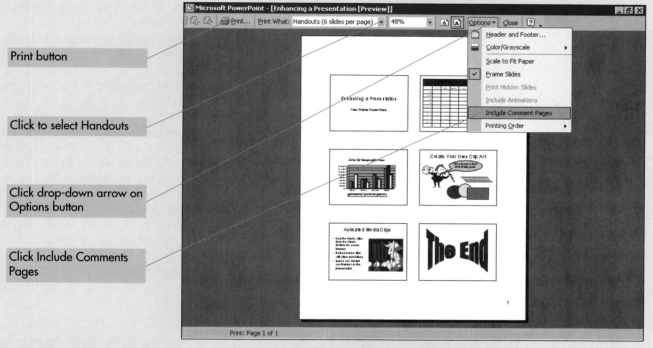

Print button

Click to select Handouts

Click drop-down arrow on Options button

Click Include Comments Pages

(k) Print the Comments Pages (step 11)

FIGURE 1.15   *Hands-on Exercise 4 (continued)*

UPDATING LINKS

The next time you open this presentation you will see a message indicating that links are present and further, that the links can be updated. You should respond by clicking the Update Links command button, which in turn will bring in the most current version of the chart to the presentation. This assumes that the Excel workbook is still in the same folder where it was created initially. If there is a problem, perhaps because the workbook has been moved or renamed, pull down the Edit menu and click the Links command to modify the link.

Microsoft PowerPoint enables you to focus on the content of a presentation without worrying about its appearance. You supply the text and supporting elements and leave the formatting to PowerPoint. The resulting presentation consists of a series of slides with a consistent design and color scheme. The presentation can be delivered in a variety of ways, such as a computer slide show, via the Web, or using overhead transparencies. It can also be printed in a variety of formats.

PowerPoint has different views, each with unique capabilities. The Normal view displays the Slide, Outline or Thumbnail images, and Notes Page views in a single window. The Slide Sorter view displays multiple slides on one screen (each slide is in miniature) and lets you see the overall flow of the presentation. The Notes Page view is best suited to printing audience handouts that display the slide and the associated speaker notes. The Slide Show view displays one slide at a time with transition and animation effects.

The outline is the easiest way to enter the text of a presentation. Text is entered continually in the outline, then promoted or demoted so that it appears on the proper level in the slide. The outline can be collapsed to show multiple slides on one screen, thus enabling you to change the order of the slides and/or move text from one slide to another.

PowerPoint provides a set of predefined slide layouts that determine the nature and position of the objects on a slide. Each layout contains one or more placeholders to determine the position of the associated object.

A template is a design specification that controls every aspect of a presentation. It specifies the formatting of the text, the fonts and colors that are used, and the design, size, and placement of the bullets.

Transitions and animations can be added to a presentation for additional interest. Transitions control the way in which one slide moves off the screen and the next slide appears. Animations control the appearance of individual elements on a single slide.

Clip art may be copied, moved, and/or sized to create modified drawings known as Office Art. The Drawing toolbar contains various tools to further enhance the clip art. WordArt is an application within Microsoft Office that creates decorative text.

Objects from other applications such as Excel charts or Word tables may be linked or embedded into a PowerPoint presentation. Linking is a dynamic technique, which means that if the underlying object changes, that change is automatically reflected in the presentation. Embedding, however, is static, and subsequent changes are not reflected in the presentation.

KEY TERMS

Animation (p. 30)
Clip art (p. 33)
Close command (p. 7)
Comments (p. 38)
Drawing toolbar (p. 4)
Embedded object (p. 38)
Exit command (p. 7)
File menu (p. 7)
File name (p. 7)
File type (p. 7)
Formatting toolbar (p. 4)
Insertion point (p. 18)
Linked object (p. 38)

Menu bar (p. 4)
Microsoft Clip Organizer (p. 33)
Microsoft WordArt (p. 40)
Normal view (p. 5)
Notes Page view (p. 5)
Open command (p. 7)
Outline (p. 5)
Outlining toolbar (p. 18)
Placeholders (p. 20)
Places bar (p. 7)
Print Command (p. 7)
Save As command (p. 13)
Save command (p. 7)

Scroll bar (p. 4)
Select-then-do (p. 18)
Slide Layout (p. 20)
Slide Show view (p. 5)
Slide Sorter view (p. 5)
Spell check (p. 14)
Standard toolbar (p. 4)
Status bar (p. 4)
Task pane (p. 5)
Template (p. 21)
Thumbnail image (p. 5)
Transition effects (p. 30)

1. How do you save changes to a PowerPoint presentation?
   (a) Pull down the File menu and click the Save command
   (b) Click the Save button on the Standard toolbar
   (c) Either (a) and (b)
   (d) Neither (a) nor (b)

2. Which of the following can be printed in support of a PowerPoint presentation?
   (a) Audience handouts
   (b) Speaker's notes
   (c) An outline
   (d) All of the above

3. Which menu contains the Undo command?
   (a) File menu
   (b) Edit menu
   (c) Tools menu
   (d) Format menu

4. Ctrl+Home and Ctrl+End are keyboard shortcuts that move to the beginning or end of the presentation in the:
   (a) Outline
   (b) Slide Sorter view
   (c) Either (a) or (b)
   (d) Neither (a) nor (b)

5. The predefined slide formats in PowerPoint are known as:
   (a) View
   (b) Slide layouts
   (c) Audience handouts
   (d) Speaker notes

6. Which menu contains the commands to save the current presentation, or to open a previously saved presentation?
   (a) The Tools menu
   (b) The File menu
   (c) The View menu
   (d) The Edit menu

7. The Open command:
   (a) Brings a presentation from disk into memory
   (b) Brings a presentation from disk into memory, then erases the presentation on disk
   (c) Stores the presentation in memory on disk
   (d) Stores the presentation in memory on disk, then erases the presentation from memory

8. The Save command:
   (a) Brings a presentation from disk into memory
   (b) Brings a presentation from disk into memory, then erases the presentation on disk
   (c) Stores the presentation in memory on disk
   (d) Stores the presentation in memory on disk, then erases the presentation from memory

9. Which of the following can be displayed in the task pane?
   (a) Animation and transition effects
   (b) Design templates and slide layouts
   (c) Both (a) and (b)
   (d) Neither (a) nor (b)

10. Where will the insertion point be after you complete the text for a bullet in the outline and press the enter key?
    (a) On the next bullet at the same level of indentation
    (b) On the next bullet at a higher level of indentation
    (c) On the next bullet at a lower level of indentation
    (d) It is impossible to determine

11. Which of the following is true about an Excel chart that is linked to both a Word document and a PowerPoint presentation?
    (a) The chart cannot be linked to any other presentations or Word documents
    (b) The chart cannot be modified since it is already linked to two documents
    (c) The chart can be modified, but any changes have to be made in two places, once in the Word document and once in the PowerPoint presentation
    (d) Any changes to the chart will be reflected automatically in both the Word document and the PowerPoint presentation.

12. What advantage, if any, is there to collapsing the outline so that only the slide titles are visible?
    (a) More slides are displayed at one time, making it easier to rearrange the slides in the presentation
    (b) Transition and build effects can be added
    (c) Graphic objects become visible
    (d) All of the above

13. Which of the following is true regarding transition and build effects?
    (a) Every slide must have the same transition effect
    (b) Every bullet must have the same build effect
    (c) Both (a) and (b)
    (d) Neither (a) nor (b)

14. Which of the following is true?
    (a) Slides can be added to a presentation after a template has been chosen
    (b) The template can be changed after all of the slides have been created
    (c) Both (a) and (b)
    (d) Neither (a) nor (b)

15. Which of the following can be changed after a slide has been created?
    (a) Its layout and transition effect
    (b) Its position within the presentation
    (c) Both (a) and (b)
    (d) Neither (a) nor (b)

ANSWERS

1. c	**6.** b	**11.** d
2. d	**7.** a	**12.** a
3. b	**8.** c	**13.** d
4. d	**9.** c	**14.** c
5. b	**10.** a	**15.** c

1. Introduction to E-Mail: The presentation in Figure 1.16 is intended to review the basics of e-mail and provide practice with modifying an existing PowerPoint presentation. Open the partially completed presentation in *Chapter 1 Practice 1* within the Exploring PowerPoint folder and do the following:

   a. Modify the title slide to include your name and e-mail address.

   b. Select the fifth slide (Mail Folders). Boldface and italicize the name of each folder on the slide.

   c. Move the last two slides (Obtaining an E-mail Account and Privacy and Terms of Agreement) before the Mail Folders slide.

   d. Apply a suitable template to the completed presentation. Add transition effects as you see fit from one slide to the next.

   e. Print the presentation in multiple ways. Print the title slide as a slide (full page) to serve as a cover page. Print audience handouts for the entire presentation (six per page). Be sure to frame the individual slides. And finally, print the presentation in outline form.

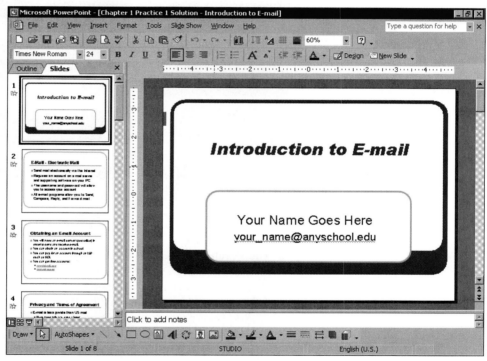

FIGURE 1.16 *Introduction to E-mail (Exercise 1)*

2. Introduction to Windows: The presentation in Figure 1.17 is intended to review the basics of Windows and provide practice with modifying an existing PowerPoint presentation. Open the partially completed presentation in *Chapter 1 Practice 2* within the Exploring PowerPoint folder and do the following:

   a. Add your name to the title page as indicated.

   b. Use the Insert Symbol command to insert the Windows logo ⊞ on the title slide. Click in the title slide at the end of the title to position the insertion point. Pull down the Insert menu, click the Symbol command, and click the Symbols tab if necessary. Select the Wingdings font, scroll until you come to the last character, then press the Insert button. Click and drag to select the newly inserted symbol, and then increase the font size as appropriate.

c. Insert a new slide after slide six (The Devices on a System) that describes the system you have at home or the system you are using at school. Add a final bullet that specifies the version of Windows under which you are running.

d. Apply a suitable template to the completed presentation. Add transition effects as you see fit from one slide to the next.

e. Print the presentation in multiple ways. Print the title slide as a slide (full page) to serve as a cover page. Print audience handouts for the entire presentation (six per page). And finally, print the presentation in outline form.

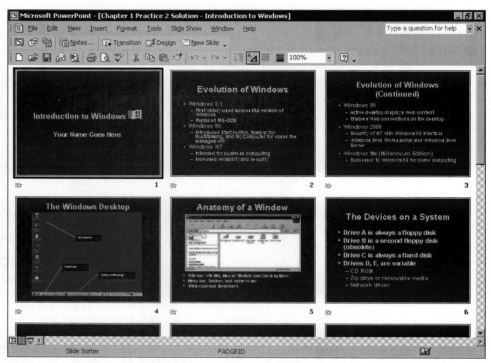

FIGURE 1.17 *Introduction to Windows (Exercise 2)*

3. The Purchase of a PC: The presentation in Figure 1.18 describes considerations in the purchase of a PC and provide practice with modifying an existing PowerPoint presentation. Open the partially completed presentation in *Chapter 1 Practice 3* within the Exploring PowerPoint folder and do the following:

a. Add your name to the title page as indicated.

b. Boldface and italicize the terms byte, kilobyte, megabyte, and gigabyte on the fourth slide.

c. Apply a suitable template to the completed presentation. Add transition effects as you see fit from one slide to the next.

d. Add a two-column bulleted slide at the end of the current presentation that describes your ideal PC in today's environment. Include the specifications for the microprocessor, RAM, fixed disk, and removable mass storage. Include additional information on the monitor, graphics card, speakers, sound card, and any other devices that you will include in the purchase.

e. Add an additional slide (after the two-column bulleted slide) that includes hyperlinks to at least three vendors. (Pull down the Insert menu and click the Hyperlink command to display the Insert Hyperlink dialog box, where you enter the text that is to appear and the associated URL.) The title of this slide should be "Purchasing on the Web".

f. Print the presentation in multiple ways. Print the title slide as a slide (full page) to serve as a cover page. Print audience handouts for the entire presentation (six per page). Finally, print the presentation in outline form.

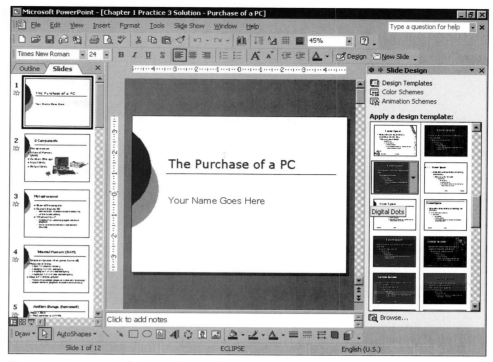

FIGURE 1.18 *The Purchase of a PC (Exercise 3)*

4. Introduction to the Internet: The presentation in Figure 1.19 is intended to review the basics of the Internet and provide practice with modifying an existing PowerPoint presentation. Open the presentation in *Chapter 1 Practice 4* within the Exploring PowerPoint folder and do the following:

   a. Add your name to the title page as indicated.

   b. Boldface and italicize the four acronyms on the fifth slide.

   c. Delete the clip art on the "Connecting to the Internet" slide. Change the layout of this slide to a two-column bulleted slide, and then describe your Internet connection(s) in the second column.

   d. Add a bulleted slide after the slide on "URL Format" that lists five specific Web sites. The first bullet should reference your school or professor. The second bullet should reference the Exploring Windows Web site. Each bullet should name the site followed by its URL—for example, The Exploring Windows Web site at www.prenhall.com/grauer.

   e. Apply a suitable template to the completed presentation. Add transition effects as you see fit from one slide to the next.

   f. Print the presentation in multiple ways. Print the title slide as a slide (full page) to serve as a cover page. Print audience handouts for the entire presentation (six per page). Be sure to frame the individual slides. And finally, print the presentation in outline form.

   g. Go through the presentation one slide at a time to learn and/or review the material. Did you learn anything new? What additional material (if any) would you include in the presentation? Summarize your thoughts in a brief note to your instructor.

   h. Use the Help command to learn how to save a presentation as a Web page for display within an Internet browser. Print one or two Help screens for your instructor to show you understand the procedure.

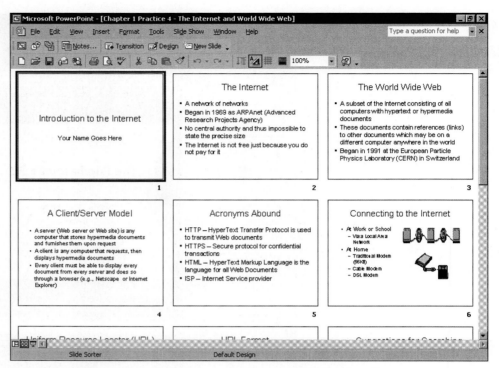

FIGURE 1.19 *Introduction to the Internet (Exercise 4)*

5. Theme Park Admissions: The presentation in Figure 1.20 is based on the Excel workbook in the file *Chapter 1 Practice 5* within the Exploring PowerPoint folder. The workbook contains two worksheets, one with tabular data, and one with a side-by-side column chart. The presentation should contain a title slide with your name (not visible in the figure), the Admissions Summary slide, a slide containing the side-by-side column chart, and a concluding slide that contains a congratulatory message. The tabular data and chart should be linked to the underlying workbook. Print the completed presentation as audience handouts, two slides per page, for your instructor.

6. My Favorite Presidents: Create a presentation similar to the one in Figure 1.21. The presentation consists of three slides—a title slide and two slides containing text and a photograph that was downloaded from the Internet. The title slide includes your name and a reference to the White House Web site (www. whitehouse.gov) as the source of your photographs.

  a. Start Internet Explorer and go to the White House Web site. Click the link to White House History and then click the link to the Presidents of the United States. Select a president, point to the picture of the president, click the right mouse button to display a shortcut menu and save the picture. Be sure you remember the location of the file when you save it on your local machine.

  b. Switch to PowerPoint. Insert a new slide and select the Text layout. Click in the title area of this slide and add the president's name and years in office. Click in the text area and press the backspace key to delete the bullet that appears automatically, then enter the text describing this president.

  c. Click and drag the sizing handles that surround the text to make the box narrower in order to allow room for the president's picture. Click outside the text area. Pull down the Insert menu, click the Picture command, then click From File to display the Insert Picture dialog box. Select the folder where you saved the file in step (a). Select the picture, then click the Insert button to insert the picture onto the slide. Move and size the picture as appropriate.

  d. Repeat these steps for a second president. Print all three slides and submit them to your instructor as proof you did this exercise.

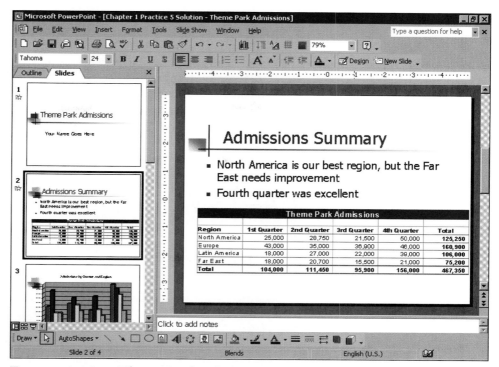

FIGURE 1.20   *Theme Park Admissions (Exercise 5)*

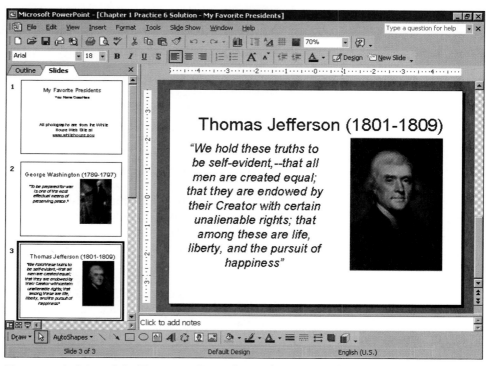

FIGURE 1.21   *My Favorite Presidents (Exercise 6)*

7. **Your Favorite Performer:** The subject of a PowerPoint presentation is limited only by your imagination. Use any Internet search engine to locate information about your favorite singer or recording group, then download information about that person or group to create a presentation such as the one in Figure 1.22. Use the technique described in the previous problem to download a picture and insert the picture into the presentation.

Print the presentation in multiple ways. Print the title slide as a full slide to serve as a cover page. Print the entire presentation as audience handouts, six per page. (Frame the slides.) Print the entire presentation as an outline.

FIGURE 1.22 *Your Favorite Performer (Exercise 7)*

8. **You Don't Have to Be an Artist:** Figure 1.23 further illustrates how you can modify existing clip art to create entirely different images. The Duck and the Computer were available in previous versions of Microsoft Office, but were removed from the Office XP version. The image is, however, available to you in the partially completed presentation that is found in *Chapter 1 Exercise 8.* Open the presentation, add a title slide, then modify the clip art as shown in Figure 1.23.

   a. The key to the exercise is to use various tools on the Drawing toolbar. Select the original clip art, click the down arrow on the Draw button, then click the Ungroup command. Click Yes to convert the picture to a Microsoft Office Drawing Object.

   b. There are now two sets of sizing handles, one around the duck, and one around the computer and table. Click in the background area of the slide to deselect both objects.

   c. Click on the duck and experiment with the various tools to flip the image horizontally or vertically. Add a title to the slide.

   d. Copy the modified slide several times, then use the appropriate tools on the Drawing toolbar to create the presentation in Figure 1.23. Add your name to the first slide, then print the completed presentation, in the form of audience handouts (six per page), for your instructor.

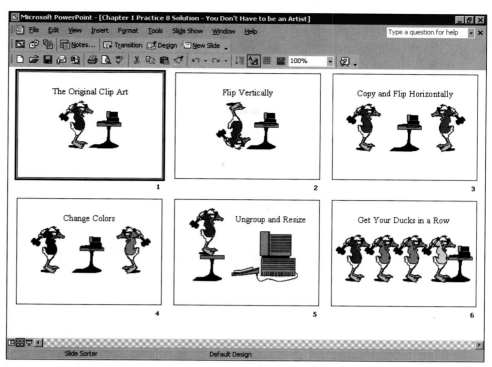

FIGURE 1.23 *You Don't Have to Be an Artist (Exercise 8)*

BUILDS ON

HANDS-ON
EXERCISE 4
PAGES 41–51

9. Exploring AutoShapes: Figure 1.24 displays a single slide containing a variety of AutoShapes. Open the presentation created in the fourth hands-on exercise.
   a. Add a blank slide immediately before the last slide.
   b. Click the AutoShapes tool on the Drawing toolbar to display the AutoShapes toolbar. Click and drag the top of the menu to make it a floating toolbar.
   c. Point to an AutoShape, then click and drag in the slide to create the shape on the slide. (You can press and hold the Shift key as you drag for special effects; for example, press and hold the Shift key as you drag the ellipse or rectangle tool to draw a circle or square, respectively. You can also use the Shift key in conjunction with the Line tool to draw a perfectly horizontal or vertical line, or a line at a 45-degree angle.)
   d. To place text inside a shape, select the shape and start typing.
   e. To change the fill color or line thickness, select the shape, then click the appropriate button on the Drawing toolbar.
   f. Use these techniques to duplicate Figure 1.24, or better yet, create your own design. Add your name to the completed slide.

10. Export an Outline to Word: The Send To command enables you to export a presentation to Microsoft Word as shown in Figure 1.25. You can send just the outline. You can also send slide miniatures to display several slides on one page with notes for each.
   a. Choose any presentation that you have created in this chapter.
   b. Pull down the File menu, click the Send To command, and choose Microsoft Word to display the Send to Microsoft Word dialog box. Click the option button to send the Outline only.
   c. Change to the Outline view in Microsoft Word and print the outline.
   d. Return to PowerPoint, click the Send To command, choose Microsoft Word, and choose the option to send Notes next to slides.
   e. Change to the Page Layout view in Word. Click in the cell next to each slide (the Word document is a table) and enter an appropriate comment.
   f. Submit the finished document to your instructor.

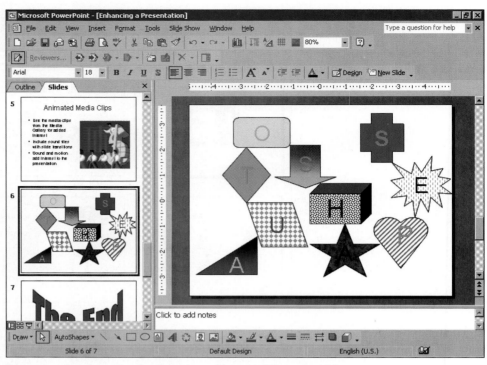

FIGURE 1.24   *Exploring AutoShapes (Exercise 9)*

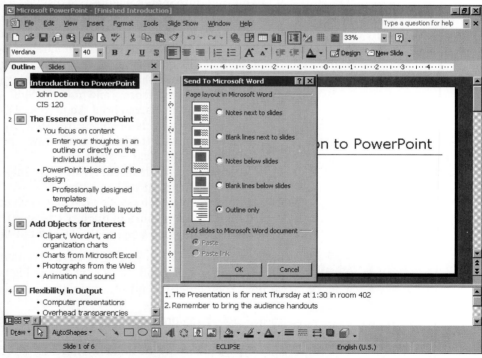

FIGURE 1.25   *Export an Outline to Word (Exercise 10)*

11. Create a New Folder: Open any presentation, pull down the File menu, and click the Save As command to display the dialog box in Figure 1.26a. Change to the Exploring PowerPoint folder, click the New Folder button, then create a new folder within this folder. Save the presentation in this folder, then close the presentation. Now click the Open button and reopen the presentation from the new folder as shown in Figure 1.26b. Creating additional folders in this fashion is very useful as you work with a large number of documents.

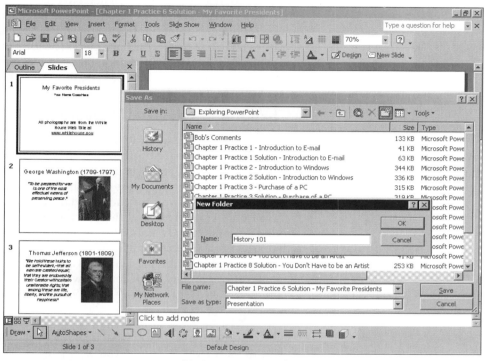

(a) Create a New Folder

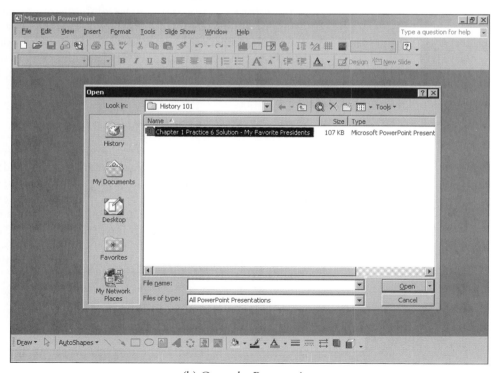

(b) Open the Presentation

FIGURE 1.26 *Create a New Folder (Exercise 11)*

Planning for Disaster

This case has nothing to do with presentations per se, but it is perhaps the most important case of all, as it deals with the question of backup. Do you have a backup strategy? Do you even know what a backup strategy is? This is a good time to learn, because sooner or later you will need to recover a file. The problem always seems to occur the night before an assignment is due. You accidentally erased a file, are unable to read from a floppy disk, or worse yet, suffer a hardware failure in which you are unable to access the hard drive. The ultimate disaster is the disappearance of your computer, by theft or natural disaster. Describe in 250 words or less the backup strategy you plan to implement in conjunction with your work in this class.

Changing Menus and Toolbars

Office XP lets you switch to a series of short menus that contain only basic commands. The additional commands are made visible by clicking the double arrow that appears at the bottom of the menu. New commands are added to the menu as they are used, and conversely, other commands are removed if they are not used. A similar strategy is followed for the Standard and Formatting toolbars, which are displayed on a single row, and thus do not show all of the buttons at one time. The intent is to simplify Office XP for the new user by limiting the number of commands that are visible. The consequence, however, is that the individual is not exposed to new commands, and hence may not use Office to its full potential. Which set of menus do you prefer? How do you switch from one set to the other?

Be Creative

One interesting way of exploring the potential of presentation graphics is to imagine it might have been used by historical figures had it been available. Choose any historical figure or current personality and create at least a six-slide presentation. You could, for example, show how Columbus might have used PowerPoint to request funding from Queen Isabella, or how Elvis Presley might have pleaded for his first recording contract. The content of your presentation should be reasonable, but you don't have to spend an inordinate amount of time on research. Just be creative and use your imagination. Use clip art as appropriate, but don't overdo it. Place your name on the title slide as technical adviser.

The National Debt

The deficit is gone, but the national debt is staggering—more than $5 trillion, or approximately $20,000 for every man, woman, and child in the United States. The annual budget is approximately $2 trillion. Use the Internet to obtain exact figures for the current year, then use this information to create a presentation on income and expenditures. Do some additional research and obtain data on the budget, the deficit, and the national debt for the years 1945, 1967, and 1980. The numbers may surprise you. For example, how does the interest expense for the current year compare to the total budget in 1967 (at the height of the Viet Nam War)? To the total budget in 1945 (at the end of World War II)?

CHAPTER 2

Gaining Proficiency: Slide Show Tools, the Web, and Slide Masters

OBJECTIVES

AFTER READING THIS CHAPTER YOU WILL BE ABLE TO:

1. Describe the Meeting Minder, Slide Navigator, and Pen; explain how these tools are used to enhance a presentation.
2. Add a table to a PowerPoint slide.
3. Add headers and footers to slides and/or audience handouts.
4. Import a Word outline as the basis of a PowerPoint presentation; export a PowerPoint presentation as a Word document.
5. Use the Rehearse Timings feature to time a presentation; create a hidden slide and explain the rationale for its use.
6. Create a presentation using the AutoContent Wizard; modify the template of an existing presentation by changing its color scheme and/or background shading.
7. Describe how the Internet and World Wide Web are integrated into Office XP; download a photograph from the Web and include it in a presentation.
8. Insert a hyperlink into a PowerPoint presentation; save a PowerPoint presentation as a Web document, then view that document in Internet Explorer.
9. Explain the role of masters in formatting a presentation; modify the slide master to include a company name.
10. Send a presentation for review; accept changes from multiple reviewers.

OVERVIEW

PowerPoint is a powerful, yet easy-to-use, application that helps you to create an attractive presentation. The delivery, however, is up to you. Many people are intimidated at the prospect of facing an audience, but you can become an effective speaker by following the basic tenets of good public speaking. You can also take advantage of the various slide show tools that are included in PowerPoint. The chapter begins, therefore, by describing different ways in which PowerPoint can help you to enhance the delivery of your presentation. It also explains how to send a presentation for review and how to incorporate the reviewers' comments electronically when they are returned.

Another way to increase the effectiveness of a presentation is to download resources from the Web in order to make your content more interesting. You might also want to save a presentation as a Web page in order to upload it to a Web server, where it can be viewed by anyone with Internet access. Both topics are covered in detail.

The last part of the chapter describes how PowerPoint can help you to develop the actual content of a presentation through the AutoContent Wizard. The resulting presentations are of a general nature, but they provide an excellent beginning. We also describe how to import an outline from Microsoft Word, and use it as the basis of a presentation. Lastly, we explain how to fine-tune a presentation through changes in its color scheme, background shading, or slide master. All told, this is a comprehensive chapter that will increase your proficiency in many ways.

SLIDE SHOW TOOLS

PowerPoint provides a series of slide show tools to help you deliver a presentation effectively. The tools are discussed briefly in conjunction with the presentation in Figure 2.1, and then described in detail in a hands-on exercise. The text on the second slide is worthy of special mention as it was entered into a table, as an alternative to the standard bulleted text slide. The table was created through the ***Insert Table command*** to provide variety within a presentation.

Look carefully under each slide and you will see a number that represents the amount of time the presenter intends to devote to the slide. The timings were entered through the ***Rehearse Timings*** feature that lets you time a presentation as you practice your delivery. The Rehearse Timings feature can also be used with the ***Set Up Show command*** to automate a presentation so that each slide will be shown for the set time period.

The icon under slide number 4 indicates that it is a ***hidden slide***, which prevents the slide from appearing during a regular slide show. This is a common practice among experienced speakers who anticipate probing questions that may arise during the presentation. The presenter prefers not to address the topic initially, but creates a slide to hold in reserve should the topic arise. The hidden slide can be displayed through the ***Slide Navigator***, a tool that enables the presenter to go directly to any slide within the presentation.

Figure 2.1b displays an ***Action Items slide*** that was created dynamically during the presentation using a tool known as the Meeting Minder. (The slide was not in the original presentation and is not in Figure 2.1a.) The ***Meeting Minder*** enables you to keep track of questions or other issues that occur during a presentation, and to summarize them at the end of the presentation. Figure 2.1b also illustrates the ability to annotate any slide using the mouse to draw on the slide (just like your favorite football announcer). This was accomplished by changing the mouse pointer from an arrow to a pen. The annotations are temporary and disappear as soon as you move to the next slide.

The text at the bottom of the slide in Figure 2.1b was entered through the ***Header and Footer command***, which places the identical text at the bottom of every slide in the presentation. (You can see the footer on the other slides by looking at the Slide Show view in Figure 2.1a.) The inclusion of a header or footer personalizes a presentation by adding items such as the date, place of the presentation, and/or the slide number.

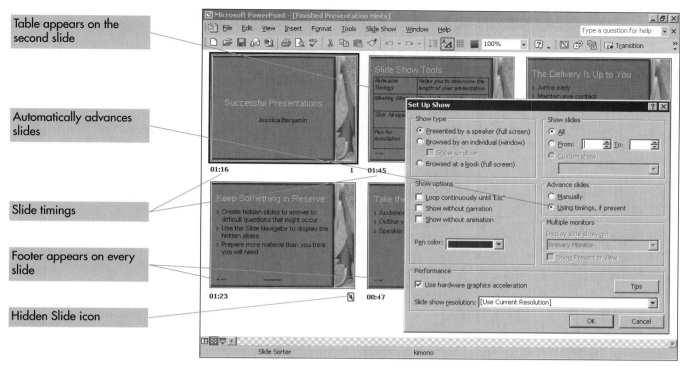

Table appears on the second slide

Automatically advances slides

Slide timings

Footer appears on every slide

Hidden Slide icon

(a) Timings and Hidden Slides

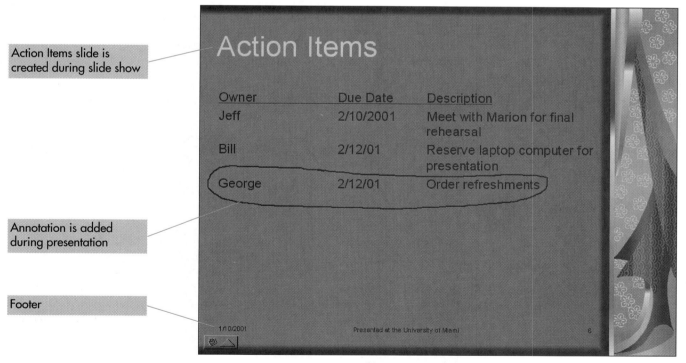

Action Items slide is created during slide show

Annotation is added during presentation

Footer

(b) Action Items and the Pen

FIGURE 2.1   *Slide Show Tools*

The American workplace is team oriented, with many people typically collaborating on the same document. Microsoft Office XP facilitates this process by enabling the revisions to be stored and accepted (or rejected) electronically. In PowerPoint, the process works as follows. You create the initial presentation, then use the ***Send To command*** to send the presentation to one or more people for review. PowerPoint automatically links to your e-mail program and sends the presentation as an attachment.

Each reviewer receives a copy of the presentation, enters his or her changes, then returns the revised presentation as an attachment in an e-mail message. You save each reviewer's attachment as its own file (such as Bob's Comments), then you open all of the reviewers' presentations to merge the comments with the original presentation. You can then merge the comments from multiple reviewers in a single session.

Figure 2.2 shows the suggested changes to the first slide in the selected presentation. The ***revisions pane*** at the right shows how the title slide would look according to the changes for each reviewer. Robert Grauer changes the title to "Successful Presentations", but retains the current template. Maryann Barber, on the other hand, retains the title, but modifies the template. You can accept either or both changes by checking the box next to each reviewer's name in the revisions pane. You can expand any proposed changes in text (such as Bob's change in title) in their own balloon and accept or reject the suggestions individually. You can also use the Undo command to cancel your changes.

The developer of the presentation goes from one slide to the next, accepting or rejecting the changes, as he or she sees fit. The ***Reviewing toolbar*** contains several buttons to aid in this process, such as the Next and Previous Item buttons to move from one revision to the next. The toolbar also provides buttons to insert, edit, or delete comments. The reviewer ends the review, which in turn closes the revisions pane and removes the reviewers' presentations from memory. You can then send the revised presentation as an e-mail attachment.

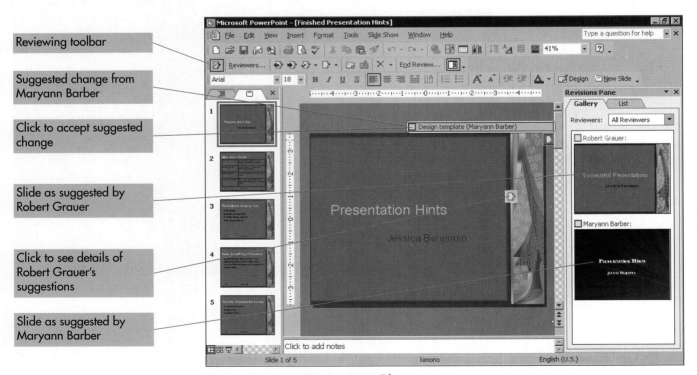

FIGURE 2.2 *Reviewing Changes*

SLIDE SHOW TOOLS

Objective To use the Rehearse Timings feature to practice your delivery; to use the Slide Navigator, pen, and Meeting Minder during a presentation. Use Figure 2.3 as a guide in the exercise.

Step 1: **Create the Table**

➤ Start PowerPoint. Click and drag the Office Assistant out of the way, or close it altogether. Open **Presentation Hints** in the **Exploring PowerPoint folder**. Click on the placeholder for the subtitle and add your name to the title slide.

➤ Pull down the **File menu**, click the **Save As command** to display the File Save dialog box, then save the presentation as **Finished Presentation Hints**.

➤ Pull down the **Insert menu** and click the **New Slide command** (or click the **New Slide button** on the Formatting toolbar). The task pane opens as shown in Figure 2.3a with a text slide selected by default.

➤ Click the **Title Only layout** to change the layout of the new slide. Click in the Title placeholder and enter the title **Slide Show Tools** as shown in the figure.

➤ Click outside the title placeholder. Pull down the **Insert menu** and click the **Table command** to display the Insert Table dialog box in Figure 2.3a.

➤ Enter **2** as the number of columns and **4** as the number of rows. Click **OK**. The table will be inserted into the document.

➤ Close the task pane. Save the presentation.

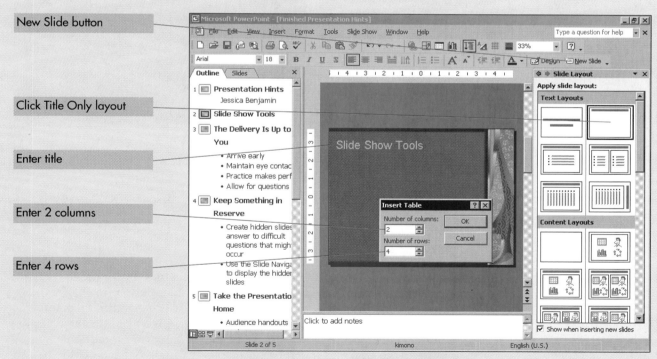

(a) Create the Table (step 1)

FIGURE 2.3 *Hands-on Exercise 1*

Step 2:   **Complete the Table**

➤ Click anywhere in the table to select the table and display a hashed border.
➤ Click and drag the vertical line dividing the two columns to the left so that the first column is narrower and the second column is wider. Drag the left and/or right border to make the table larger or smaller as necessary.
➤ Enter the text into the table as shown in Figure 2.3b. Text is entered into each cell independently of the other cells.
➤ Click in a cell, type the appropriate text, then press the **Tab key** to move to the next cell. Complete the table as shown in the figure.
➤ Click and drag to select multiple cells simultaneously, then use the various buttons on the Formatting toolbar to format the text in these cells as you see fit. Click outside the table to deselect it.
➤ Save the presentation.

Click drop-down arrow to change font size

Italic button

Enter text

Click and drag to change column width

Tables and Borders toolbar

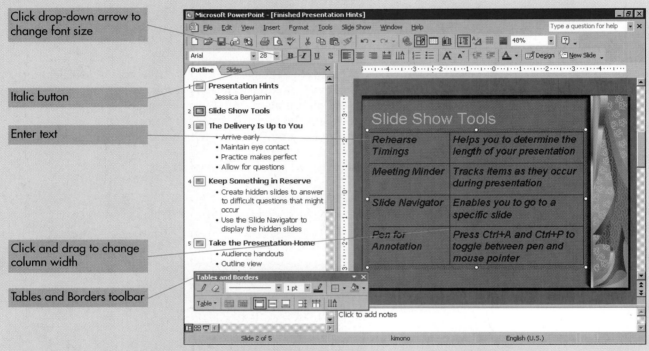

(b) Complete the Table (step 2)

FIGURE 2.3   *Hands-on Exercise 1 (continued)*

THE TABLE AND BORDERS TOOLBAR

The Tables and Borders toolbar contains a variety of tools for use in creating and/or modifying a table. Click the Border Color button (to change the color) or click the Border Width down arrow (to change the thickness), then use the mouse (the pointer changes to a pencil) to paint the table borders according to the new settings. Click the down arrow on the Table button to see the commands that are available. If you do not see the toolbar, pull down the View menu, click (or point to) the Toolbars command, then click the Table and Borders toolbar.

Step 3:   **Add the Slide Footer**

➤ Pull down the **View menu** and click the **Header and Footer command** to display the Header and Footer dialog box in Figure 2.3c.
➤ Click the **Slide tab**. Click the check box for the Date and Time, then click the **Option button** to update the date automatically. The presentation will always show the current date when this option is in effect. (Alternatively, you can clear the check box to enter a fixed date.)
➤ Check the Slide Number and Footer check boxes as shown. Click in the text box associated with the footer and enter the appropriate text to reflect your school or university.
➤ Check the box, **Don't show on title slide**, to suppress the footer on the first slide. Click the **Apply to All button** to accept these settings and close the Header and Footer dialog box.
➤ Save the presentation.

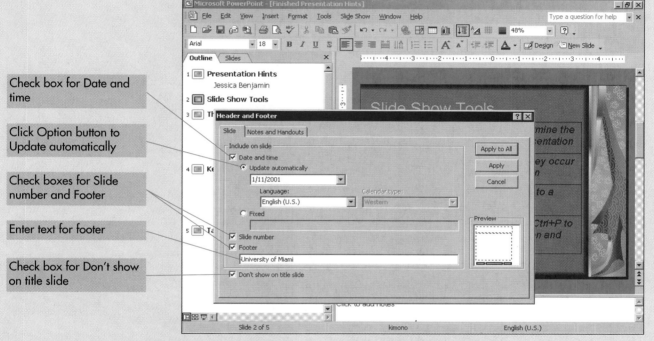

Check box for Date and time

Click Option button to Update automatically

Check boxes for Slide number and Footer

Enter text for footer

Check box for Don't show on title slide

(c) Add the Slide Footer (step 3)

FIGURE 2.3   *Hands-on Exercise 1 (continued)*

CUSTOMIZE THE TABLE LAYOUT

Click and drag to select one or more cells within a table, then pull down the Format menu and click the Tables command to display the Format Table dialog box. You can change the border, fill, or text alignment by clicking the appropriate tab within the dialog box, then executing the appropriate command. Click the Undo command if the result is different from what you intended. You might also want to set a time limit, because there are almost too many options from which to choose.

Step 4: **Send for Review**

➤ Pull down the **File menu**, click (or point to) the **Send To command**, then choose **Mail Recipient (for Review)**. Your e-mail program will open automatically and display a new message as shown in Figure 2.3d. (Skip this step if your e-mail program does not appear, as might happen in a computer lab.)

➤ The subject, attachment, and text of the note are entered automatically for you. The name of the current presentation, "Finished Presentation Hints," appears in both the subject line and the attachment.

➤ Enter the name of a recipient (e.g., a fellow student). You can enter the names of multiple individuals if you want more than one person to review the presentation. Sign your name in the message area and click the **Send button**.

➤ Normally, you would need the reviewer to return the presentation to you with his or her comments.

➤ We have, however, supplied a presentation for you with comments from our reviewer, so that you do not have to wait for a response.

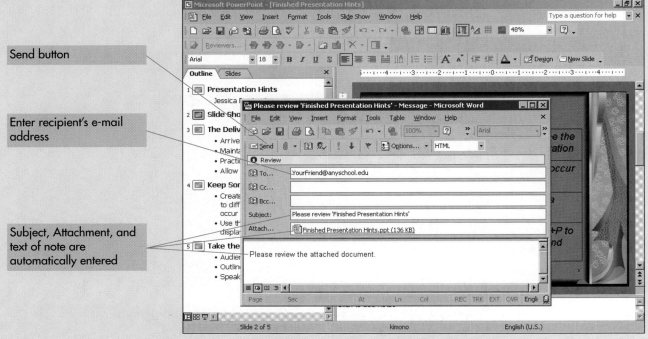

Send button

Enter recipient's e-mail address

Subject, Attachment, and text of note are automatically entered

(d) Send for Review (step 4)

FIGURE 2.3 *Hands-on Exercise 1 (continued)*

SEND THE PRESENTATION AS AN ATTACHMENT

Send the completed presentation as an attachment, as opposed to sending it for review. Pull down the File menu, click the Send To command, then choose the second option to send the open presentation as an attachment to an e-mail message. This is an option with which you are probably familiar and is similar in concept to mailing a Word document or Excel workbook. (PowerPoint presentations are generally large files, and thus you may want to compress the file before sending it.)

Step 5: **Compare and Merge Presentations**

➤ Pull down the **Tools menu** and click the **Compare and Merge Presentations command**. Locate the **Bob's Comments** presentation (which represents a review of your presentation) in the Exploring PowerPoint folder. Click the **Merge button**.

➤ The Revisions Pane opens as shown in Figure 2.3e. If necessary, click the **Outline** and **Gallery tabs** in the left and right panes, respectively.

➤ Click the icon to the right of the title slide to see suggestions from the reviewer (Bob, in this example). Check the box to accept all changes to the title slide.

➤ Click the **Next Item button** on the Reviewing toolbar to move to the next revision. This takes you to the third slide, title "The Delivery is Up to You". Check the box to accept all changes on this slide.

➤ Continue to click the **Next Item button** and accept all suggested changes until you reach the last slide. PowerPoint indicates that you have reached the end of the presentation and asks if you want to continue. Click **Cancel** since you have reviewed all of the changes.

➤ Click the **End Review button** on the Reviewing toolbar. Click **Yes** when asked whether to end the review and close the Revisions Pane. Save the presentation.

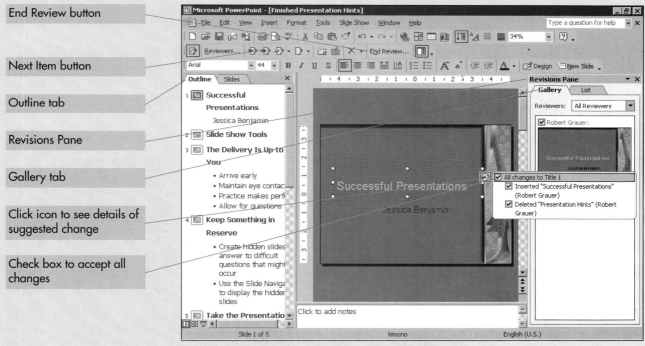

(e) Compare and Merge Presentations (step 5)

FIGURE 2.3   *Hands-on Exercise 1 (continued)*

INSERT COMMENTS INTO THE PRESENTATION

Pull down the Insert menu and click the Comments command (or click the Insert Comments button on the Reviewing toolbar) to insert a comment. The comments are for information only and do not change the actual presentation. Click the Comments and Changes button on the Reviewing toolbar to toggle the comment (and reviewer remarks) on and off.

Step 6: **Rehearse the Presentation**

➤ Press **Ctrl+Home** to return to the first slide. Pull down the **Slide Show menu** and click the **Rehearse Timings command**.

➤ The first slide appears in the Slide Show view. The Rehearsal toolbar is displayed in the upper-left corner of the screen. Speak as though you were presenting the slide, then click the mouse to register the elapsed time for that slide and move to the next slide.

➤ The second slide in the presentation should appear as shown in Figure 2.3f. Speak as though you were presenting the slide and, as you do, watch the Rehearsal toolbar:

- The time for the specific slide (1 minute and 45 seconds) is displayed in the Slide Time box. The cumulative time for the presentation (3 minutes and 01 second) is also shown.
- Click the **Repeat button** to redo the timing for the slide.
- Click the **Pause button** to (temporarily) stop the clock. Click the **Pause button** a second time to resume the clock.
- Click the **Next button** to record the timing and move to the next slide.

➤ Continue rehearsing the show until you reach the end of the presentation. You should see a dialog box at the end of the presentation that indicates the total time of the slide show.

➤ Click **Yes** when asked whether you want to record the new timings. PowerPoint returns to the Slide Sorter view and records the timings under each slide.

➤ Pull down the **Slide Show menu** and click the **Set Up Show command** to display the Set Up Show dialog box.

➤ Check the option button to advance slides **Manually** (otherwise the slides will be automatically advanced according to the times you just recorded). Click **OK** to accept the settings and close the dialog box.

➤ Save the presentation.

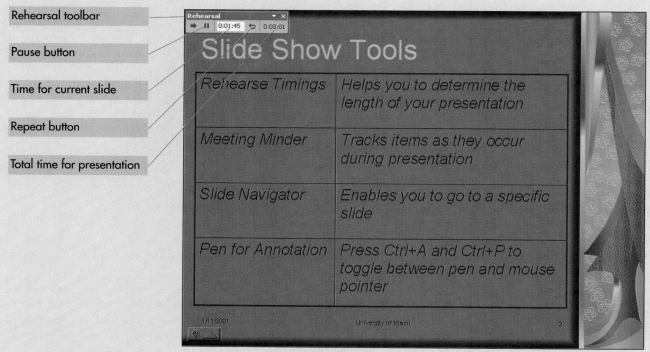

(f) Rehearse the Presentation (step 6)

FIGURE 2.3   *Hands-on Exercise 1 (continued)*

Step 7: **Hide a Slide**

➤ If necessary, click the **down arrow** on the Zoom Control box to zoom to 100%. The slides are larger and easier to read.
➤ Select (click) the fourth slide (Keep Something in Reserve) then click the **Hide Slide button** as shown in Figure 2.3g. The slide remains in the presentation, but it will *not* be displayed during the slide show.
➤ The Hide Slide button functions as a toggle switch. Click it once and the slide is hidden. Click the command a second time and the slide is no longer hidden. Leave the slide hidden.
➤ Click Slide 1, then click the **Slide Show view button** and move quickly through the presentation. You will not see the slide titled Keep Something in Reserve because it has been hidden. (You can still access this slide through the Slide Navigator, as described in step 9.)
➤ Save the presentation.

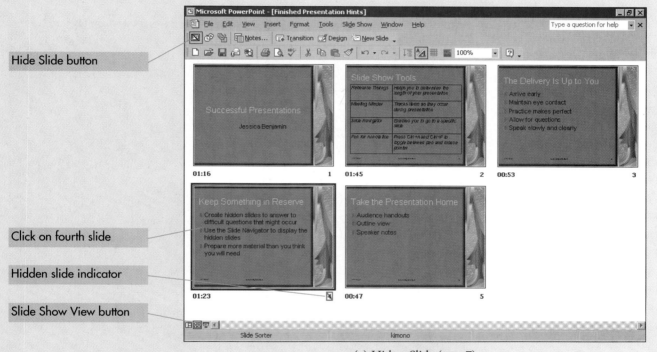

(g) Hide a Slide (step 7)

FIGURE 2.3   *Hands-on Exercise 1 (continued)*

PACK AND GO

Are you positive that PowerPoint is installed on the computer you will use to deliver your presentation? If not, you need to pack up your presentation, together with the PowerPoint Viewer, so that you will be able to present it on another computer, even one without PowerPoint. Pull down the File menu, click the Pack and Go command to start the Wizard, then follow the onscreen instructions. The Wizard packs all of the files and fonts that are used in your presentation into a single file, then saves the file on a floppy disk or network drive. Unpack your presentation on the other end and enjoy the show. See practice exercise 9 at the end of the chapter.

Step 8: **The Meeting Minder**

➤ You should still be on slide one. Click the **Slide Show View button** above the Status bar to show the presentation.

➤ You should see the title slide with your name as shown in Figure 2.3h. Point anywhere on the slide, and click the **right mouse button** to display a shortcut menu containing the various slide show tools.

➤ Click **Meeting Minder** to display the Meeting Minder dialog box, then click the **Action Items tab** as shown in Figure 2.3h.

➤ Click in the Description text box and enter **Meet with Marion for final rehearsal**. Click in the Assigned To: text box and enter **Jeff**. Click **Add**. Enter the second and third items in similar fashion. Click **OK**.

➤ Click the mouse button to move from one slide to the next (you can enter an action item from any slide) until you reach the end of the presentation (the slide titled Action Items).

➤ A new slide has been created containing the action items you just supplied.

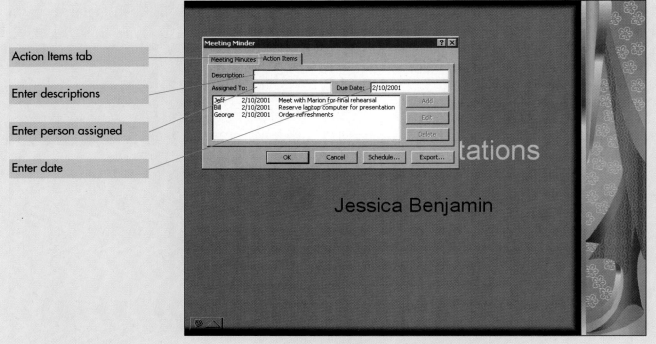

(h) The Meeting Minder (step 8)

FIGURE 2.3 *Hands-on Exercise 1 (continued)*

EMBED TRUETYPE FONTS

Have you ever created a presentation on one computer, then tried to show it on another, and noticed that the fonts had changed? It's an easy problem to avoid—all you have to do is take the fonts with you. Pull down the File menu, click the Save As command, click the Tools button, click Save Options, then check the Embed TrueType Fonts check box. Your presentation will increase slightly in size, but your fonts will be the same on every computer. See practice exercise 8 at the end of the chapter.

Step 9:   **The Slide Navigator**

➤ You should be positioned on the last slide (Action Items). Click the action button at the lower left of the slide or right click anywhere on the slide. Either way, you should see a menu with various commands that pertain to slide show options.

➤ Select (click) the **Go command**, then click **Slide Navigator** to display the Slide Navigator dialog box as shown in Figure 2.3i.

➤ The titles of all slides (including the hidden slide) are displayed in the Slide Navigator dialog box. The number of the hidden slide, however, is enclosed in parentheses to indicate it is a hidden slide.

➤ Select the hidden slide and click the **Go To button** (or double click the slide) to display this slide on the screen. The Slide Navigator is the only way to display a hidden slide.

➤ Hidden slides are very useful to keep something in reserve. See practice exercise 5 at the end of the chapter.

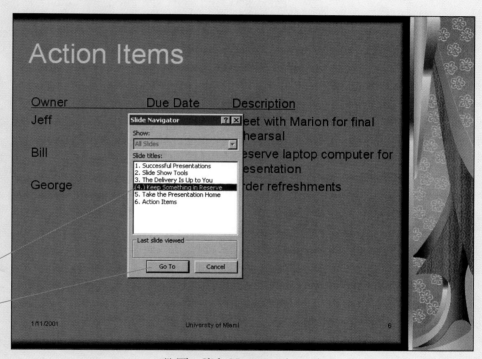

(i) The Slide Navigator (step 9)

FIGURE 2.3   *Hands-on Exercise 1 (continued)*

SETTING UP A SLIDE SHOW

You can start a slide show on any slide, advance the slides automatically according to preset timings (established through the Rehearse Timings commands), and/or loop through the slide show continually until the user presses the Esc key. Pull down the Slide Show menu, click the Set Up Show command to display the associated dialog box, then experiment with the various options. Click OK to accept the settings and close the dialog box.

Step 10: **Annotate a Slide**

➤ You should see the slide in Figure 2.3j. Click the **right mouse button** to display the shortcut menu, click **Pointer Options**, then click **Pen** from the submenu. The mouse pointer changes from an arrow to a pencil.

➤ Click and drag on the slide to annotate the slide as shown in Figure 2.3j. The annotation is temporary and will be visible only on this slide.

➤ Press **N** (or the **PgDn key**) to move to the next slide, then press **P** (or the **PgUp key**) to return to the previous slide. The annotation is gone.

➤ Press the **PgDn key** continually to move through the remaining slides. You can also click the **right mouse button** to display the shortcut menu, then click **End Show** to end the presentation.

➤ Pull down the **File menu**. Click **Print** to display the Print dialog box. Click the **drop-down arrow** in the **Print What** drop-down list box. Click **Handouts** (6 slides per page). Check the boxes to **Frame Slides** and **Print Hidden Slides**.

➤ Check that the **All option button** is selected under Print Range. You will print every slide in the presentation, including the hidden slide and the slide containing the action items. Click **OK**.

➤ Save the presentation. Exit PowerPoint if you do not want to continue with the next exercise at this time.

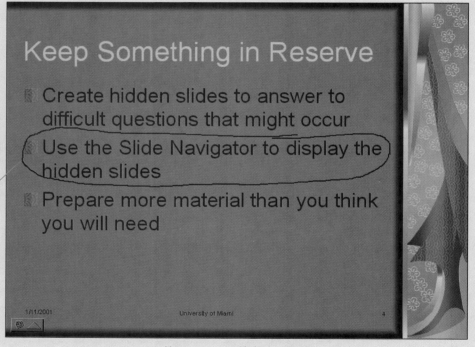

(j) Annotate a Slide (step 10)

FIGURE 2.3 *Hands-on Exercise 1 (continued)*

THE PEN AND THE ARROW

Press Ctrl+P or Ctrl+A at any time to change to the pencil or arrow, respectively. You can also change the color of the pen. Right click any slide to display a context-sensitive menu, click Pointer Options, then choose Pen Color.

The *Internet* and *World Wide Web* are thoroughly integrated into all applications in Microsoft Office in three important ways. First, you can download resources from any Web page for inclusion in a PowerPoint presentation, as you will see in our next hands-on exercise. Second, you can insert hyperlinks into any Office document, then click those links to display the associated Web page in your Web browser. And finally, you can convert any Office document into a Web page for display on your Web server or local area network.

Figure 2.4 illustrates how resources from the Internet can be used to enhance a PowerPoint presentation. The title slide in Figure 2.4a displays a photograph that was downloaded from the Smithsonian Institution's collection of online photographs. The photograph is displayed as an object on a slide and is typical of how most people use a photograph within a presentation. The slide in Figure 2.4b is much more dramatic, and indeed does not even look like a PowerPoint slide. It too displays a photograph, but as background, rather than an object. The text has been entered into a *text box* using the appropriate tool on the Drawing toolbar. (You can right click the text box after it has been created, so that the box will expand and wrap text automatically if additional text is entered.)

Regardless of how you choose to use a photograph, your first task is to access the Web and locate the resource. Thus, you start your Web browser, then you use a search engine to locate the required information (e.g., a photograph of a dinosaur). Once this is done, right click on the photograph to display the context-sensitive menu in the figure, then click the Save Picture As command to download the file to your hard drive. Next, you start PowerPoint where you use the *Insert Picture command* to insert the picture that was just downloaded into a presentation. You can also use the *Insert Hyperlink command* to insert a *hyperlink* onto a slide, which you can click during the slide show, and provided you have an Internet connection, your Web browser will display the associated page.

Copyright Protection

A *copyright* provides legal protection to a written or artistic work, giving the author exclusive rights to its use and reproduction, except as governed under the fair use exclusion. Anything on the Internet should be considered copyrighted unless the document specifically says it is in the *public domain*, in which case the author has relinquished his or her copyright.

Does this mean you cannot use statistics and other facts that you find while browsing the Web? Does it mean you cannot download an image to include in a report? The answer to both questions depends on the amount of the material and on your intended use of the information. It is considered *fair use*, and thus not an infringement of copyright, to use a portion of the work for educational, nonprofit purposes, or for the purpose of critical review or commentary. In other words, you can use a quote, downloaded image, or other information from the Web, provided you cite the original work in your footnotes and/or bibliography. Facts themselves are not covered by copyright, but be sure to cite the original source.

POWERPOINT AND WORD

It's easy to develop the text of your presentation entirely within PowerPoint. On the other hand, you may have already outlined the presentation in Microsoft Word, in which case you can import that outline into PowerPoint, then create a presentation based on the imported outline. Conversely, you can export a PowerPoint presentation to Word as an outline.

Photograph inserted as an object

Text box

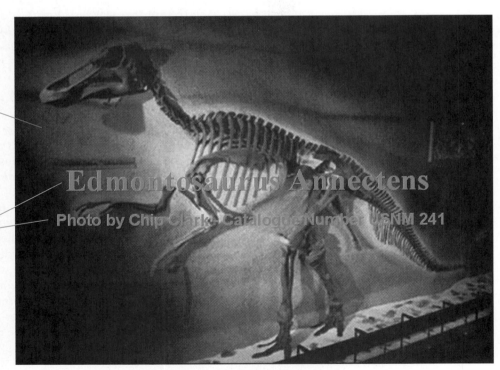

The Smithsonian National Museum of Natural History

Photo by Chip Clark — Catalogue number USNM 2580

(a) Title Slide

Photograph used as slide background

Text box

Edmontosaurus Annectens
Photo by Chip Clark Catalogue Number USNM 241

(b) Photograph as Background

FIGURE 2.4   *The Web as a Resource*

THE INTERNET AS A RESOURCE

Objective   To import slides from an outline; to download a picture from the Internet and use it in a PowerPoint presentation. Use Figure 2.5 as a guide in the exercise. The exercise requires that you have an Internet connection.

Step 1:   **Insert the Word Outline**

➤ Start PowerPoint, which in turn opens a new blank presentation with the title slide already selected. Close the task pane.

➤ Enter **Extinction of the Dinosaurs** as the title of the presentation and your name as the author. Save the presentation as **Extinction of the Dinosaurs** in the **Exploring PowerPoint folder**.

➤ Pull down the **Insert menu** and click the **Slides from Outline command** to display the Insert Outline dialog box in Figure 2.5a.

➤ Click the **drop-down arrow** on the Look in list box to select the Exploring PowerPoint folder. Select the **Extinction of the Dinosaurs** Word document and click the **Insert button**.

➤ The Word document is imported into the presentation and converted to individual slides. Any paragraph that has been formatted in the Heading 1 style is converted to the title of a PowerPoint slide.

➤ Save the presentation.

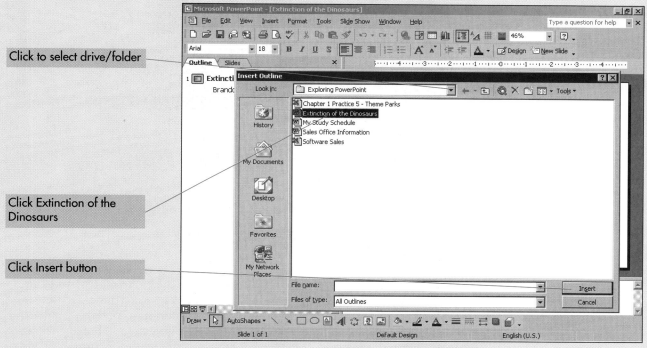

Click to select drive/folder

Click Extinction of the Dinosaurs

Click Insert button

(a) Insert the Word Outline (step 1)

FIGURE 2.5   *Hands-on Exercise 2*

Step 2: **Complete the Outline**

➤ You should see the text of the presentation as shown in Figure 2.5b. Click on the fourth slide that describes the origin of the word *dinosaur*.

➤ Right click the word "deinos" that is flagged as a misspelling because it is not in the English dictionary. Click **Ignore All** to accept the term without flagging it as a misspelling. Accept the spelling of "sauros" in similar fashion.

➤ Select (double click) **deinos**, then click the **Bold** and **Italics buttons** on the Formatting toolbar. (You can also use the Ctrl+B and Ctrl+I keyboard shortcuts that apply to all Office applications.)

➤ Use the **Format Painter** (see boxed tip) to copy this formatting to "sauros" and to "Sir Richard Owen".

➤ Click outside the placeholder to continue working.

➤ Save the presentation.

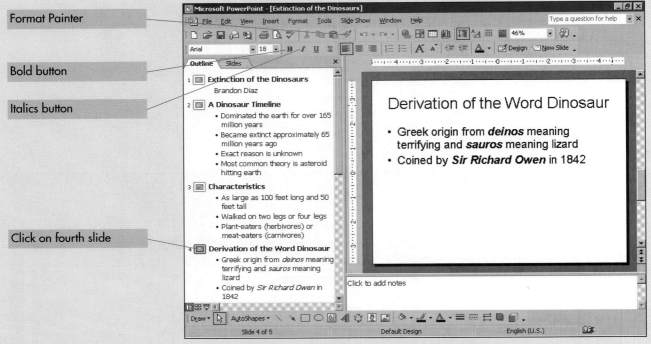

(b) Complete the Outline (step 2)

FIGURE 2.5   *Hands-on Exercise 2 (continued)*

THE FORMAT PAINTER

The Format Painter copies the formatting of the selected text to other places in a presentation. Select the text with the formatting you want to copy, then click or double click the Format Painter button on the Standard toolbar. Clicking the button will paint only one selection. Double clicking the button will paint multiple selections until the feature is turned off by again clicking the Format Painter button. Either way, the mouse pointer changes to a paintbrush, which you can drag over text to give it the identical formatting characteristics as the original selection.

Step 3: **Search the Web**

> ➤ Start Internet Explorer. Click the **Search button** on the Internet Explorer toolbar to open the Search pane. The option button to find a Web page is selected by default. Enter **Dinosaur photographs** in the Find a Web page text box, then click the **Search button**.
> ➤ The results of our search are displayed underneath the Search text box as shown in Figure 2.5c, but you will undoubtedly see a different set of links.
> ➤ Click the link to the **National Museum of Natural History** if it appears. Alternatively, you can click any link that seems promising, or you can click the **Next button** in the Search pane to repeat the search using a different engine.
> ➤ Try to find a page that contains one or more photographs. You can also enter the address (**www.nmnh.si.edu/paleo/dino**) directly to duplicate the remainder of the exercise.
> ➤ Click the **Close button** for the Search pane.

Search button

Close button

Enter search text

Click Search button

Click link to desired site

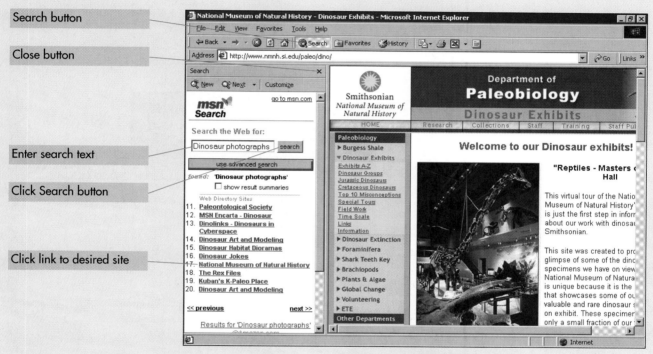

(c) Search the Web (step 3)

FIGURE 2.5 *Hands-on Exercise 2 (continued)*

CUSTOMIZE THE SEARCH ASSISTANT

You can customize the Search Assistant to change the categories that appear and/or the providers in each category. Start Internet Explorer and click the Search button to open the Search pane, then click the Customize button to display the Customize Search Settings page. Check or clear the category boxes to determine the categories that appear. Check or clear the check boxes to select or eliminate the providers in each category. Select a provider name, then click the up/down arrow to change the order in which the providers are listed, then click the OK button to record your changes.

Step 4: **Download the Photograph**

➤ Select any picture on the site, click the **right mouse button** to display a shortcut menu, then click the **Save Picture As command** to display the Save As dialog box in Figure 2.5d.

➤ Click the **drop-down arrow** in the Save in list box to specify the drive and folder in which you want to save the graphic (e.g., the Exploring PowerPoint folder on drive C).

➤ The file name and file type are entered automatically. You can change the name, but do not change the file type.

➤ Click the **Save button** to download the image. Remember the file name and location, as you will need to access the file later in the exercise. The Save As dialog box closes automatically as soon as the picture has been downloaded.

➤ You need to download at least two pictures for your presentation; thus, repeat the process to download a second picture.

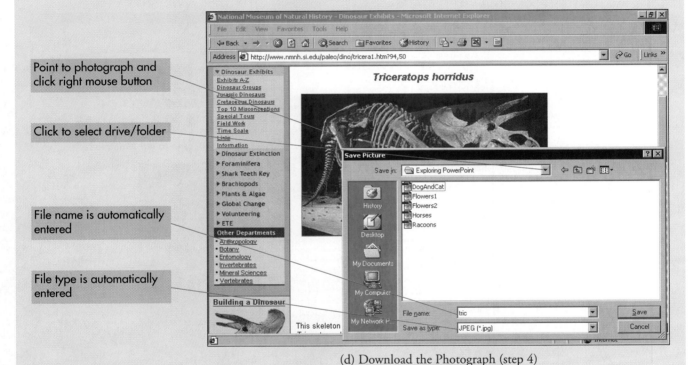

(d) Download the Photograph (step 4)

FIGURE 2.5 *Hands-on Exercise 2 (continued)*

MULTITASKING

Multitasking, the ability to run multiple applications at the same time, is one of the primary advantages of the Windows environment. Switching from one application to another is easy—just click the appropriate button on the Windows taskbar. (If the taskbar is not visible on your screen, it is because the Auto Hide feature is in effect—just point to the bottom edge of the window, and the taskbar will come into view.) You can also use the classic Alt+Tab shortcut. Press and hold the Alt key as you click the Tab key repeatedly to display icons for the open applications, then release the Tab key when the desired application is selected.

Step 5: **Insert the Photograph**

➤ Click the **PowerPoint button** on the taskbar, then press **Ctrl+Home** to display the first slide. Click below the placeholder for your name in the title slide. Pull down the **Insert menu**, point to (or click) **Picture**, then click **From File** to display the Insert Picture dialog box shown in Figure 2.4e.

➤ Click the **down arrow** on the Views button to select the **Preview view**. Click the **down arrow** on the Look in text box to select the drive and folder where you previously saved the pictures (e.g., the Exploring PowerPoint folder on drive C).

➤ Select (click) any photograph and a preview should appear within the Insert Picture dialog box. Click the **Insert button**.

➤ Click and drag the photograph to the bottom right side of the slide. Click the slide title and drag the placeholder to the top of the slide.

➤ Click the placeholder for your name and drag it underneath the title. Click and drag the picture underneath your name. Size the picture as necessary.

➤ Save the presentation.

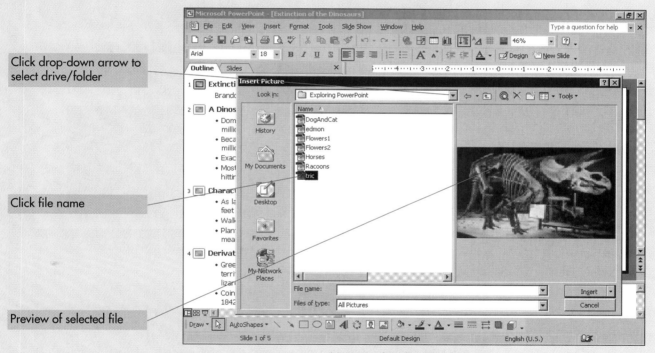

Click drop-down arrow to select drive/folder

Click file name

Preview of selected file

(e) Insert the Photograph (step 5)

FIGURE 2.5 *Hands-on Exercise 2 (continued)*

CROPPING A PICTURE

The Crop tool lets you eliminate (crop) part of a picture. Select (click) the picture to display the Picture toolbar and sizing handles. (If you do not see the Picture toolbar, pull down the View menu, click the Toolbars command, then click the Picture toolbar.) Click the Crop tool (the ScreenTip will display the name of the tool), then click and drag a sizing handle to crop the part of the picture you want to eliminate.

Step 6: **Move and Size the Objects**

➤ Your title slide should be similar to Figure 2.5f. Click the **Text Box tool**, then click and drag below the picture to create a text box. Enter the text as shown in Figure 2.5f. If necessary, change to an appropriate font and point size.

➤ Move and size the objects on the slide as necessary. To size an object:
   • Click the object to display the sizing handles.
   • Drag a corner handle (the mouse pointer changes to a double arrow) to change the length and width of the object simultaneously.
   • Drag a handle on the horizontal or vertical border to change one dimension.

➤ To move an object:
   • Click the object to display the sizing handles.
   • Point to any part of the object except a sizing handle (the mouse pointer changes to a four-sided arrow), then click and drag to move the object.

➤ Save the presentation.

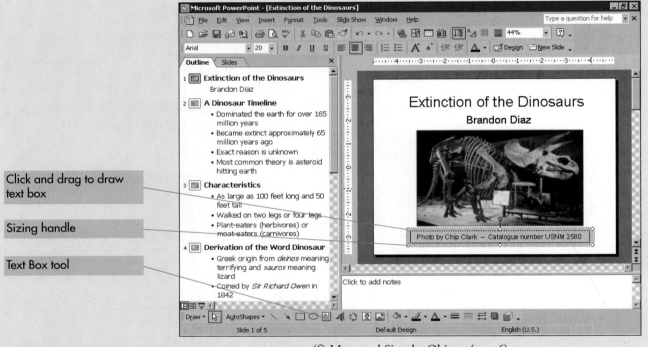

Click and drag to draw text box

Sizing handle

Text Box tool

(f) Move and Size the Objects (step 6)

FIGURE 2.5 *Hands-on Exercise 2 (continued)*

ENTER THE URL AUTOMATICALLY

Use the Copy command to enter the URL into a presentation and ensure that it is entered correctly. Click in the Address bar of Internet Explorer to select the URL, then pull down the Edit menu and click the Copy command (or use the Ctrl+C shortcut). Switch to the PowerPoint presentation, click on the slide where you want to insert the URL, then pull down the Edit menu and click Paste (or press Ctrl+V). (The Cut command does not apply here, but it can be executed by the Ctrl+X keyboard shortcut. The "X" is supposed to remind you of a pair of scissors.)

Step 7: **The Picture as Background**

➤ Click the **New Slide button** to display slide layouts in the task pane. Click the blank slide layout.
➤ Pull down the **Format menu** and click the **Background command** to display the Background dialog box in Figure 2.5g.
➤ Click the **down arrow** in the Background fill list box, click **Fill Effects** to display the Fill Effects dialog box, click the **Picture tab**, then click the **Select Picture button** to display the Select Picture dialog box.
➤ Click the **down arrow** on the Look in text box to select the drive and folder where you saved the picture, select the photograph, then click the **Insert button** so that the photograph appears in the Fill Effects dialog box.
➤ Click **OK** to accept the picture and close the Fill Effects dialog box. Click the **Apply button** on the Background dialog box. The photograph should now appear as the background for your slide.
➤ Save the presentation.

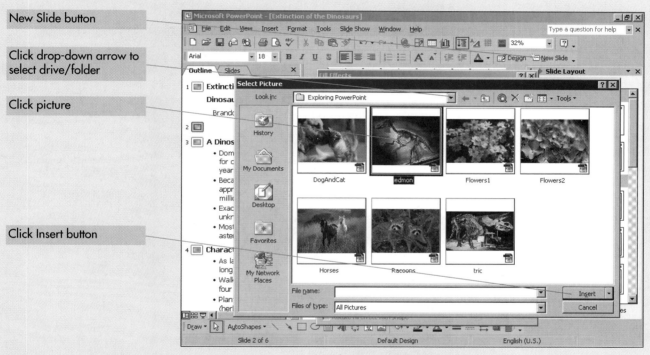

New Slide button

Click drop-down arrow to select drive/folder

Click picture

Click Insert button

(g) The Picture as Background (step 7)

FIGURE 2.5 *Hands-on Exercise 2 (continued)*

IT'S A DIFFERENT LOOK

The slide you just created does not look like a PowerPoint slide, but it is, and it will make a tremendous impact during your next presentation. Use your imagination to expand the technique to an entire presentation. You could, for example, do a report on Impressionist paintings and show one painting per slide. You can also add a second (and smaller) photograph (perhaps of the artist) on the slide that will show both artist and painting. See practice exercise 2 at the end of the chapter.

Step 8: **Add a Text Box**

➤ Click the **Text Box tool** on the Drawing toolbar, then click and drag on the right side of the slide to create a text box. Enter the dinosaur name as shown in Figure 2.5h. If necessary, change to an appropriate font and point size, such as **48 point Times New Roman bold**.

➤ Click the **Text Box tool** a second time, then click and drag below the picture to create a second text box. Enter the text as shown in the figure. We used the same font as in the previous text box (Times New Roman), but chose a smaller size (**24 point**). Save the presentation.

➤ Pull down the **File menu** and click the **Print command** to display the Print dialog box. Select **Handouts** in the Print What dialog box and choose **6 slides per page**. Click **OK**.

➤ Pull down the **File menu** a second time and click the **Print command**. Print an outline of the presentation.

➤ Close Internet Explorer. Exit PowerPoint if you do not want to continue with the next exercise at this time.

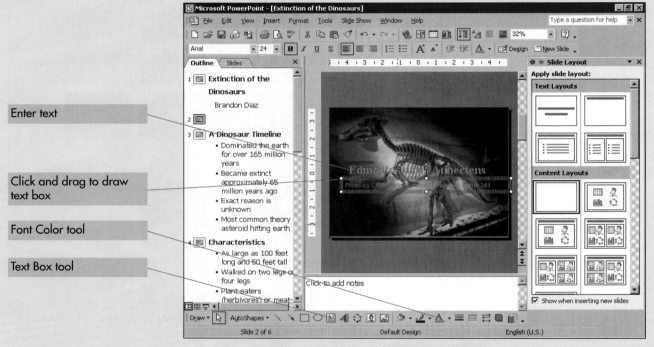

(h) Add a Text Box (step 8)

FIGURE 2.5 *Hands-on Exercise 2 (continued)*

CHANGE THE ALIGNMENT

Use the Left, Center, or Right-Align buttons to change the alignment of any bullet, slide title, or text box. Just click anywhere in the item, then click the appropriate button on the Formatting toolbar. You can also use the corresponding keyboard shortcuts (Ctrl+L, Ctrl+E, Ctrl+R), for left, center, or right alignment. The shortcuts also work in Microsoft Word.

Perhaps you have already created a home page and have uploaded it to the World Wide Web. If so, you know that the process is not difficult, and have experienced the satisfaction of adding your documents to the Web. If not, this is a good time to learn. This section describes how to insert hyperlinks into a PowerPoint presentation, and then shows you how to convert a PowerPoint presentation into a series of Web pages for display on the Web or local area network.

All Web pages are written in a language called ***HTML (HyperText Markup Language)***. Initially, the only way to create a Web page was to learn HTML. Microsoft Office simplifies the process because you can create the document in any Office application, then simply save it as a Web page. In other words, you start PowerPoint in the usual fashion and enter the text of the presentation with basic formatting. However, instead of saving the document in the default format (as a PowerPoint presentation), you use the ***Save As Web Page command*** to convert the presentation to HTML.

PowerPoint does the rest and generates the HTML statements for you. You can continue to enter text and/or change the formatting for existing text just as you can with an ordinary presentation. Hyperlinks can be inserted at any time, either through the Insert Hyperlink command or through the corresponding button on the Standard toolbar.

Figure 2.6 displays the title slide of a presentation entitled "Widgets of America" as viewed in ***Internet Explorer***, rather than in PowerPoint. The Internet Explorer window is divided into two vertical frames and is similar to the Normal view in PowerPoint. The left frame displays the title of each slide, and these titles function as links; that is, you can click any title in the left frame, and the corresponding slide will be displayed in the right pane. You can also click and drag the border separating the panes to change the size of the panes. Note, too, the address in the Address bar of Internet Explorer that indicates the presentation is stored on a local drive, as opposed to a Web server.

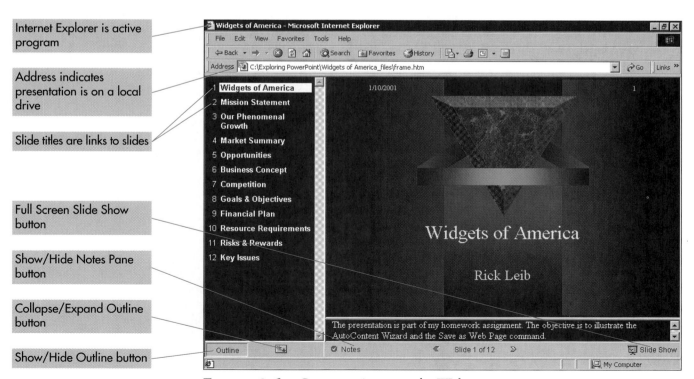

FIGURE 2.6   *Presentations on the Web*

The *navigation controls* at the bottom of the window provide additional options for viewing within Internet Explorer. (The controls were created automatically in conjunction with the Save As Web Page command when the presentation was saved initially.) The Show/Hide Outline button at the bottom left of the window toggles the left (outline) pane on and off. The Expand/Collapse Outline button appears to the right of the outline when the outline is visible and lets you vary the detail of the outline. The Show/Hide Notes button toggles a notes pane on and off at the bottom of the slide. The left and right arrows move to the previous and next slide, respectively. And finally, the Full Screen Slide Show button at the lower right creates a slide show on the Internet that is identical to the slide show viewed within PowerPoint.

ROUND TRIP HTML

All applications in Microsoft Office enable you to open an HTML document in the Office application that created it. In other words, you can start with a PowerPoint presentation, use the Save As Web Page command to convert the presentation to a series of HTML documents, then view those documents in a Web browser. You can then reopen the HTML document in PowerPoint (the original Office application) and have full access to all PowerPoint commands if you want to modify the document.

Uploading a Presentation

Creating a Web document is only the beginning in that you need to place the pages on the Web so that other people will be able to access it. This in turn requires you to obtain an account on a Web server, a computer with Internet access and adequate disk space to hold the various pages you create. To do so, you need to check with your system administrator at school or work, or with your local Internet provider, to determine how to submit your page when it is complete. It's not difficult, and you will be pleased to see your work on the Internet.

Realize, however, that even if you do not place your presentation on the Web, you can still view it locally on your PC. This is the approach we follow in the next hands-on exercise, which enables you to create an HTML document and see the results of your effort. Your document is stored on a local drive (e.g., on drive A or drive C) rather than on a Web server, but it can still be viewed through Internet Explorer (or any other browser). After you have completed the exercise, you (and/or your instructor) can determine if it is worthwhile to place your page on your school's or university's server, where it can be accessed by anyone.

SCHEDULING A BROADCAST

You can broadcast a presentation, including sound and video, over the Web or a local area network using the NetMeeting and NetShow capabilities within Microsoft Office. Pull down the Slide Show menu, click Online Broadcast, click the Schedule a Live Broadcast command, then follow the onscreen instructions. Attendees can be located anywhere, but will need Internet Explorer 4.0 or higher to view the broadcast. You can also subscribe to a presentation, and be notified via e-mail of any changes, provided that the Office Server Extensions have been installed on your Web server. See practice exercise 10 at the end of the chapter.

One of the hardest things about creating a presentation is getting started. You have a general idea of what you want to say, but the words do not come easily to you. The *AutoContent Wizard* offers a potential solution. It asks you a series of questions, then it uses your answers to suggest a presentation. The presentation is not complete, but it does provide an excellent beginning.

The AutoContent Wizard is accessed through the New Presentation view in the task pane and is illustrated in Figure 2.7. The Wizard prompts you for the type of presentation in Figure 2.7a, for the style of the presentation in Figure 2.7b, and for additional information in Figure 2.7c. The Wizard then has all the information it needs and proceeds to create a presentation for you. It even chooses a design template as illustrated by the title slide in Figure 2.7d. The template contains a color scheme and custom formatting to give your presentation a certain "look." You can change the design at any time to give your presentation a completely different look while retaining its content.

The real benefit of the Wizard, however, is the outline shown in Figure 2.7e, which corresponds to the topic you selected earlier (Marketing Plan). The outline is very general, as it must be, but it provides the essential topics to include in your presentation. You work with the outline provided by the AutoContent Wizard just as you would with any other outline. You can type over existing text, add or delete slides, move slides around, promote or demote items, and so on. In short, you don't use the AutoContent outline exactly as it is presented; instead you use the outline as a starting point, then modify it to fit the needs of your presentation. The Wizard has accomplished its goal, however, by giving you a solid beginning.

The presentation created by the AutoContent Wizard is based on one of several presentations that are provided with PowerPoint. You can use the Wizard as just described, or you can bypass the Wizard entirely and select the outline directly from the *General Templates link* in the New Presentation task pane. Either way you wind up with a professional presentation with respect to design and content. Naturally, you have to modify the content to fit your needs, but you have jump-started the creative process. You simply open the presentation, then you modify the existing text as necessary, while retaining the formatting in the selected template.

Figure 2.8 displays the title slides of several sample presentations that are included with PowerPoint. The presentations vary considerably in content and design. There is a presentation for recommending a strategy in Figure 2.8a, a business plan in Figure 2.8b, and even a presentation to communicate bad news in Figure 2.8c. The presentation in Figure 2.8d is one of several that were developed by the Dale Carnegie Foundation and is designed to introduce and thank a speaker. The presentations in Figure 2.8e and 2.8f are for an employee orientation and a project overview, respectively. Animation and branching are also built into several of the presentations.

CHOOSE AN APPROPRIATE DESIGN

A design should enhance a presentation without calling attention to itself. It should be consistent with your message, and as authoritative or informal as the situation demands. Choosing the right template requires common sense and good taste. What works in one instance will not necessarily work in another. You would not, for example, use the same template to proclaim a year-end bonus as you would to announce a fourth-quarter loss and impending layoffs. Set a time limit, or else you will spend too much time on the formatting and lose sight of the content.

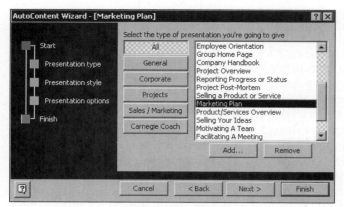

(a) Presentation Type

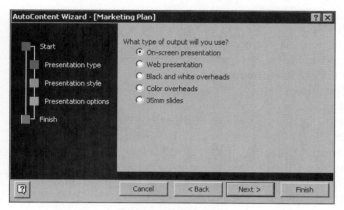

(b) Presentation Style

(c) Presentation Options

(d) Title Slide and Selected Template

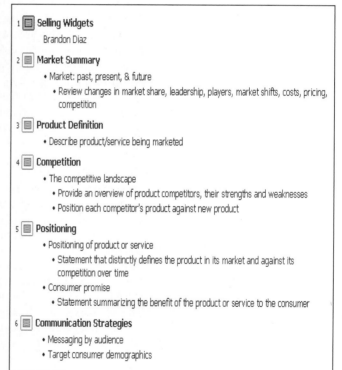

(e) Suggested Outline (additional slides not shown)

FIGURE 2.7 *The AutoContent Wizard*

(a) Recommending a Strategy

(b) Business Plan

(c) Communicating Bad News

(d) Thanking a Speaker

(e) Employee Orientation

(f) Project Overview

FIGURE 2.8 *Suggested Presentations*

PRESENTATIONS ON THE WEB

Objective   To use the AutoContent Wizard as the basis of a PowerPoint presentation; to insert a hyperlink into a presentation, and save the presentation as a series of Web pages. Use Figure 2.9 as a guide in the exercise.

Step 1:   **The AutoContent Wizard**

> Start PowerPoint and (if necessary) open the task pane. Click the link **From AutoContent Wizard** in the New area.
> You should see the first screen in the AutoContent Wizard. Click the **Next button** (within the Wizard's dialog box) to select the presentation type as shown in Figure 2.9a. Click the **Corporate button**.
> Choose a presentation that has been installed. We chose **Business Plan**. (Additional presentations may be found on the Office CD, but require installation.) Click **Next**.
> The option button for **On-screen presentation** is selected by default. Click **Next**. (You can click the Back button at any time to retrace your steps.)
> Click in the Presentation title text box and enter **Widgets of America** as the name of the presentation. Clear the boxes for **Date last updated** and **Slide Number**. Click **Next**.
> The Wizard indicates it has all of the necessary information to create your presentation. Click **Finish**.

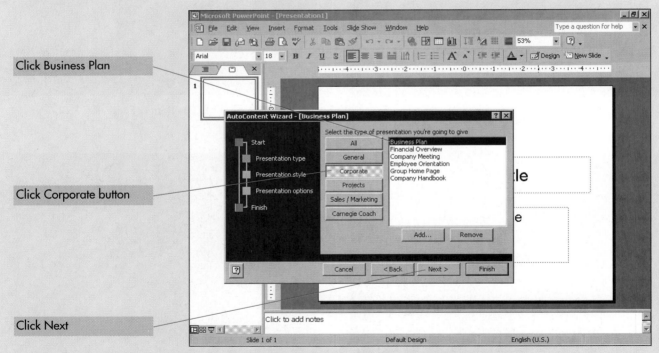

(a) The AutoContent Wizard (step 1)

FIGURE 2.9   *Hands-on Exercise 3*

Step 2: **Add Speaker Notes**

➤ Your presentation should be displayed in the Normal view as shown in Figure 2.9b. If necessary, click and drag to select the author's name and substitute your own. (The author's name is entered by default and corresponds to the person or organization in whose name the program is registered.)

➤ Click in the speaker notes area and enter an appropriate note. You can use our text, or make up your own. Click on the slide. Press the **PgDn key** to move to the second slide that describes the mission statement for your organization.

➤ Press the **PgDn key** repeatedly to view the slides in the presentation and gain an appreciation for the work of the AutoContent Wizard.

➤ Click the icon of one or more slides that you do not think are relevant to the presentation. Note that when you click the icon, the entire slide is selected. Press the **Del key** to delete the slide from the presentation.

➤ Save the presentation.

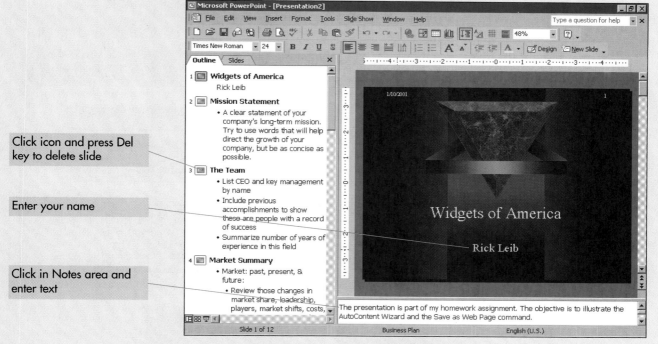

Click icon and press Del key to delete slide

Enter your name

Click in Notes area and enter text

(b) Add Speaker Notes (step 2)

FIGURE 2.9 *Hands-on Exercise 3 (continued)*

DELETING SLIDES

Slides may be deleted in either the Normal (tri-pane) view or the Slide Sorter view. Select (click) the Slide icon in the outline of the Normal view to select one slide (or click and drag to select multiple slides), then press the Del key. You can also click the Slides tab in the Normal view, then press and hold the Ctrl key to select multiple slides prior to pressing the Del key. Use the same technique in the Slide Sorter view.

Step 3:   **Save the Presentation**

➤ Pull down the **File menu**. Click the **Save As Web Page command** to display the Save As dialog box. If necessary, click the **drop-down arrow** in the Save In list box to select the appropriate drive, such as drive C or drive A.

➤ Open the **Exploring PowerPoint folder**. Check that the name of the Web page is **Widgets of America**.

➤ Click the **Change Title button** to display the Set Page Title dialog box in Figure 2.9c. Enter **Widgets of America** and click **OK**. (The entry in this dialog box is displayed on the title bar of the Web browser.) Click **Save** to save the page.

➤ The title bar changes to the name of the Web page (Widgets of America), but the display does not change in any other way. Thus, you can continue to work in PowerPoint and modify the Web page through ordinary PowerPoint commands.

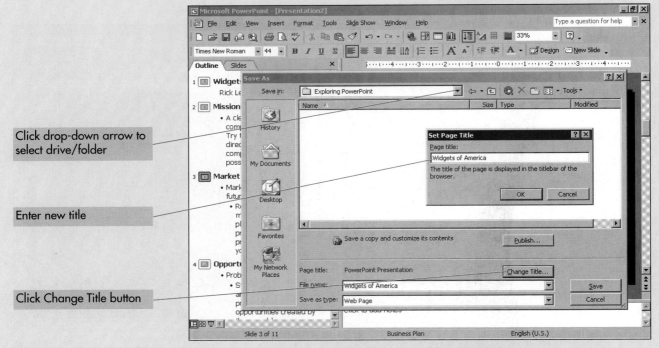

Click drop-down arrow to select drive/folder

Enter new title

Click Change Title button

(c) Save the Presentation (step 3)

FIGURE 2.9   *Hands-on Exercise 3 (continued)*

PUBLISHING OPTIONS

Click the Publish button in the Save As dialog box to display the Publish As Web Page dialog box, where you can view and/or modify the various options associated with an HTML document. The default publishing options work well, but you have total control over your Web pages. Note, too, that you can click the down arrow on the Save In list box to access the FTP capability within PowerPoint 2002 to save directly onto a Web server. (It may be easier, however, to use a standalone FTP program.)

Step 4: **Insert the Hyperlink**

➤ You can enter text in either the Outline pane or the Slide pane. Click at the end of the first bullet on slide two in the outline and press the **enter key** to create a new bullet.

➤ Press **Shift+Tab** to promote the item and start a new slide. Enter the text **Our Phenomenal Growth** as the title of the slide. Press **enter**, then press the **Tab key** to enter the bulleted text in Figure 2.9d.

➤ Click and drag to select the words **Click here** (to make the phrase the actual hyperlink), then click the **Insert Hyperlink button** on the Standard toolbar to display the Insert Hyperlink dialog box.

➤ Click **Browsed Pages**, then click in the Address text box. Enter the address of our web page at **www.prenhall.com/grauer** (the http:// is assumed).

➤ Click **OK** to create the hyperlink, which should appear as underlined text on the slide. The hyperlink is not active until you switch to the Slide Show view.

➤ Save the presentation.

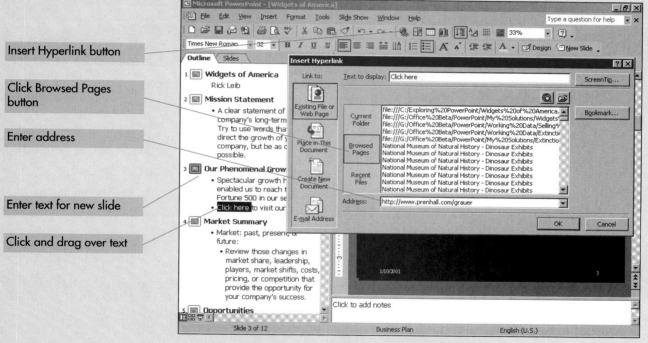

Insert Hyperlink button

Click Browsed Pages button

Enter address

Enter text for new slide

Click and drag over text

(d) Insert the Hyperlink (step 4)

FIGURE 2.9   *Hands-on Exercise 3 (continued)*

ADD NUMBERED OR GRAPHICAL BULLETS

Why settle for simple bullets when you can have numbers or pictures? Click and drag to select the bullets on a slide, then click the Numbering button on the Formatting toolbar to change to numbered bullets. You can also right click the selected bullets to display a context-sensitive menu, then click the Bullets and Numbering command to display the associated dialog box, where you can customize the bullets by selecting symbols, pictures, and/or special characters.

Step 5: **Open the Web Page**

➤ You can view the Web page you just created even if it has not been saved on a Web server. Start **Internet Explorer** if it is not already open, or click its button on the Windows taskbar.

➤ Pull down the **File menu** and click the **Open command** to display the Open dialog box in Figure 2.9e. Click the **Browse button**, then select the drive and folder (e.g., Exploring PowerPoint on drive C) where you saved the Web page.

➤ Select the **Widgets of America HTML document** and click **Open**. Click **OK** to open the presentation.

➤ You should see the presentation that was created earlier, except that you are viewing it in Internet Explorer rather than PowerPoint. The Address bar reflects the local address (in the Exploring PowerPoint folder) of the presentation.

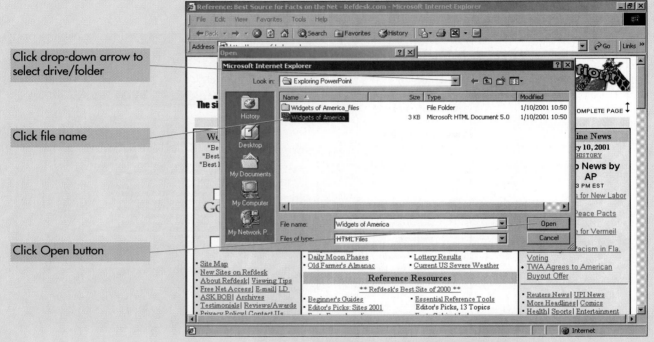

Click drop-down arrow to select drive/folder

Click file name

Click Open button

(e) Open the Web Page (step 5)

FIGURE 2.9 *Hands-on Exercise 3 (continued)*

AN EXTRA FOLDER

Look carefully at the contents of the Exploring PowerPoint folder within the Open dialog box. You see the Widgets of America HTML document that you just created, as well as a folder that was created automatically by the Save As Web Page command. The latter contains the various objects that are referenced by the HTML pages within the presentation. Be sure to copy the contents of this folder to the Web server in addition to your Web page if you decide to post the page.

Step 6: **View the Presentation**

➤ Click the **Show/Hide Outline button** at the bottom left to show or hide the outline. Click the **Expand/Collapse Outline button** (when the outline is visible) to vary the detail of the outline.
➤ Click the **Notes button** to show/hide the Notes pane at the bottom of the window. The title page is the only slide that contains a note.
➤ Click the **Full Screen Slide Show button** at the lower right of the Internet Explorer window to start the slide show. This is the identical slide show that you would see if you were viewing the presentation from within PowerPoint.
➤ If necessary, press the **Esc key** to stop the show and return to the view in Figure 2.9f. Click **Our Phenomenal Growth** in the outline to view the slide.
➤ Click the hyperlink that you created earlier.

Click Our Phenomenal Growth

Click hyperlink

Full Screen Slide Show button

Notes button

Collapse/Expand Outline button

Show/Hide Outline button

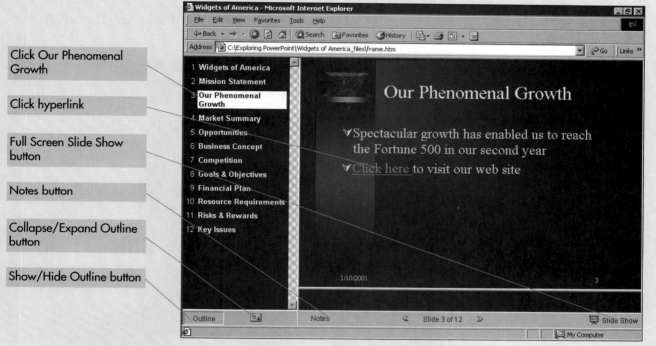

(f) View the Presentation (step 6)

FIGURE 2.9   *Hands-on Exercise 3 (continued)*

HYPERLINKS BEFORE AND AFTER (INTERNET EXPLORER)

Hyperlinks are displayed in different colors, depending on whether (or not) the associated page has been displayed. You can change the default colors, however, to suit your personal preference. Pull down the Tools menu, click the Internet Options command to display the Internet Options dialog box, and click the General tab. Click the Colors button, then click the colored box next to the visited or unvisited links to display a color palette. Select (click) the desired color, click OK to close the palette, click OK to close the Colors dialog box, then click OK to close the Internet Options dialog box.

Step 7: **The Exploring Office Home Page**

➤ You should see the Exploring Office home page as shown in Figure 2.9g. If you do not see the page, it is most likely because you did not create the link correctly in the original presentation. Correct the hyperlink as follows:

- Click the **PowerPoint button** on the Windows taskbar and return to slide three (the slide that is to contain the hyperlink).
- Point to the link in the Slide or Outline view, click the **right mouse button** to display a context-sensitive menu. Click the **Edit Hyperlink command** to display the Edit Hyperlink dialog box.
- Be sure you enter the correct address, **www.prenhall.com/grauer** (the http:// is assumed). Click **OK**. Save the presentation.
- Click the **Internet Explorer button** on the taskbar to return to the browser. Click the **Refresh button** on the Internet Explorer toolbar to view the corrected page, then try the link a second time.

➤ Close Internet Explorer. Exit PowerPoint if you do not want to continue with the next exercise at this time.

The address of our Web page

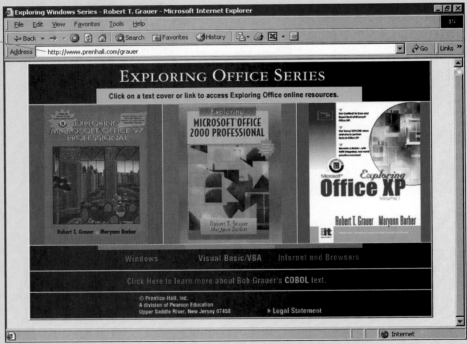

(g) The Exploring Windows Home Page (step 7)

FIGURE 2.9 *Hands-on Exercise 3 (continued)*

PRESENTATION PROPERTIES

How much time have you spent on the presentation in total? How many revisions have you made? How many words are there in the entire presentation? The answers to these and other questions are found in the presentation properties. Pull down the File menu, click the Properties command, and click the Statistics tab, then use that information to tell your instructor how hard you worked on this assignment. (You must execute this command from within PowerPoint, rather than from Internet Explorer.)

A template is a design specification that controls every aspect of a presentation. It specifies the background design, the formatting of the text, the fonts and colors that are used, and the design, size, and placement of the bullets. You can change the look of a presentation at any time by applying a different template. Changing from one template to another changes the appearance of the presentation in every way, while maintaining the content.

What if, however, you want to make subtle changes to the template? In other words, you are content with the overall design, but you want to change one or more of its elements. You don't want a radical change, but you want to fine-tune the presentation by modifying its color scheme and/or background shading. Or perhaps you want to add a consistent element to every slide, such as a corporate name or corporate logo.

The Color Scheme

A *color scheme* is a set of eight balanced colors that is associated with a template. It consists of a background color, a color for the title of each slide, a color for lines and text, and five additional colors to provide accents to different elements, such as shadows and fill colors. Each template has a default color scheme, which is applied when the template is selected. Each template also has a set of alternate color schemes from which to choose.

Figure 2.10a displays the title slide of a presentation. The Competition template is selected and the default color scheme is in effect. Figure 2.10b displays the Color Scheme dialog box with the suggested color schemes for this template. To choose one of the other color schemes, select the color scheme, then click the Apply All command button to apply the new color scheme to the entire presentation.

You have additional flexibility in that you can change any of the individual colors within a color scheme. Select the desired color scheme, click the Custom tab, select the color you wish to change (e.g., the color of the background), then click the Change Color command button. View your presentation with the modified color scheme, then click the Undo button if you want to return to the default design.

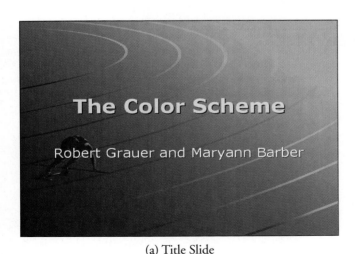

(a) Title Slide

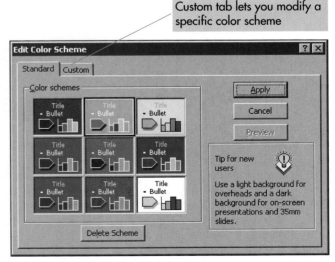

(b) Standard Color Schemes

FIGURE 2.10   *The Color Scheme*

The ***Background command*** in the Format menu lets you modify the background and/or shading of a slide, enabling you to truly fine-tune a presentation. Figure 2.11a displays the Fill Effects dialog box that changes the original title slide in Figure 2.11b to its modified form in Figure 2.11c. The difference is subtle and is due to changing the shading style from Diagonal down in the original slide to Horizontal shading in the modified version. The average person will not notice. (The Fill Effects dialog box also provides access to the Picture tab that creates an entirely different look, by using a picture as the background.)

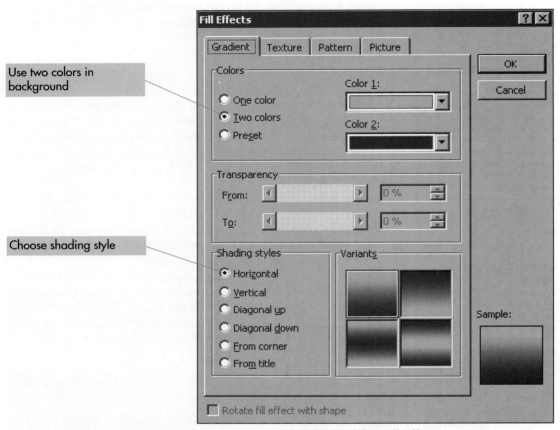

(a) Modified Fill Effects

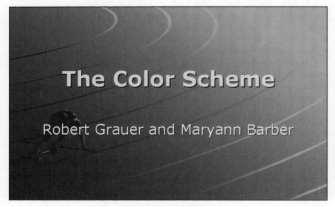

(b) Original Slide

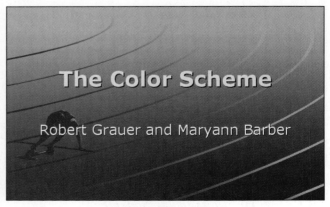

(c) Modified Slide

FIGURE 2.11   *Customize the Background*

PowerPoint Masters

PowerPoint lets you change the color scheme or background, but these changes typically have a minimal effect. The best ways to customize a presentation is to add a unifying element to each slide, such as a corporate name or logo. You could add the element to every slide, but that would be unnecessarily tedious. It is much easier to add the element to the *slide master,* which defines the formatting and other elements that appear on the individual slides. Any change to the slide master is automatically reflected in every slide except for the title slide (which has its own title master). In similar fashion, any change to the Handouts master or Notes master affects the corresponding elements.

Consider, for example, the slide master shown in Figure 2.12, which contains a placeholder for the title of the slide and a second placeholder for the bulleted text. Change the position or formatting of either object, and you automatically change it on every slide. The slide master also contains additional placeholders at the bottom of the slide for the date, footer, and slide number. Change the position and/or content of any of these elements on the master slide, and the corresponding element will be changed throughout the presentation. Thus, you could add the name of the organization in the footer area of the master slide, and have it appear on every slide in the presentation. In similar fashion, any change to the font, bullets, font color, point size, or alignment within a placeholder would also carry through to all of the individual slides.

You can add clip art to the master, as was done in Figure 2.12, and the clip art in turn will appear on every slide. Note, too, the left pane in the figure, which contains two masters, called the slide and title masters, respectively. The slide master affects every slide except the title slide, whereas the title master pertains to just the title slide. Its use is limited, therefore, unless you have multiple title slides in a presentation. (See practice exercise 6 at the end of the chapter.)

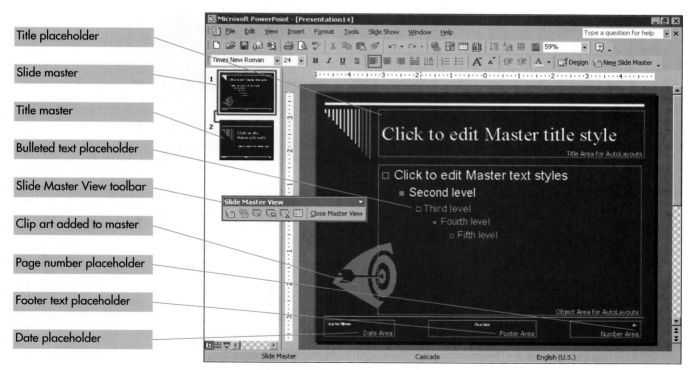

FIGURE 2.12 *The Slide Master*

FINE-TUNING A PRESENTATION

Objective To create a presentation based on an existing PowerPoint presentation; to change color schemes and backgrounds. Use Figure 2.13 as a guide.

Step 1: **Open an Existing Presentation**

> ➤ Start PowerPoint. If necessary, pull down the **File menu** and click **New** to open the task pane. Click the link to **General Templates** to open the Templates dialog box as shown in Figure 2.13a.
> ➤ Click the **Presentations tab** within the dialog box, then click the **Details button** so that you can see the title of each presentation more clearly. Scroll until you can select the **Recommending a Strategy** presentation.
> ➤ Click **OK** to open the presentation. Save the presentation as **Recommending a Strategy** in the Exploring PowerPoint folder.

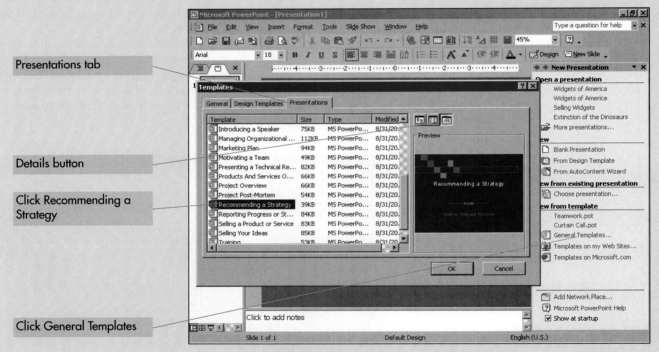

Presentations tab

Details button

Click Recommending a Strategy

Click General Templates

(a) Open an Existing Presentation (step 1)

FIGURE 2.13 *Hands-on Exercise 4 (continued)*

SORT BY NAME, DATE, OR FILE SIZE

The files in the Save As and Open dialog boxes can be displayed in ascending or descending sequence by name, date modified, or size. Change to the Details view, then click the heading of the desired column; for example, click the Modified column to list the files according to the date they were last changed. Click the column heading a second time to reverse the sequence—that is, to switch from ascending to descending and vice versa.

Step 2: **Modify the Outline**

➤ Click and drag to select **Ideas for Today and Tomorrow**. Enter the names of your group (e.g., Tom, Dick, and Harry) as shown in Figure 2.13b.
➤ Scroll through the slides that are included in the default presentation. The outline is very general, as it must be, but it provides the essential topics in recommending a strategy.
➤ Change the text as appropriate. We do not provide specific instructions, but you should modify at least two slides.
➤ Click at the end of any line, either a title or a bulleted item. Press **enter** to create a new line at the same level. Press **Tab** to indent or **Shift+Tab** to move back one level. Enter the text on the new line.
➤ Save the presentation.

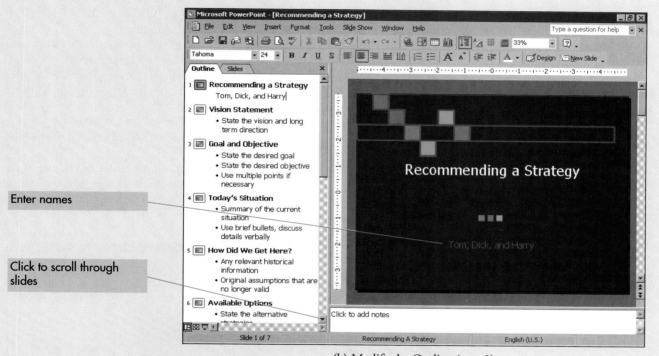

Enter names

Click to scroll through slides

(b) Modify the Outline (step 2)

FIGURE 2.13 *Hands-on Exercise 4 (continued)*

INSERTING SLIDES FROM OTHER PRESENTATIONS

You work hard to develop individual slides, and thus you may find it useful to reuse a slide from one presentation to the next. Pull down the Insert menu, click the Slides from Files command to display the Slide Finder dialog box, then browse until you locate the presentation containing the slide you want to use. Open the presentation to view the slides it contains. Select the slides individually, or press and hold the Shift key to select multiple slides, click Insert, then close the Slide Finder dialog box.

Step 3:   **Change the Slide Master**

➤ Pull down the **View menu**, click **Master**, then click **Slide Master** to display the slide master as shown in Figure 2.13c. (The Header and Footer dialog box is not yet visible.) Click the Slide Master in the left pane.

➤ Click the border of the number area at the bottom right of the slide to select this element. Press the **Del key** to delete this element.

➤ Pull down the **Insert menu**, click (or point to) **Picture**, then click **Clip Art**. The task pane opens and displays the Insert Clip Art Search pane.

➤ Click in the **Search text box**. Type **idea** to search for any clip art image that is indexed with this key word.

➤ Set the options to search in all collections and for all media types, then click the **Search button** or press **enter**.

➤ The images are displayed in the Results box. Select (click) an image to display a drop-down arrow to its right. Click the arrow to display a context-sensitive menu. Click **Insert** to insert the image into the document.

➤ Click and drag the inserted image to the lower-left part of the slide as shown in Figure 2.13c, then size the image as necessary. Close the task pane.

➤ Pull down the **View menu**. Click **Header and Footer** to display the Header and Footer dialog box. The **Date and Time** check box is selected. Click the option button to **Update Automatically**.

➤ Select the **Footer** check box, then enter the name of your school. Check the box to suppress the display on the title slide. Click the **Apply to All command button** to accept these settings.

➤ Click the **Normal view button** on the status bar, then press the **PgDn key** once or twice to move from slide to slide. You should see today's date and the name of your school at the bottom of each slide except for the title slide.

➤ Save the presentation.

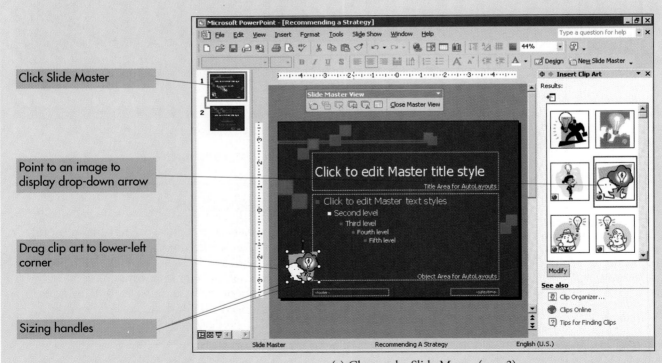

(c) Change the Slide Master (step 3)

FIGURE 2.13   *Hands-on Exercise 4 (continued)*

Step 4: **Change the Color Scheme**

➤ Open the task pane. Click the **down arrow** in the task pane, then click **Slide Design—Color Schemes** as shown in Figure 2.13d.

➤ Point to a different color scheme, then click the **down arrow** that appears to display a context-sensitive menu. Click **Apply to All masters**.

➤ Click **Edit Color Schemes** at the bottom of the task pane to see the different elements that define every color scheme. Select (click) a color, then click the **Change Color button** to choose a different color. Click **OK**, then click **Apply**.

➤ Click the **Undo button** if you are disappointed with the result. The default color schemes are quite good, and it is often difficult to improve on their appearance.

➤ Save the presentation.

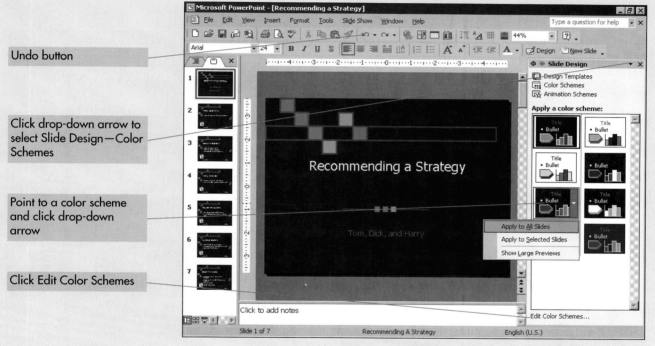

Undo button

Click drop-down arrow to select Slide Design—Color Schemes

Point to a color scheme and click drop-down arrow

Click Edit Color Schemes

(d) Change the Color Scheme (step 4)

FIGURE 2.13 *Hands-on Exercise 4 (continued)*

MULTIPLE SLIDE MASTERS ARE POSSIBLE

Most presentations use only a single template, but there are occasions when you want to include multiple designs in the same presentation. Choose the design you want in the task pane, click the down arrow next to that design, then select the command to apply the design to the selected slide(s). To include another design, go to a different slide, select a different design, and click the down arrow to repeat the process. See practice exercise 6 at the end of the chapter.

Step 5: **Customize the Background**

➤ Pull down the **Format menu**. Click **Background** to display the Background dialog box in Figure 2.13e.

➤ Click the **drop-down arrow** to display the various types of backgrounds, then click **Fill Effects** to display the Fill Effects dialog box in Figure 2.13e.

➤ If necessary, click the **Gradient tab**. Click the option button for **Two colors**. Click the **From title option button** as the Shading Style.

➤ You can see the effect of these changes in the Sample box. Experiment with additional changes, then click **OK** to accept the changes and close the Fill Effects dialog box.

➤ Click **Apply to All** to apply the changes to all slides and close the Custom Background dialog box. Use the **Undo command** to return to the initial design if you are disappointed with your modification.

➤ Save the presentation.

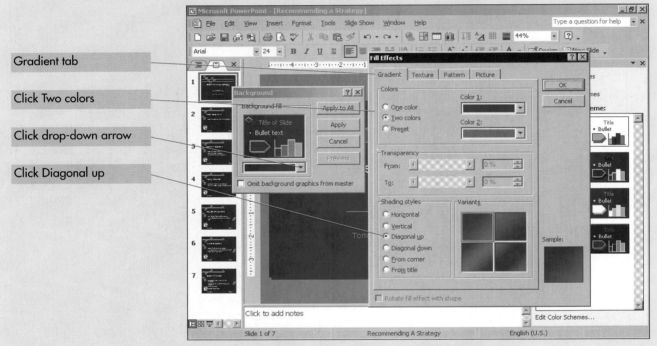

(e) Customize the Background (step 5)

FIGURE 2.13 *Hands-on Exercise 4 (continued)*

SET A TIME LIMIT

We warn you—it's addictive and it's not always productive. Yes, it's fun to experiment with different color schemes and backgrounds, but it is all too easy to spend too much time fine-tuning the design. The PowerPoint templates were designed by professionals, and thus you may not be able to improve on their efforts. Concentrate on the content of your presentation rather than its appearance. Impose a limit on the amount of time you will spend on formatting. End the session when the limit is reached.

Step 6: **Print the Audience Handouts**

➤ Pull down the **File menu**. Click **Print** to display the Print dialog box in Figure 2.13f. Set the print options to match those in the figure:
  • Click the **All option button** as the print range.
  • Click the **down arrow** on the Print What list box to select **Handouts**. Specify six slides per page in the Handouts area.
  • Check the box to **Frame slides**.
  • Click **OK**.
➤ Submit the audience handouts to your instructor as proof that you did the exercise. Save the presentation.
➤ Exit PowerPoint. Congratulations on a job well done.

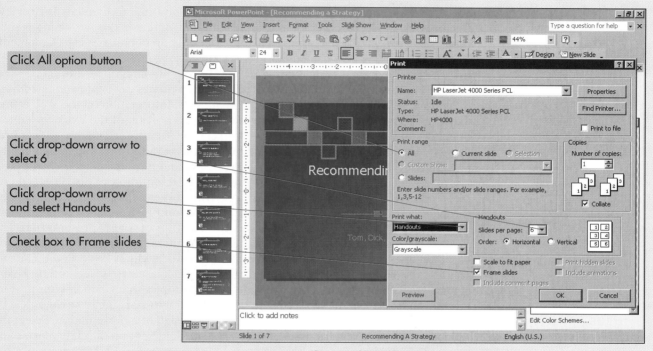

Click All option button

Click drop-down arrow to select 6

Click drop-down arrow and select Handouts

Check box to Frame slides

(f) Print the Audience Handouts (step 6)

FIGURE 2.13 *Hands-on Exercise 4 (continued)*

PRINT IN A VARIETY OF FORMATS

Use the flexibility inherent in the Print command to print a presentation in a variety of formats. Pull down the File menu, click the Print command to display the Print dialog box, and then select the desired output. Print handouts for your audience that contain the slide miniatures, or give your audience an outline of the entire presentation. Print the Notes Pages for yourself as a guide in preparing for the presentation. And finally, you can print the slides themselves, one per page, on overhead transparency masters as backup in case the computer is not available.

PowerPoint provides several slide show tools to help the speaker deliver a presentation. The Header and Footer command helps you to personalize a presentation by inserting a common element on every slide, such as the date, time, or place of the presentation and/or a corporate logo. The Rehearse Timings feature lets you time each slide as you practice.

Other tools are provided for use during the actual presentation. The Slide Navigator lets you branch directly to any slide, whereas the Pen will annotate a slide for added emphasis. The Meeting Minder enables you to create a list of action items for follow-up after the presentation. The list of items appears as a slide within the presentation. Hidden slides can also be included and displayed at the option of the speaker.

A presentation can be sent electronically to multiple individuals for review. Each reviewer receives a copy of the presentation, enters his or her changes, then returns the revised presentation as an attachment in an e-mail message. Comments from multiple reviewers can be merged in a single session.

The Internet and World Wide Web are thoroughly integrated into all applications in Microsoft Office. Photographs and other resources can be downloaded from the Web for inclusion in a PowerPoint presentation. Information on the Web is protected by copyright, but you are permitted to use a portion of the work for educational or nonprofit uses under the fair use exclusion. Be sure to cite the work appropriately. The Insert Hyperlink command adds a hyperlink to a slide, which can be accessed during a presentation, provided you have an Internet connection. The Save As Web Page command converts a PowerPoint presentation to an HTML document, after which it can be uploaded to a Web server, where it can be accessed through an Internet Browser such as Internet Explorer or Netscape Navigator.

The AutoContent Wizard facilitates the creation of a new presentation. The Wizard asks a series of questions, then it uses your answers to suggest a presentation based on one of several general presentations included within PowerPoint. The end result of the Wizard is an outline based on the topic you selected. The outline is very general, as it must be, but it provides the essential topics to include in your presentation. The AutoContent Wizard is the best way to jump-start the creative process.

The slide master enables you to modify the design of a presentation. Select the slide master from the View menu, then change any element on the slide master and you automatically change that element on every slide in the presentation. PowerPoint also lets you fine-tune a presentation by changing its color scheme or background shading. Bear in mind, however, that it is often difficult (and time consuming) to improve on the original templates, and that this type of effort is often counterproductive.

KEY TERMS

Action Items slide (p. 66)
AutoContent Wizard (p. 91)
Background command (p. 87)
Color Scheme (p. 101)
Copyright (p. 79)
Fair Use (p. 79)
Header and Footer command
  (p. 66)
Hidden slides (p. 66)
HTML (p. 89)

Hyperlink (p. 79)
Insert Hyperlink command (p. 79)
Insert Picture command (p. 79)
Insert Table command (p. 69)
Internet (p. 79)
Internet Explorer (p. 89)
Meeting Minder (p. 66)
Navigation controls (p. 90)
Public domain (p. 79)
Rehearse Timings (p. 66)

Reviewing toolbar (p. 68)
Revisions Pane (p. 68)
Save As Web Page command (p. 89)
Send To command (p. 68)
Slide master (p. 103)
Slide Navigator (p. 77)
Text box (p. 88)
World Wide Web (p. 79)

1. Which of the following is true about hidden slides?
   (a) Hidden slides are invisible in every view
   (b) Hidden slides cannot be accessed during a slide show
   (c) Both (a) and (b)
   (d) Neither (a) nor (b)

2. Which view displays the timings for individual slides after the timings have been established by rehearsing the presentation?
   (a) Slide show
   (b) Normal view
   (c) Slide Sorter view
   (d) Notes pages

3. Which of the following is true about annotating a slide?
   (a) The annotations are permanent; that is, once entered on a slide, they cannot be erased
   (b) The annotations are entered using the pen during the slide show
   (c) Both (a) and (b)
   (d) Neither (a) nor (b)

4. The AutoContent Wizard:
   (a) Creates a single, all-purpose presentation that can be customized as necessary for specific situations
   (b) Inserts a clip art image on every slide according to its content
   (c) Selects the best color scheme and background shading for a presentation according to its content
   (d) None of the above

5. How do you insert a corporate logo on every slide in a presentation?
   (a) Select the image, change to the Slide Sorter view, then paste the image on every slide
   (b) Insert the image on the title slide, then pull down the View menu, and specify every slide
   (c) Insert the image on the slide master
   (d) Insert the image on the title and handouts masters

6. Which of the following is true?
   (a) PowerPoint supplies many different templates, but each template has only one color scheme
   (b) PowerPoint supplies many different templates, and each template in turn has multiple color schemes
   (c) You cannot change the template of a presentation once it has been selected
   (d) You cannot change the color scheme of a presentation once it has been selected

7. Which of the following is true?
   (a) A color scheme specifies eight different colors, one color for each element in a presentation
   (b) You can change any color within a color scheme
   (c) A given template may have many different color schemes
   (d) All of the above

8. How do you insert a hyperlink into a PowerPoint presentation?
   (a) Pull down the Insert menu and click the Hyperlink command
   (b) Click the Insert Hyperlink button on the Standard toolbar
   (c) Both (a) and (b)
   (d) Neither (a) nor (b)

9. What is the easiest way to switch back and forth between PowerPoint and Internet Explorer, given that both are open?
   (a) Click the appropriate button on the Windows taskbar
   (b) Click the Start button, click the Programs command, then choose the appropriate program
   (c) Minimize all applications to display the Windows desktop, then double click the icon for the appropriate application
   (d) All of the above are equally convenient

10. Which slide can be created dynamically as a presentation is shown?
   (a) A hidden slide
   (b) Action Items
   (c) Reviewer comments
   (d) None of the above (slides must be created prior to the slide show)

11. Internet Explorer can display a Web page that is stored on:
   (a) A local area network
   (b) A Web server
   (c) Drive A or drive C of a stand-alone PC
   (d) All of the above

12. How do you save a PowerPoint presentation as a Web page?
   (a) Click the Save button on the Standard toolbar
   (b) Pull down the File menu and click the Save As Web Page command
   (c) Both (a) and (b)
   (d) Neither (a) nor (b)

13. Which of the following requires an Internet connection?
   (a) Using Internet Explorer to view the Microsoft home page
   (b) Using Internet Explorer to view a Web page that is stored locally
   (c) Both (a) and (b)
   (d) Neither (a) nor (b)

14. Which of the following is a true statement regarding the review of a presentation by others?
   (a) A presentation must have multiple reviewers
   (b) The review process is initiated by sending a presentation as an ordinary e-mail attachment
   (c) Each reviewer's comments must be examined in a separate session
   (d) The comments of multiple reviewers can be merged in a single session

15. Which of the following are created as navigation controls for use with Internet Explorer when viewing a PowerPoint presentation?
   (a) An Outline button to toggle the left (outline) pane on and off
   (b) A Notes button to toggle a notes pane on and off
   (c) A full screen slide show button to display the presentation as it would appear in a PowerPoint slide show
   (d) All of the above

ANSWERS

1. d	**6.** b	**11.** d
2. c	**7.** d	**12.** b
3. b	**8.** b	**13.** a
4. d	**9.** a	**14.** d
5. c	**10.** b	**15.** d

1. **The AutoContent Wizard:** The most difficult part of a presentation is getting started. PowerPoint anticipates the problem and provides several existing presentations on a variety of topics.
   a. Start PowerPoint. Pull down the File menu, click New, then click the link From AutoContent Wizard that appears in the task pane. Select a generic presentation, then answer the various questions that the wizard asks.
   b. You should end up with a presentation similar to the one shown in Figure 2.14 except that we have changed the title. Add your name, class, and date to the title page.
   c. Choose any topic you like, then complete the generic presentation that was created by the wizard. You will have to change the title of various slides, delete some existing slides, and possibly add new slides.
   d. Print the completed presentation for your instructor as follows. Print the first slide as a slide to use as a cover page. Print the entire presentation as audience handouts (6 per page). Do not forget to frame the slides. And finally, print the outline of the presentation.
   e. Submit all of the pages to your instructor.

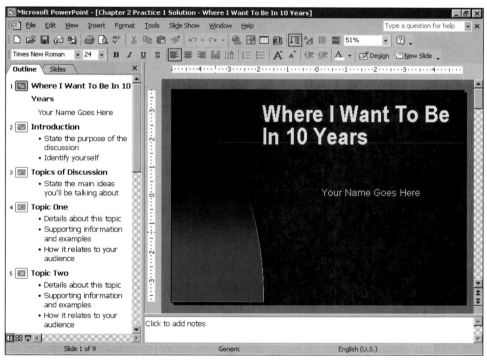

FIGURE 2.14   *The AutoContent Wizard (Exercise 1)*

2. **My Photo Album:** The presentation in Figure 2.15 is based on photographs that were obtained from the Microsoft Media Gallery, but could just as easily have been created with your own pictures from a digital camera. It uses the Format Background command and specifies the various pictures as background effects. The end result is anything but the typical PowerPoint presentation.
   a. Determine the photographs you will use for the presentation, each of which should be saved as a separate file. We have supplied a few photographs within the practice files in the Exploring PowerPoint folder. You can obtain other photographs from the Clip Organizer.

b. To use the Clip Organizer, pull down the Insert menu, click Picture, and click Clip Art to display the Clip Organizer within the task pane. Do not specify any search text (because you are looking for any picture), and change the media type to photographs only. Insert the picture onto a slide, right click the picture from the slide, and use the Save As command to save the picture as a separate file that you can use for a background.

c. Print the audience handouts (six per page) for your instructor. You must specify color (even if you do not have a color printer) within the Color/Grayscale list box within the Print dialog box in order to see the slide backgrounds.

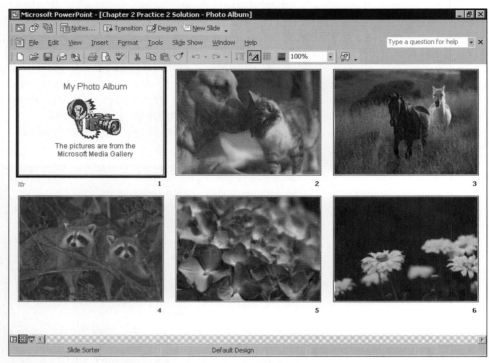

FIGURE 2.15 *My Photo Album (Exercise 2)*

BUILDS ON

PRACTICE EXERCISE 2 PAGES 113–114

3. Presentations as Web Pages: The Save As Web Page command converts a PowerPoint presentation to its HTML equivalent. You can view the resulting document locally (on a PC or local area network), or you can upload it to a Web server, where it can be seen by anyone with Internet access. Choose any presentation from this chapter (we selected the photo album from the previous chapter) and save it as Web Page as shown in Figure 2.16.

Start Internet Explorer and open your presentation (or open it directly from within Windows Explorer). Do you think this is a more effective show than from within PowerPoint? Summarize your thoughts in a brief note to your instructor.

4. Landmarks Around the World: Search the Web to select three different landmarks, download a picture of each landmark, then create a short presentation, consisting of a title slide plus three additional slides similar to the one in Figure 2.17. Write a sentence or two that describes each landmark. Use the Insert Hyperlink command to include a reference to the Web page where you obtained each picture.

Print the presentation in multiple ways. Print the title slide as a full slide to serve as a cover page. Print the entire presentation as audience handouts, six per page. (Be sure to frame the slides.) Print the entire presentation as an outline.

FIGURE 2.16 *Presentations as Web Pages (Exercise 3)*

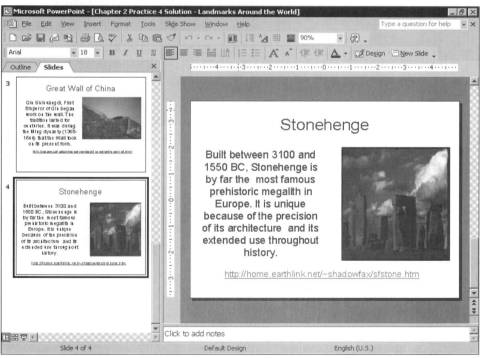

FIGURE 2.17 *Landmarks Around the World (Exercise 4)*

5. Hidden Slides (A Card Trick): You didn't expect a card trick in a book on PowerPoint, but we think you will enjoy this exercise. Open the presentation in *Chapter 2 Practice 5* and follow the instructions. You will see the slide in Figure 2.18. Concentrate on a card and then click the mouse as instructed. Your card will be removed from the stack, and only five cards will remain. Try it as often as you like, choosing a different card each time. We will continue to "read your mind" and will always remove your card from the pile.

We were going to keep the solution to ourselves, but decided instead to include the explanation on a hidden slide. Your task is to unhide the solution, then build a hyperlink to that slide from the title slide.

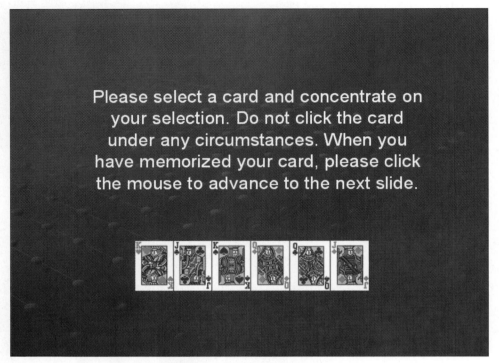

FIGURE 2.18 *Hidden Slides (Exercise 5)*

6. Multiple Masters: The ability to include multiple design templates within a single presentation is a feature that the PowerPoint community has always wanted. It has been added to PowerPoint 2002. Start a new presentation and create the title slide using the default design. Go to the Slide Sorter view and copy that slide five times to create a six-slide presentation.

Select the first slide in the presentation and apply a design template such as Crayons, the design we chose for our presentation. Modify the text on this slide to include the name of the template. Repeat the process for each of the remaining slides, choosing a different design for each slide. Change to the Slide Sorter view to see an overview of your presentation in which the six different designs are visible simultaneously.

PowerPoint also provides the ability to manage the master list as shown in Figure 2.19. Create the presentation as described above, then pull down the View menu and select the Slide Master view. This in turn displays the Slide Master View toolbar, where you can add, delete, or modify the various slide masters that are included in the presentation. (There is nothing specific that you need to do with this screen at this time.) Print the audience handouts (six slides per page) for your instructor as proof you completed the exercise. Be sure to frame the individual slides.

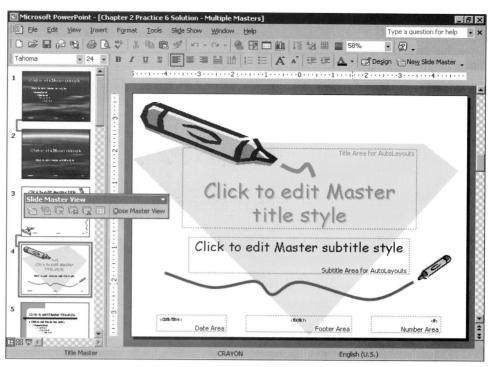

FIGURE 2.19 *Multiple Masters (Exercise 6)*

BUILDS ON

CHAPTER 1
HANDS-ON
EXERCISE 4
PAGES 41–51

7. Navigating within a Presentation: The hyperlinks in a presentation can refer to Web sites and/or they can refer to other slides within a presentation as shown in Figure 2.20. The title slide contains a link to every other slide in the presentation to create a table of contents for the presentation. The title slide also contains a set of navigation buttons that are found on every other slide to enable easy navigation from one slide to the next.

   a. Return to Chapter 1 and complete the fourth hands-on exercise to create the presentation in Figure 2.20.

   b. Modify the title slide to contain a list of the other slides as shown in Figure 2.20. Select the description of each slide, pull down the Insert menu, and select the Hyperlink command. Click the icon for a place in this document and select the appropriate slide to complete the hyperlink.

   c. The navigation (action) buttons that appear at the bottom of the slide are added to the slide master so that they (the buttons) will appear on every slide. Change to the slide master, click the Slide Show menu, click Action Buttons, then select the button you want. Click and drag to create the button on the slide master, then supply the necessary link (such as the next slide).

   d. Go to the Slide Show view and test the navigation. Print the audience handouts (six per page) of the completed presentation for your instructor.

8. Embed TrueType Fonts: The fonts available for inclusion in a presentation are those fonts that have been installed on the specific computer, as opposed to the fonts that are included within Microsoft Office. Thus, if you customize a presentation to include a nonstandard font, that font may be lost if you take the presentation to another computer. You can avoid the problem by embedding the fonts within a presentation.

   Open any presentation and change the title slide to include an unusual font. Pull down the Tools menu and click the Options command to display the Options dialog box in Figure 2.21. Check the box to embed TrueType fonts, then click OK to accept the setting and close the dialog box. Save the presentation, then take it to a different computer. You should see the same font as on the original computer.

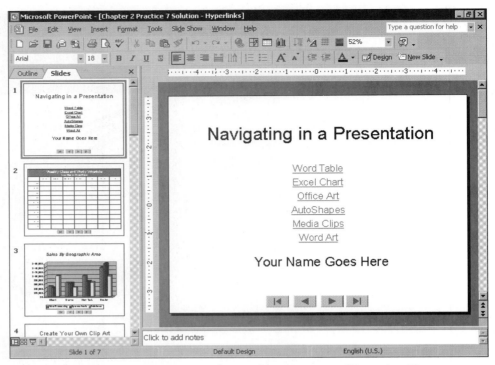

FIGURE 2.20 *Navigating within a Presentation (Exercise 7)*

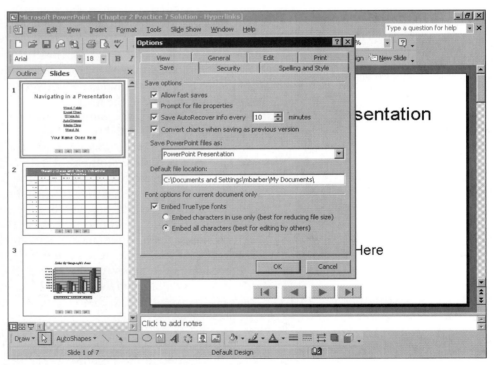

FIGURE 2.21 *Embed TrueType Fonts (Exercise 8)*

9. Pack and Go: Your presentation looks great on your computer, but you just found out that PowerPoint is not installed in the conference room where you are to deliver the presentation. There is a solution. Open any presentation, pull down the File menu, and click the Pack and Go Wizard command to start the wizard as shown in Figure 2.22, and follow the instructions. The end result is an executable file that will show your presentation on any computer, regardless of whether PowerPoint has been installed on that machine.

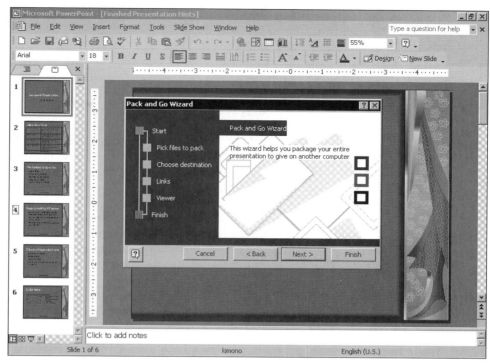

FIGURE 2.22 *Pack and Go (Exercise 9)*

10. Scheduling a Broadcast: Choose any presentation that was completed in the chapter. Pull down the Slide Slow menu, click On Line Broadcast, then click Schedule a Live Broadcast to display the Schedule Presentation Broadcast dialog box. Click the Settings button to display the dialog box in Figure 2.23. Complete the appropriate settings and then schedule the broadcast and notify your audience by e-mail when the presentation will be shown. (You must have access to a presentation server in order to deliver the live broadcast.)

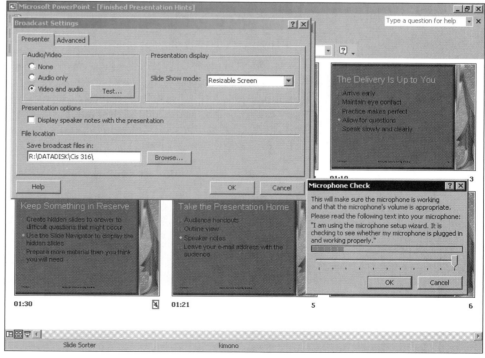

FIGURE 2.23 *Scheduling a Broadcast (Exercise 10)*

FTP for Windows

Microsoft Office simplifies the process of uploading a page to a Web server by including a basic FTP capability. That is the good news. The bad news is that the capability is limited when compared to standalone FTP programs. One advantage of the latter, for example, is the ability to display the progress of a file transfer. In PowerPoint, for example, you click the Save button to upload your presentation, then you wait several seconds (or longer) before the system displays any additional information. An FTP program, however, will display the progress of the file transfer as it takes place.

Use your favorite search engine to locate an FTP program. There are many such programs available, and many permit a free trial period. Locate a specific program, then compare its capabilities to the FTP capability in Office. Summarize your findings in a short note to your instructor.

The Annual Report

Corporate America spends a small fortune to produce its annual reports, which are readily available to the public. Choose any company and obtain a copy of its most recent annual report via the Internet. Use the information in the annual report as the basis for a PowerPoint presentation. PowerPoint is one step ahead of you and offers a suggested financial report through the AutoContent Wizard.

Two Different Clipboards

The Office clipboard is different from the Windows clipboard, but both clipboards share some functionality. Thus, whenever you copy an object to the Office clipboard, it is also copied to the Windows clipboard. However, each successive copy operation *adds* an object to the Office clipboard (up to a maximum of 24 objects), whereas it *replaces* the contents of the Windows clipboard. The Office clipboard also has its own task pane. Experiment with the Office clipboard from different applications, then summarize your findings in a brief note to your instructor.

The Fortune 500

Use the Fortune 500 Web site as the basis of a presentation on America's five largest corporations. Display the names of the corporations in a table, together with the annual sales and a hyperlink to the company's Web site. Complete the presentation by creating five additional slides, one for each company. You need not follow our outline exactly, but we think you will find the Fortune 500 an interesting source of information.

Essentials of
Microsoft® Windows®

OBJECTIVES

AFTER READING THIS SUPPLEMENT YOU WILL BE ABLE TO:

1. Describe the objects on the Windows desktop; use the icons on the desktop to start the associated applications.
2. Explain the significance of the common user interface; identify the elements that are present in every window.
3. Explain in general terms the similarities and differences between various versions of Windows.
4. Use the Help command to learn about Windows.
5. Format a floppy disk.
6. Differentiate between a program file and a data file; explain the significance of the icons that appear next to a file in My Computer and Windows Explorer.
7. Explain how folders are used to organize the files on a disk; use the View menu and/or the Folder Options command to change the appearance of a folder.
8. Distinguish between My Computer and Windows Explorer with respect to viewing files and folders; explain the advantages of the hierarchical view available within Windows Explorer.
9. Use Internet Explorer to download a file; describe how to view a Web page from within Windows Explorer.
10. Copy and/or move a file from one folder to another; delete a file, then recover the deleted file from the Recycle Bin.

OVERVIEW

Microsoft® Windows is a computer program (actually many programs) that controls the operation of a computer and its peripherals. The Windows environment provides a common user interface and consistent command structure for every application. You have seen the interface many times, but do you really understand it? Can

1

you move and copy files with confidence? Do you know how to back up the Excel spreadsheets, Access databases, and other Office documents that you work so hard to create? If not, now is the time to learn. This section is written for you, the computer novice, and it assumes no previous knowledge.

We begin with an introduction to the Windows desktop, the graphical user interface that enables you to work in intuitive fashion by pointing at icons and clicking the mouse. We identify the basic components of a window and describe how to execute commands and supply information through different elements in a dialog box. We introduce you to My Computer, an icon on the Windows desktop, and show you how to use My Computer to access the various components of your system. We also describe how to access the Help command.

The supplement concentrates, however, on disk and file management. We present the basic definitions of a file and a folder, then describe how to use My Computer to look for a specific file or folder. We introduce Windows Explorer, which provides a more efficient way of finding data on your system, then show you how to move or copy a file from one folder to another. We discuss other basic operations, such as renaming and deleting a file. We also describe how to recover a deleted file (if necessary) from the Recycle Bin.

There are also four hands-on exercises, which enable you to apply the conceptual discussion in the text at the computer. The exercises refer to a set of practice files (data disk) that we have created for you. You can obtain these files from our Web site (www.prenhall.com/grauer) or from a local area network if your professor has downloaded the files for you.

THE DESKTOP

Windows 95 was the first of the so-called "modern Windows" and was followed by Windows NT, Windows 98, Windows 2000, Windows Me (Millennium edition), and most recently, by Windows XP. Each of these systems is still in use. Windows 98 and its successor, Windows Me, are geared for the home user and provide extensive support for games and peripheral devices. Windows NT, and its successor Windows 2000, are aimed at the business user and provide increased security and reliability. Windows XP is the successor to all current breeds of Windows. It has a slightly different look, but maintains the conventions of its various predecessors. Hence we have called this module "Essentials of Microsoft Windows" and refer to Windows in a generic sense. (The screens were taken from Windows 2000 Professional, but could just as easily have been taken from other versions of the operating system.)

All versions of Windows create a working environment for your computer that parallels the working environment at home or in an office. You work at a desk. Windows operations take place on the *desktop* as shown in Figure 1. There are physical objects on a desk such as folders, a dictionary, a calculator, or a phone. The computer equivalents of those objects appear as icons (pictorial symbols) on the desktop. Each object on a real desk has attributes (properties) such as size, weight, and color. In similar fashion, Windows assigns properties to every object on its desktop. And just as you can move the objects on a real desk, you can rearrange the objects on the Windows desktop.

Figure 1a displays the typical desktop that appears when Windows is installed on a new computer. It has only a few objects and is similar to the desk in a new office, just after you move in. This desktop might have been taken from any of five systems—Windows 95, Windows NT, Windows 98, Windows 2000, or Windows Me—and is sometimes called "Classic Windows." The icons on this desktop are opened by double clicking. (It is possible to display an alternate desktop with underlined icons that are opened by single clicking, but that option is rarely used.) Figure 1b shows the new Windows XP desktop as it might appear on a home computer, where individual accounts are established for different users.

Double click an icon to open it

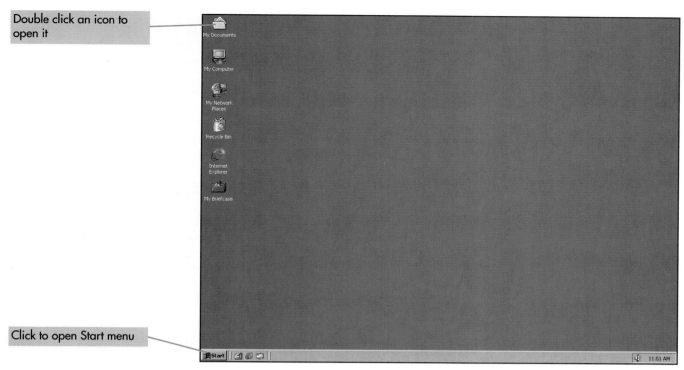

(a) Windows 95, Windows NT, Windows 98, Windows Me, and Windows 2000

Click to open Start menu

Individual desktops are established for different users

(b) Windows XP

FIGURE 1   *The Different Faces of Windows*

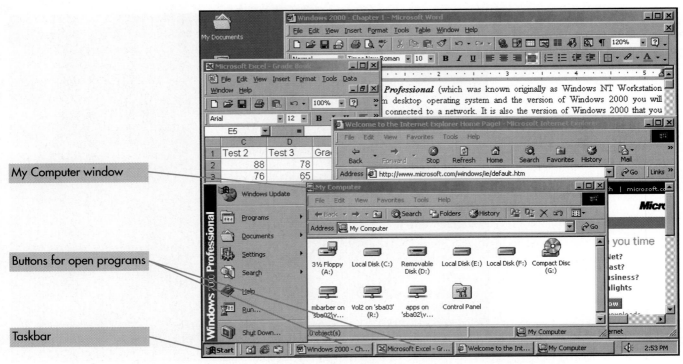

My Computer window

Buttons for open programs

Taskbar

(c) A Working Desktop (all versions of Windows)

FIGURE 1   *The Different Faces of Windows (continued)*

Do not be concerned if your desktop is different from ours. Your real desk is arranged differently from those of your friends, just as your Windows desktop will also be different. Moreover, you are likely to work on different systems—at school, at work, or at home, and thus it is important that you recognize the common functionality that is present on all desktops. The *Start button*, as its name suggests, is where you begin. Click the Start button and you see a menu that lets you start any program installed on your computer.

Look now at Figure 1c, which displays an entirely different desktop, one with four open windows that is similar to a desk in the middle of a working day. Each window in Figure 1c displays a program that is currently in use. The ability to run several programs at the same time is known as *multitasking*, and it is a major benefit of the Windows environment. Multitasking enables you to run a word processor in one window, create a spreadsheet in a second window, surf the Internet in a third window, play a game in a fourth window, and so on. You can work in a program as long as you want, then change to a different program by clicking its window.

You can also change from one program to another by using the taskbar at the bottom of the desktop. The *taskbar* contains a button for each open program, and it enables you to switch back and forth between those programs by clicking the appropriate button. The taskbar in Figure 1a does not contain any buttons (other than the Start button) since there are no open applications. The taskbar in Figure 1c, however, contains four additional buttons, one for each open window.

The icons on the desktop are used to access programs or other functions. The *My Computer* icon is the most basic. It enables you to view the devices on your system, including the drives on a local area network to which you have direct access. Open My Computer in either Figure 1a or 1b, for example, and you see the objects in the My Computer window of Figure 1c. The contents of My Computer depend on the hardware of the specific computer system. Our system, for example, has one floppy drive, three local (hard or fixed) disks, a removable disk (an Iomega Zip drive), a CD-ROM, and access to various network drives. The My Computer window also contains the Control Panel folder that provides access to functions that control other elements of your computing environment. (These capabilities are not used by beginners, are generally "off limits" in a lab environment, and thus are not discussed further.)

The other icons on the desktop are also noteworthy. The *My Documents* folder is a convenient place in which to store the documents you create. *My Network Places* extends the view of your computer to include the other local area networks (if any) that your computer can access, provided you have a valid username and password. The *Recycle Bin* enables you to restore a file that was previously deleted. The Internet Explorer icon starts *Internet Explorer*, the Web browser that is built into the Windows operating system.

THE DOJ (DEPARTMENT OF JUSTICE) VERSUS MICROSOFT

A simple icon is at the heart of the multibillion dollar lawsuit brought by 19 states against Microsoft. In short, Microsoft is accused of integrating its Internet Explorer browser into the Windows operating system with the goal of dominating the market and eliminating the competition. Is Internet Explorer built into every current version of Microsoft Windows? Yes. Can Netscape Navigator run without difficulty under every current version of Microsoft Windows? The answer is also yes. As of this writing the eventual outcome of the case against Microsoft has yet to be determined.

THE COMMON USER INTERFACE

All Windows applications share a *common user interface* and possess a consistent command structure. This means that every Windows application works essentially the same way, which provides a sense of familiarity from one application to the next. In other words, once you learn the basic concepts and techniques in one application, you can apply that knowledge to every other application. Consider, for example, Figure 2, which shows open windows for My Computer and My Network Places, and labels the essential elements in each.

The contents of the two windows are different, but each window has the same essential elements. The *title bar* appears at the top of each window and displays the name of the window, My Computer and My Network Places in Figure 2a and 2b, respectively. The icon at the extreme left of the title bar identifies the window and also provides access to a control menu with operations relevant to the window such as moving it or sizing it. The *minimize button* shrinks the window to a button on the taskbar, but leaves the window in memory. The *maximize button* enlarges the window so that it takes up the entire desktop. The *restore button* (not shown in either figure) appears instead of the maximize button after a window has been maximized, and restores the window to its previous size. The *close button* closes the window and removes it from memory and the desktop.

The *menu bar* appears immediately below the title bar and provides access to *pull-down menus*. One or more *toolbars* appear below the menu bar and let you execute a command by clicking a button as opposed to pulling down a menu. The *status bar* at the bottom of the window displays information about the window as a whole or about a selected object within a window.

A vertical (or horizontal) *scroll bar* appears at the right (or bottom) border of a window when its contents are not completely visible and provides access to the unseen areas. A scroll bar does not appear in Figure 2a since all of the objects in the window are visible at the same time. A vertical scroll bar is found in Figure 2b, however, since there are other objects in the window.

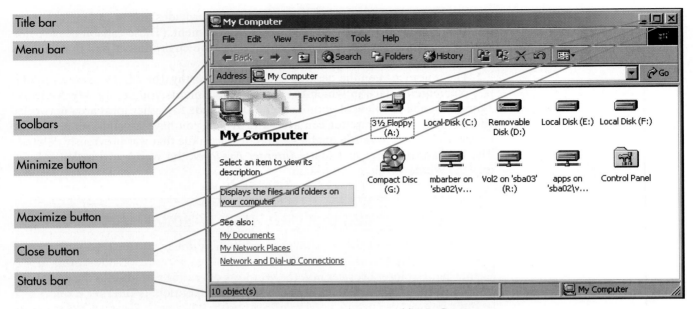

Title bar

Menu bar

Toolbars

Minimize button

Maximize button

Close button

Status bar

(a) My Computer

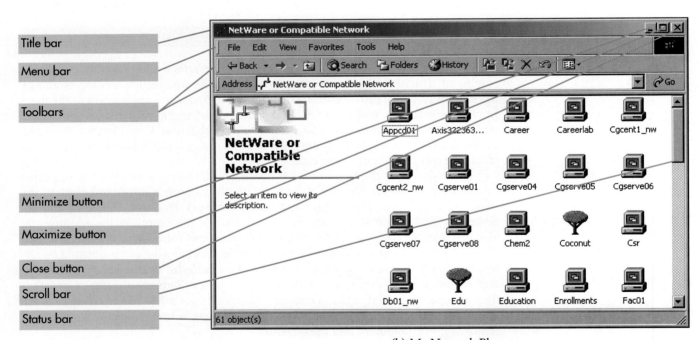

Title bar

Menu bar

Toolbars

Minimize button

Maximize button

Close button

Scroll bar

Status bar

(b) My Network Places

FIGURE 2 *Anatomy of a Window*

Moving and Sizing a Window

A window can be sized or moved on the desktop through appropriate actions with the mouse. To *size a window*, point to any border (the mouse pointer changes to a double arrow), then drag the border in the direction you want to go—inward to shrink the window or outward to enlarge it. You can also drag a corner (instead of a border) to change both dimensions at the same time. To *move a window* while retaining its current size, click and drag the title bar to a new position on the desktop.

Pull-Down Menus

The menu bar provides access to *pull-down menus* that enable you to execute commands within an application (program). A pull-down menu is accessed by clicking the menu name or by pressing the Alt key plus the underlined letter in the menu name; for example, press Alt+V to pull down the View menu. (You may have to press the Alt key in order to see the underlines.) Three pull-down menus associated with My Computer are shown in Figure 3.

Commands within a menu are executed by clicking the command or by typing the underlined letter. Alternatively, you can bypass the menu entirely if you know the equivalent keystrokes shown to the right of the command in the menu (e.g., Ctrl+X, Ctrl+C, or Ctrl+V to cut, copy, or paste as shown within the Edit menu). A dimmed command (e.g., the Paste command in the Edit menu) means the command is not currently executable; some additional action has to be taken for the command to become available.

An ellipsis (...) following a command indicates that additional information is required to execute the command; for example, selection of the Format command in the File menu requires the user to specify additional information about the format-

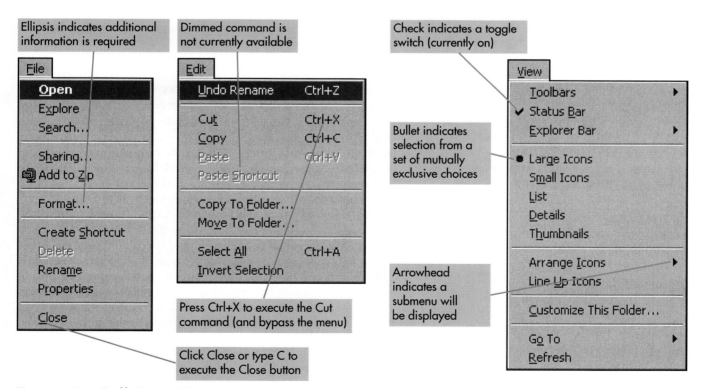

FIGURE 3 *Pull-Down Menus*

ting process. This information is entered into a dialog box (discussed in the next section), which appears immediately after the command has been selected.

A check next to a command indicates a toggle switch, whereby the command is either on or off. There is a check next to the Status Bar command in the View menu of Figure 3, which means the command is in effect (and thus the status bar will be displayed). Click the Status Bar command and the check disappears, which suppresses the display of the status bar. Click the command a second time and the check reappears, as does the status bar in the associated window.

A bullet next to an item (e.g., Large Icons in Figure 3) indicates a selection from a set of mutually exclusive choices. Click another option within the group (e.g., Small Icons) and the bullet will disappear from the previous selection (Large Icons) and appear next to the new selection (Small Icons).

An arrowhead after a command (e.g., the Arrange Icons command in the View menu) indicates that a submenu (also known as a cascaded menu) will be displayed with additional menu options.

Dialog Boxes

A *dialog box* appears when additional information is necessary to execute a command. Click the Print command in Internet Explorer, for example, and you are presented with the Print dialog box in Figure 4, requesting information about precisely what to print and how. The information is entered into the dialog box in different ways, depending on the type of information that is required. The tabs at the top of the dialog box provide access to different sets of options. The General and Paper tabs are selected in Figures 4a and 4b, respectively.

Option (Radio) buttons indicate mutually exclusive choices, one of which must be chosen, such as the page range in Figure 4a. You can print all pages, the selection (highlighted text), the current page, or a specific set of pages (such as pages 1–4), but you can choose one and only one option. Click a button to select an option, which automatically deselects the previously selected option.

A *text box* enters specific information such as the pages that will be printed in conjunction with selecting the radio button for pages. A flashing vertical bar (an I-beam) appears within the text box when the text box is active, to mark the insertion point for the text you will enter.

A *spin button* is another way to enter specific information such as the number of copies. Click the Up or Down arrow to increase or decrease the number of pages, respectively. You can also enter the information explicitly by typing it into a spin box, just as you would a text box.

Check boxes are used instead of option buttons if the choices are not mutually exclusive or if an option is not required. The Collate check box is checked in Figure 4a, whereas the Print to file box is not checked. Individual options are selected and cleared by clicking the appropriate check box, which toggles the box on and off.

A *list box* such as the Size is list box in Figure 4b displays some or all of the available choices, any one of which is selected by clicking the desired item. Just click the Down arrow on the list box to display the associated choices such as the paper source in Figure 4b. (A scroll bar appears within an open list box if all of the choices are not visible and provides access to the hidden choices.)

The *Help button* (a question mark at the right end of the title bar) provides help for any item in the dialog box. Click the button, then click the item in the dialog box for which you want additional information. The Close button (the X at the extreme right of the title bar) closes the dialog box without executing the command.

Tabs provide access to
different sets of options

Spin buttons

Check box is clear if
option is not required

Option buttons indicate
mutually exclusive choices

Text box enters
specific information

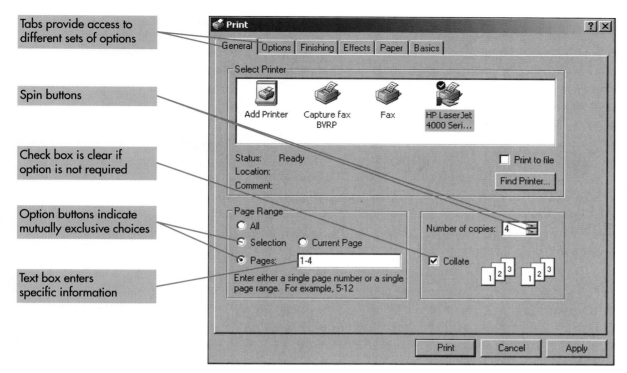

(a) General Tab

Help button

Close button

List box displays some
or all available choices

Click down arrow to
display associated choices

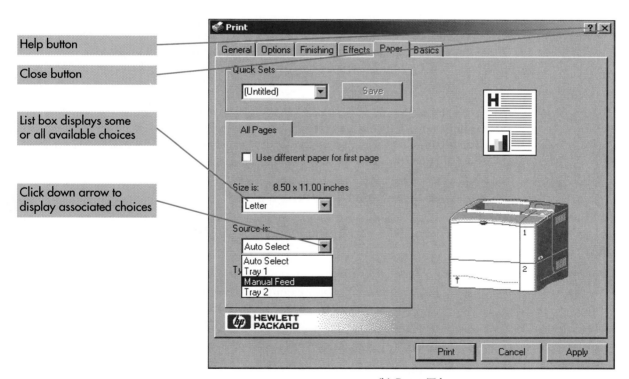

(b) Paper Tab

FIGURE 4   *Dialog Boxes*

All dialog boxes also contain one or more **command buttons**, the function of which is generally apparent from the button's name. The Print button, in Figure 4a, for example, initiates the printing process. The Cancel button does just the opposite, and ignores (cancels) any changes made to the settings, then closes the dialog box without further action. An ellipsis (three dots) on a command button indicates that additional information will be required if the button is selected.

THE MOUSE

The mouse is indispensable to Windows and is referenced continually in the hands-on exercises throughout the text. There are five basic operations with which you must become familiar:

- To *point* to an object, move the mouse pointer onto the object.
- To *click* an object, point to it, then press and release the left mouse button.
- To *right click* an object, point to the object, then press and release the right mouse button. Right clicking an object displays a context-sensitive menu with commands that pertain to the object.
- To *double click* an object, point to it and then quickly click the left button twice in succession.
- To *drag* an object, move the pointer to the object, then press and hold the left button while you move the mouse to a new position.

You may also encounter a mouse with a wheel between the left and right buttons that lets you scroll through a document by rotating the wheel forward or backward. The action of the wheel, however, may change, depending on the application in use. In any event, the mouse is a pointing device—move the mouse on your desk and the mouse pointer, typically a small arrowhead, moves on the monitor. The mouse pointer assumes different shapes according to the location of the pointer or the nature of the current action. You will see a double arrow when you change the size of a window, an I-beam as you insert text, a hand to jump from one help topic to the next, or a circle with a line through it to indicate that an attempted action is invalid.

The mouse pointer will also change to an hourglass to indicate Windows is processing your command, and that no further commands may be issued until the action is completed. The more powerful your computer, the less frequently the hourglass will appear.

The Mouse versus the Keyboard

Almost every command in Windows can be executed in different ways, using either the mouse or the keyboard. Most people start with the mouse and add keyboard shortcuts as they become more proficient. There is no right or wrong technique, just different techniques, and the one you choose depends entirely on personal preference in a specific situation. If, for example, your hands are already on the keyboard, it is faster to use the keyboard equivalent. Other times, your hand will be on the mouse and that will be the fastest way. Toolbars provide still other ways to execute common commands.

In the beginning, you may wonder why there are so many different ways to do the same thing, but you will eventually recognize the many options as part of Windows' charm. It is not necessary to memorize anything, nor should you even try; just be flexible and willing to experiment. The more you practice, the faster all of this will become second nature to you.

All versions of Windows include extensive documentation with detailed information about virtually every function in Windows. It is accessed through the ***Help command*** on the Start menu, which provides different ways to search for information.

The ***Contents tab*** in Figure 5a is analogous to the table of contents in an ordinary book. The topics are listed in the left pane and the information for the selected topic is displayed in the right pane. The list of topics can be displayed in varying amounts of detail, by opening and closing the various book icons that appear. (The size of the left pane can be increased or decreased by dragging the border between the left and right pane in the appropriate direction.)

A closed book such as "Troubleshooting and Maintenance" indicates the presence of subtopics, which are displayed by opening (clicking) the book. An open book, on the other hand, such as "Internet, E-mail, and Communications," already displays its subtopics. Each subtopic is shown with one of two icons—a question mark to indicate "how to" information, or an open book to indicate conceptual information. Either way, you can click any subtopic in the left pane to view its contents in the right pane. Underlined entries in the right pane (e.g., Related Topics) indicate a hyperlink, which in turn displays additional information. Note, too, that you can print the information in the right pane by pulling down the Options menu and selecting the Print command.

The ***Index tab*** in Figure 5b is analogous to the index of an ordinary book. You enter the first several letters of the topic to look up, such as "floppy disk," choose a topic from the resulting list, and then click the Display button to view the information in the right pane. The underlined entries in the right pane represent hyperlinks, which you can click to display additional topics. And, as in the Contents window, you can print the information in the right pane by pulling down the Options menu and selecting the Print command.

The ***Search tab*** (not shown in Figure 5) displays a more extensive listing of entries than does the Index tab. It lets you enter a specific word or phrase and then it returns every topic containing that word or phrase.

The ***Favorites tab*** enables you to save the information within specified help topics as bookmarks, in order to return to those topics at a later date, as explained in the following hands-on exercise.

FORMATTING A FLOPPY DISK

You will soon begin to work on the computer, which means that you will be using various applications to create different types of documents. Each document is saved in its own file and stored on disk, either on a local disk (e.g., drive C) if you have your own computer, or on a floppy disk (drive A) if you are working in a computer lab at school.

All disks have to be formatted before they can hold data. The formatting process divides a disk into concentric circles called tracks, and then further divides each track into sectors. You don't have to worry about formatting a hard disk, as that is done at the factory prior to the machine being sold. You typically don't even have to format a floppy disk, since most floppies today are already formatted when you buy them. Nevertheless, it is very easy to format a floppy disk and it is a worthwhile exercise. Be aware, however, that formatting erases any data that was previously on a disk, so be careful not to format a disk with important data (e.g., one containing today's homework assignment). Formatting is accomplished through the ***Format command***. The process is straightforward, as you will see in the hands-on exercise that follows.

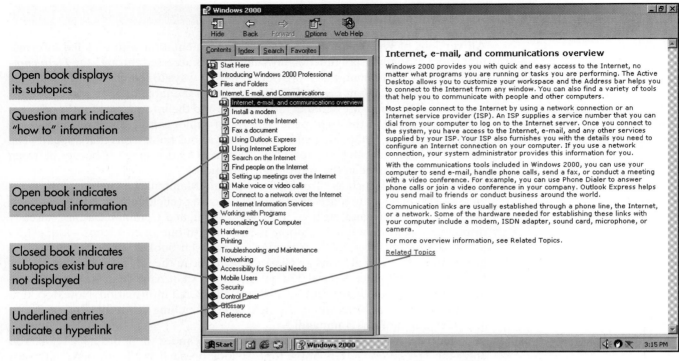

Open book displays its subtopics

Question mark indicates "how to" information

Open book indicates conceptual information

Closed book indicates subtopics exist but are not displayed

Underlined entries indicate a hyperlink

(a) Contents Tab

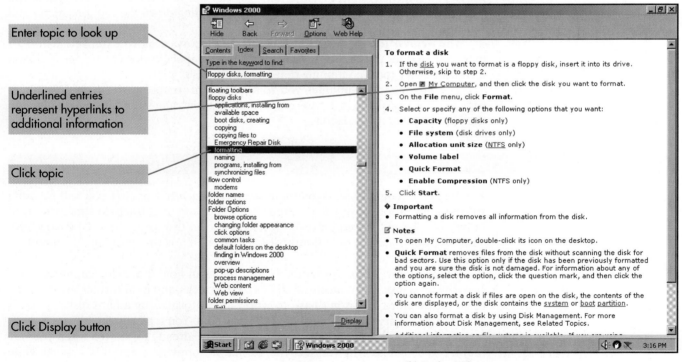

Enter topic to look up

Underlined entries represent hyperlinks to additional information

Click topic

Click Display button

(b) Index Tab

FIGURE 5   *The Help Command*

WELCOME TO WINDOWS

Objective   To turn on the computer, start Windows, and open My Computer; to move and size a window; to format a floppy disk and use the Help command. Use Figure 6 as a guide in the exercise.

Step 1:   **Open My Computer**

➤ Start the computer by turning on the various switches appropriate to your system. Your system will take a minute or so to boot up, after which you may be asked for a **user name** and **password**.

➤ Enter this information, after which you should see the desktop in Figure 6a. It does not matter if you are using a different version of Windows.

➤ Close the Getting Started with Windows 2000 window if it appears. Do not be concerned if your desktop differs from ours.

➤ The way in which you open My Computer (single or double clicking) depends on the options in effect as described in step 2. Either way, however, you can **right click** the **My Computer icon** to display a context-sensitive menu, then click the **Open command**.

➤ The My Computer window will open on your desktop, but the contents of your window and/or its size and position will be different from ours. You are ready to go to work.

Right click My Computer and click Open from the context-sensitive menu

Click to close Getting Started with Windows 2000 window

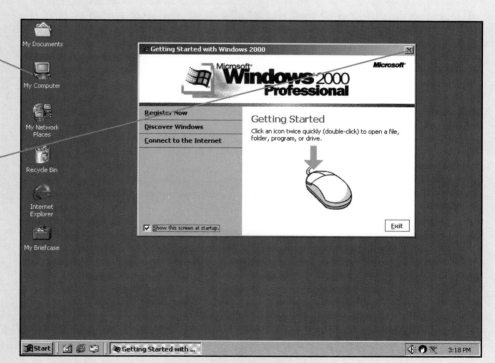

(a) Open My Computer (step 1)

FIGURE 6   *Hands-on Exercise 1*

Step 2: **Set the Folder Options**

➤ Pull down the **Tools menu** and click the **Folder Options command** to display the Folder Options dialog box. Click the **General tab**, then set the options as shown in Figure 6b. (Your network administrator may have disabled this command, in which case you will use the default settings.)
  • The Active desktop enables you to display Web content directly on the desktop. We suggest that you disable this option initially.
  • Enabling Web content in folders displays the template at the left side of the window. The Windows classic option does not contain this information.
  • Opening each successive folder within the same window saves space on the desktop as you browse the system. We discuss this in detail later on.
  • The choice between clicking underlined items and double clicking an icon (without the underline) is personal. We prefer to double click.
➤ Click **OK** to accept the settings and close the Folder Options dialog box. The My Computer window on your desktop should be similar to ours.

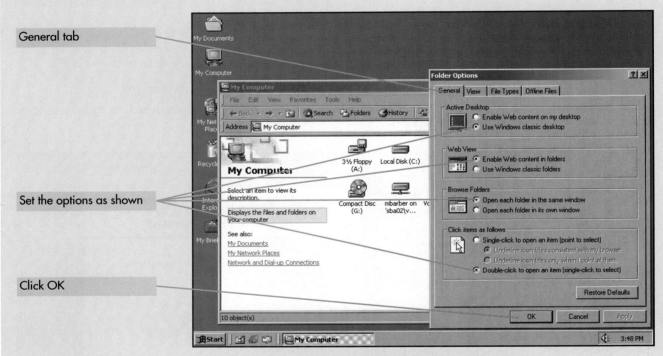

(b) Set the Folder Options (step 2)

FIGURE 6 *Hands-on Exercise 1 (continued)*

IT'S DIFFERENT IN WINDOWS 98

The Folder Options command is under the View menu in Windows 98, whereas it is found in the Tools menu in Windows 2000. Thus, to go from clicking to double clicking in Windows 98, pull down the View menu, click Folder Options, click the General tab, then choose Web style or Classic style, respectively. The procedure to display Web content in a folder is also different in Windows 98; you need to pull down the View menu and toggle the As Web Page command on.

Step 3:   **Move and Size a Window**

➤ If necessary, pull down the **View menu** and click **Large Icons** so that your My Computer window more closely resembles the window in Figure 6c.

➤ Move and size the My Computer window on your desktop to match the display in Figure 6c.

 • To change the width or height of the window, click and drag a border (the mouse pointer changes to a double arrow) in the direction you want to go.

 • To change the width and height at the same time, click and drag a corner rather than a border.

 • To change the position of the window, click and drag the title bar.

➤ Click the **minimize button** to shrink the My Computer window to a button on the taskbar. My Computer is still active in memory, however. Click the **My Computer button** on the taskbar to reopen the window.

➤ Click the **maximize button** so that the My Computer window expands to fill the entire screen. Click the **restore button** (which replaces the maximize button and is not shown in Figure 6c) to return the window to its previous size.

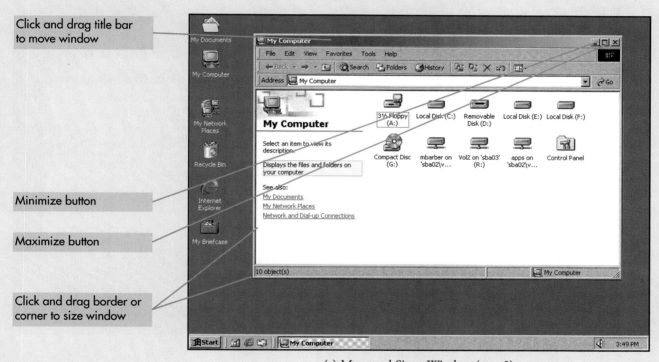

Click and drag title bar to move window

Minimize button

Maximize button

Click and drag border or corner to size window

(c) Move and Size a Window (step 3)

FIGURE 6   *Hands-on Exercise 1 (continued)*

MINIMIZING VERSUS CLOSING AN APPLICATION

Minimizing an application leaves the application open in memory and available at the click of the taskbar button. Closing it, however, removes the application from memory, which also causes it to disappear from the taskbar. The advantage of minimizing an application is that you can return to the application immediately. The disadvantage is that leaving too many applications open simultaneously may degrade performance.

Step 4: **Use the Pull-Down Menus**

➤ Pull down the **View menu**, then click the **Toolbars command** to display a cascaded menu as shown in Figure 6d. If necessary, check the commands for the **Standard Buttons** and **Address Bar**, and clear the commands for Links and Radio.

➤ Pull down the **View menu** to make or verify the following selections. (You have to pull down the View menu each time you make an additional change.)
  • The **Status Bar command** should be checked. The Status Bar command functions as a toggle switch. Click the command and the status bar is displayed; click the command a second time and the status bar disappears.)
  • Click the **Details command** to change to this view. Notice that the different views are grouped within the menu and that only one view at a time can be selected.

➤ Pull down the **View menu** once again, click (or point to) the **Explorer Bar command**, and verify that none of the options is checked.

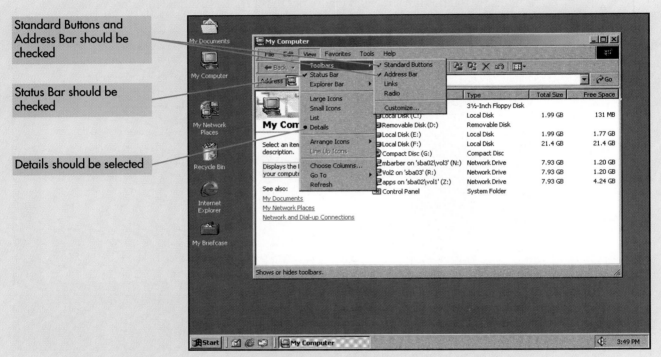

Standard Buttons and Address Bar should be checked

Status Bar should be checked

Details should be selected

(d) Use the Pull-Down Menus (step 4)

FIGURE 6 *Hands-on Exercise 1 (continued)*

DESIGNATING THE DEVICES ON A SYSTEM

The first (usually only) floppy drive is always designated as drive A. (A second floppy drive, if it were present, would be drive B.) The first hard (local) disk on a system is always drive C, whether or not there are one or two floppy drives. Additional local drives, if any, a Zip (removable storage) drive, a network drive, and/or the CD-ROM are labeled from D on.

Step 5:   **Format a Floppy Disk**

➤ Place a floppy disk in drive A. Select (click) drive A, then pull down the **File menu** and click the **Format command** to display the dialog box in Figure 6e.
   • Set the **Capacity** to match the floppy disk you purchased (1.44MB for a high-density disk and 720KB for a double-density disk).
   • Click the **Volume label text box** if it's empty or click and drag over the existing label. Enter a new label (containing up to 11 characters).
   • You can check the **Quick Format box** if the disk has been previously formatted, as a convenient way to erase the contents of the disk.
➤ Click the **Start button**, then click **OK** after you have read the warning. The formatting process erases anything that is on the disk, so be sure that you do not need anything on the disk you are about to format.
➤ Click **OK** after the formatting is complete. Close the Format dialog box, then save the formatted disk for use with various exercises later in the text.
➤ Close the My Computer window.

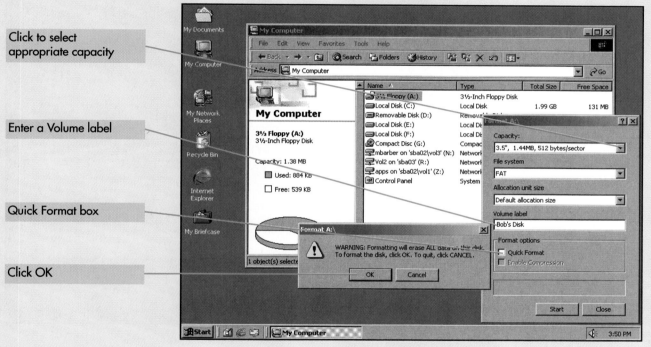

Click to select appropriate capacity

Enter a Volume label

Quick Format box

Click OK

(e) Format a Floppy Disk (step 5)

FIGURE 6   *Hands-on Exercise 1 (continued)*

THE HELP BUTTON

The Help button (a question mark) appears in the title bar of almost every dialog box. Click the question mark, then click the item you want information about (which then appears in a pop-up window). To print the contents of the pop-up window, click the right mouse button inside the window, and click Print Topic. Click outside the pop-up window to close the window and continue working.

Step 6: **The Help Command**

➤ Click the **Start button** on the taskbar, then click the **Help command** to display the Help window in Figure 6f. Maximize the Help window.

➤ Click the **Contents tab**, then click a closed book such as **Hardware** to open the book and display the associated topics. Click any one of the displayed topics such as **Hardware overview** in Figure 6f.

➤ Pull down the **Options menu** and click the **Print command** to display the Print Topics dialog box. Click the option button to print the selected topic, click **OK**, then click the **Print button** in the resulting dialog box.

➤ Click the **Index tab**, type **format** (the first several letters in "Formatting disks," the topic you are searching for). Double click the subtopic "overview". Pull down the **Options menu** and click the **Print command** to print this information as well.

➤ Submit the printed information to your instructor. Close the Help window.

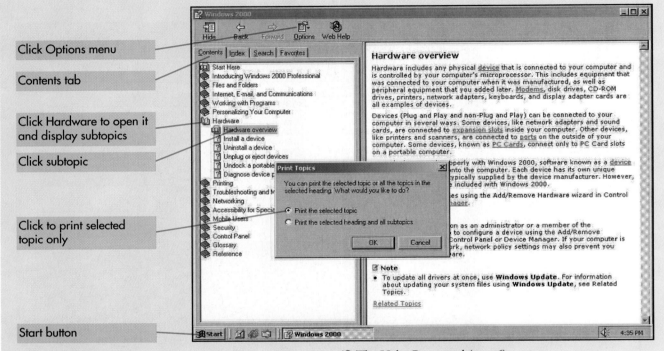

(f) The Help Command (step 6)

FIGURE 6 *Hands-on Exercise 1 (continued)*

THE FAVORITES TAB

Do you find yourself continually searching for the same Help topic? If so, you can make life a little easier by adding the topic to a list of favorite Help topics. Start Help, then use the Contents, Index, or Search tabs to locate the desired topic. Now click the Favorites tab in the Help window, then click the Add button to add the topic. You can return to the topic at any time by clicking the Favorites tab, then double clicking the bookmark to display the information.

Step 7:   **Shut Down the Computer**

> ➤ It is very important that you shut down your computer properly as opposed to just turning off the power. This enables Windows to properly close all of its system files and to save any changes that were made during the session.
> ➤ Click the **Start button**, click the **Shut Down command** to display the Shut Down Windows dialog box in Figure 6g. Click the **drop-down arrow** to display the desired option, then click **OK**.
> > • Logging off ends your session, but leaves the computer running at full power. This is the typical option you select in a laboratory setting.
> > • Shutting down the computer ends the session and also closes Windows so that you can safely turn the power off. (Some computers will automatically turn the power off for you if this option is selected.)
> > • Restarting the computer ends your sessions, then closes and restarts Windows to begin a new session.
> ➤ Welcome to Windows 2000!

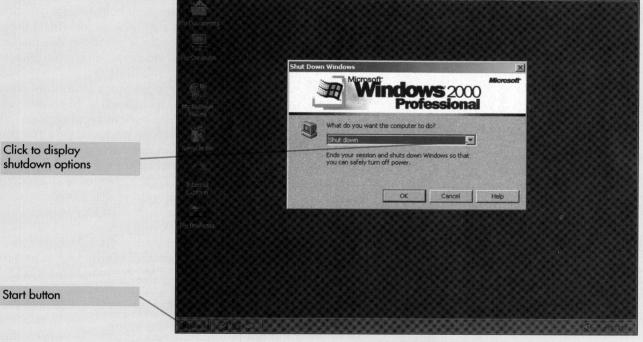

Click to display shutdown options

Start button

(g) Shut Down the Computer (step 7)

FIGURE 6   *Hands-on Exercise 1 (continued)*

THE TASK MANAGER

The Start button is the normal way to exit Windows. Occasionally, however, an application may "hang"—in which case you want to close the problem application but leave Windows open. Press Ctrl+Alt+Del to display the Windows Security dialog box, then click the Task Manager command button. Click the Applications tab, select the problem application, and click the End Task button.

A *file* is a set of instructions or data that has been given a name and stored on disk. There are two basic types of files, *program files* and *data files*. Microsoft Word and Microsoft Excel are examples of program files. The documents and workbooks created by these programs are examples of data files.

A *program file* is an executable file because it contains instructions that tell the computer what to do. A *data file* is not executable and can be used only in conjunction with a specific program. As a typical student, you execute (run) program files, then you use those programs to create and/or modify the associated data files.

Every file has a *file name* that identifies it to the operating system. The file name may contain up to 255 characters and may include spaces. (File names cannot contain the following characters: \, /, :, *, ?, ", <, >, or |. We suggest that you try to keep file names simple and restrict yourself to the use of letters, numbers, and spaces.) Long file names permit descriptive entries such as *Term Paper for Western Civilization* (as distinct from a more cryptic *TPWCIV* that was required under MS-DOS and Windows 3.1).

Files are stored in *folders* to better organize the hundreds (thousands, or tens of thousands) of files on a hard disk. A Windows folder is similar in concept to a manila folder in a filing cabinet into which you put one or more documents (files) that are somehow related to each other. An office worker stores his or her documents in manila folders. In Windows, you store your files (documents) in electronic folders on disk.

Folders are the keys to the Windows storage system. Some folders are created automatically; for example, the installation of a program such as Microsoft Office automatically creates one or more folders to hold the various program files. Other folders are created by the user to hold the documents he or she creates. You could, for example, create one folder for your word processing documents and a second folder for your spreadsheets. Alternatively, you can create a folder to hold all of your work for a specific class, which may contain a combination of word processing documents and spreadsheets. The choice is entirely up to you, and you can use any system that makes sense to you. Anything at all can go into a folder—program files, data files, even other folders.

Figure 7 displays the contents of a hypothetical Homework folder with six documents. Figure 7a enables Web content, and so we see the colorful logo at the left of the folder, together with links to My Documents, My Network Places, and My Computer. Figure 7b is displayed without the Web content, primarily to gain space within the window. The display or suppression of the Web content is determined by a setting in the Folder Options command.

Figures 7a and 7b are displayed in different views. Figure 7a uses the *Large Icons view*, whereas Figure 7b is displayed in the *Details view*, which shows additional information for each file. (Other possible views include Small Icons, List, and Thumbnail.) The file icon, whether large or small, indicates the *file type* or application that was used to create the file. The History of Computers file, for example, is a Microsoft Word document. The Grade Book is a Microsoft Excel workbook.

Regardless of the view and options in effect, the name of the folder (Homework) appears in the title bar next to the icon of an open folder. The minimize, maximize, and Close buttons appear at the right of the title bar. A menu bar with six pull-down menus appears below the title bar. The Standard Buttons toolbar appears below the menu, and the Address Bar (indicating the drive and folder) appears below the toolbar. A status bar appears at the bottom of both windows, indicating that the Homework folder contains six objects (documents) and that the total file size is 525KB.

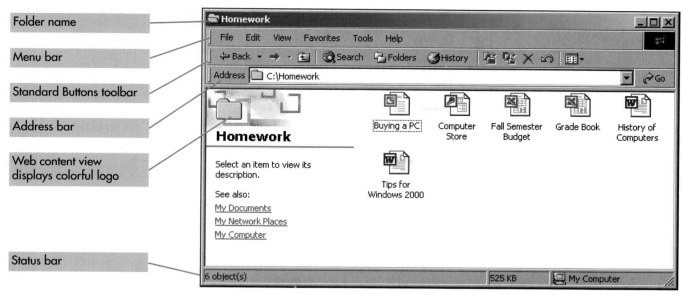

Folder name

Menu bar

Standard Buttons toolbar

Address bar

Web content view
displays colorful logo

Status bar

(a) Large Icons View with Web Content Enabled

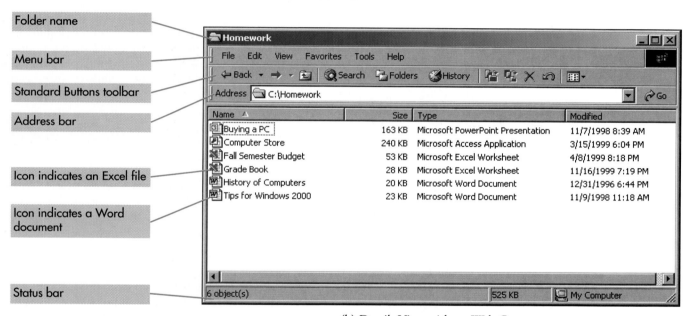

Folder name

Menu bar

Standard Buttons toolbar

Address bar

Icon indicates an Excel file

Icon indicates a Word
document

Status bar

(b) Details View without Web Content

FIGURE 7   *The Homework Folder*

CHANGE THE VIEW

Look closely at the address bar in Figures 7a and 7b to see that both figures display the Homework folder on drive C, although the figures are very different in appearance. Figure 7a displays Web content to provide direct links to three other folders, and the contents of the Homework folder are displayed in the Large Icons view to save space. Figure 7b suppresses the Web content and uses the Details view to provide the maximum amount of information for each file in the Homework folder. You are free to choose whichever options you prefer.

My Computer enables you to browse through the various drives and folders on a system in order to locate a document and go to work. Let's assume that you're looking for a document called "History of Computers" that you saved previously in the Homework folder on drive C. To get to this document, you would open My Computer, from where you would open drive C, open the Homework folder, and then open the document. It's a straightforward process that can be accomplished in two different ways, as shown in Figure 8.

The difference between the two figures is whether each drive or folder is opened in its own window, as shown in Figure 8a, or whether the same window is used for every folder, as in Figure 8b. (This is another option that is set through the Folder Options command.) In Figure 8a you begin by double clicking the My Computer icon on the desktop to open the My Computer window, which in turn displays the devices on your system. Next, you double click the icon for drive C to open a second window that displays the folders on drive C. From there, you double click the icon for the Homework folder to open a third window containing the documents in the Homework folder. Once in the Homework folder, you can double click the icon of an existing document, which starts the associated application and opens the document.

The process is identical in Figure 8b except that each object opens in the same window. The Back arrow on the Standard Buttons toolbar is meaningful in Figure 8b because you can click the button to return to the previous window (drive C), then click it again to go back to My Computer. Note, however, that the button is dimmed in all three windows in Figure 8a because there is no previous window, since each folder is opened in its own window.

THE EXPLORING OFFICE PRACTICE FILES

There is only one way to master the file operations inherent in Windows and that is to practice at the computer. To do so requires that you have a series of files with which to work. We have created these files for you, and we reference them in the next several hands-on exercises. Your instructor will make these files available to you in a variety of ways:

- The files can be downloaded from our Web site, assuming that you have access to the Internet and that you have a basic proficiency with Internet Explorer. Software and other files that are downloaded from the Internet are typically compressed (made smaller) to reduce the amount of time it takes to transmit the file. In essence, you will download a *compressed file* (which may contain multiple individual files) from our Web site and then uncompress the file onto a local drive as described in the next hands-on exercise.
- The files might be on a network drive, in which case you can use My Computer (or Windows Explorer, which is discussed later in the chapter) to copy the files from the network drive to a floppy disk. The procedure to do this is described in the third hands-on exercise.
- There may be an actual "data disk" in the computer lab. Go to the lab with a floppy disk, then use the Copy Disk command (on the File menu of My Computer) to duplicate the data disk and create a copy for yourself.

It doesn't matter how you obtain the practice files, only that you are able to do so. Indeed, you may want to try different techniques in order to gain additional practice with Windows.

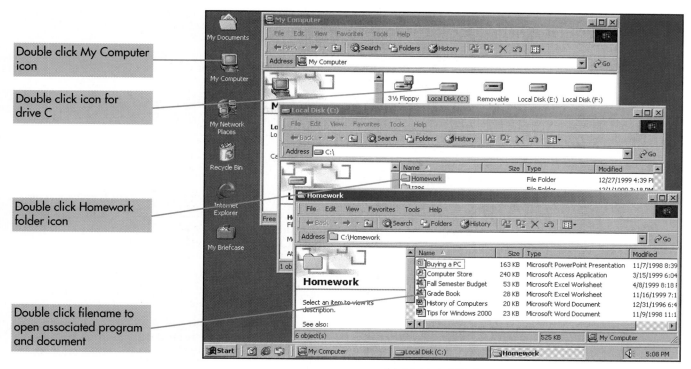

Double click My Computer icon

Double click icon for drive C

Double click Homework folder icon

Double click filename to open associated program and document

(a) Multiple Windows

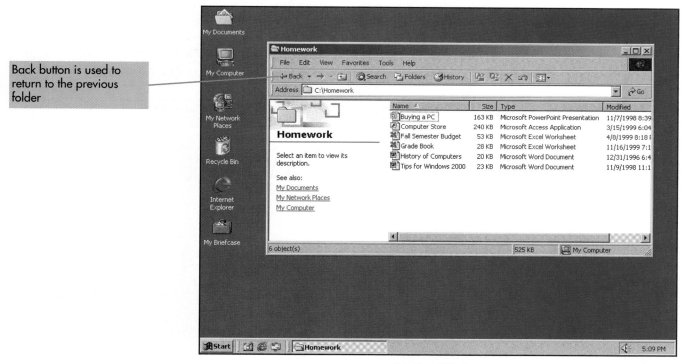

Back button is used to return to the previous folder

(b) One Window

FIGURE 8 *Browsing My Computer*

THE PRACTICE FILES VIA THE WEB

Objective   To download a file from the Web. The exercise requires a formatted floppy disk and access to the Internet. Use Figure 9 as a guide in the exercise.

Step 1:   **Start Internet Explorer**

➤ Start Internet Explorer, perhaps by double clicking the **Internet Explorer icon** on the desktop, or by clicking the **Start button**, clicking the **Programs command**, then locating the command to start the program. If necessary, click the **maximize button** so that Internet Explorer takes the entire desktop.

➤ Enter the address of the site you want to visit:
  • Pull down the **File menu**, click the **Open command** to display the Open dialog box, and enter **www.prenhall.com/grauer** (the http:// is assumed). Click **OK**.
  • *Or,* click in the **Address bar** below the toolbar, which automatically selects the current address (so that whatever you type replaces the current address). Enter the address of the site you want to visit, **www.prenhall.com/grauer** (the http:// is assumed). Press **enter**.

➤ You should see the *Exploring Office Series* home page as shown in Figure 9a. Click the book for **Office XP**, which takes you to the Office XP home page.

➤ Click the **Student Resources link** (at the top of the window) to go to the Student Resources page.

Enter address of site

Click book for Office XP

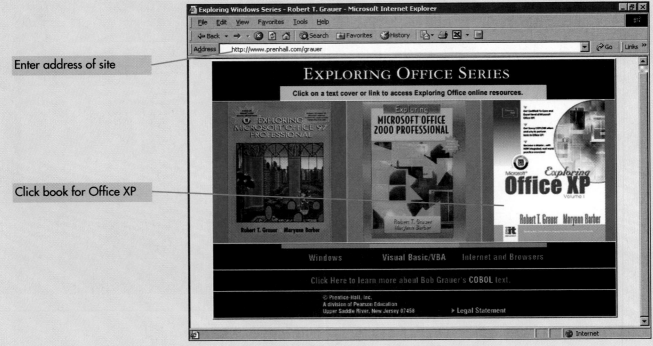

(a) Start Internet Explorer (step 1)

FIGURE 9   *Hands-on Exercise 2*

Step 2: **Download the Practice Files**

➤ Click the link to **Student Data Disk** (in the right frame), then scroll down the page until you can see **Essentials of Microsoft Windows**.

➤ Click the indicated link to download the practice files. The Save As dialog box is not yet visible.

➤ You will see the File Download dialog box asking what you want to do. Click **Save**. The Save As dialog box appears as shown in Figure 9b.

➤ Place a formatted floppy disk in drive A, click the **drop-down arrow** on the Save in list box, and select (click) **drive A**. Click **Save** to begin downloading the file.

➤ The File Download window will reappear on your screen and show you the status of the downloading operation. If necessary, click **Close** when you see the dialog box indicating that the download is complete.

➤ Close Internet Explorer.

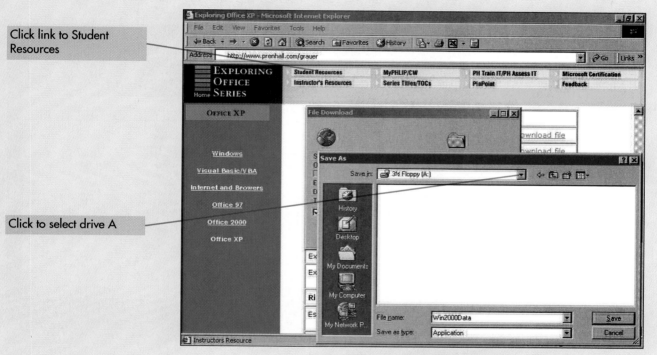

Click link to Student Resources

Click to select drive A

(b) Download the Practice Files (step 2)

FIGURE 9   *Hands-on Exercise 2 (continued)*

REMEMBER THE LOCATION

It's easy to download a file from the Web. The only tricky part, if any, is remembering where you have saved the file. This exercise is written for a laboratory setting, and thus we specified drive A as the destination, so that you will have the file on a floppy disk at the end of the exercise. If you have your own computer, however, it's faster to save the file to the desktop or in a temporary folder on drive C. Just remember where you save the file so that you can access it after it has been downloaded.

Step 3: **Open My Computer**

➤ Double click the My Computer icon on the desktop to open My Computer. If necessary, customize My Computer to match Figure 9c.
   • Pull down the **View menu** and change to the **Details view**.
   • Pull down the **View menu** a second time, click (or point to) the **Toolbars command**, then check the **Standard buttons** and **Address Bar** toolbars.
➤ Pull down the **Tools menu** and click the **Folder Options command** to verify the settings in effect so that your window matches ours. Be sure to **Enable Web content in folders** (in the Web View area), to **Open each folder in the same window** (in the Browse Folders area), and **Double Click to open an item** (in the Click Items area). Click **OK**.
➤ Click the icon for **drive A** to select it. The description of drive A appears at the left of the window.
➤ Double click the icon for **drive A** to open this drive. The contents of the My Computer window are replaced by the contents of drive A.

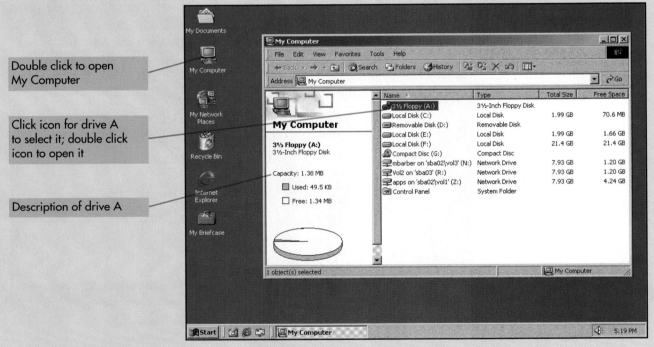

Double click to open My Computer

Click icon for drive A to select it; double click icon to open it

Description of drive A

(c) Open My Computer (step 3)

FIGURE 9   *Hands-on Exercise 2 (continued)*

THE RIGHT MOUSE BUTTON

Point to any object on the Windows desktop or within an application window, then click the right mouse button to see a context-sensitive menu with commands pertaining to that object. You could, for example, right click the icon for drive A, then select the Open command from the resulting menu. The right mouse button is one of the most powerful Windows shortcuts and one of its best-kept secrets. Use it!

Step 4:   **Install the Practice Files**

➤ You should see the contents of drive A as shown in Figure 9d. (If your desktop displays two windows rather than one, it is because you did not set the folder options correctly. Pull down the **Tools menu**, click the **Folder Options command**, and choose the option to **Open each folder in the same window**.)

➤ Double click the **Win2000data file** to install the data disk. You will see a dialog box thanking you for selecting the *Exploring Windows* series. Click **OK**.

• Check that the Unzip To Folder text box specifies **A:** to extract the files to the floppy disk. (You may enter a different drive and/or folder.)

• Click the **Unzip button** to extract the practice files and copy them onto the designated drive. Click **OK** after you see the message indicating that the files have been unzipped successfully. Close the WinZip dialog box.

➤ The practice files have been extracted to drive A and should appear in the Drive A window. If you do not see the files, pull down the **View menu** and click the **Refresh command.**

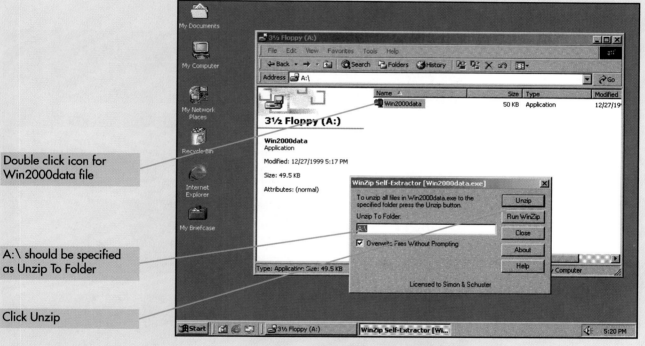

(d) Install the Practice Files (step 4)

FIGURE 9   *Hands-on Exercise 2 (continued)*

DOWNLOADING A FILE

Software and other files are typically compressed to reduce the amount of storage space the files require on disk and/or the time it takes to download the files. In essence, you download a compressed file (which may contain multiple individual files), then you uncompress (expand) the file on your local drive in order to access the individual files. After the file has been expanded, it is no longer needed and can be deleted.

Step 5: **Delete the Compressed File**

➤ If necessary, pull down the **View menu** and click **Details** to change to the Details view in Figure 9e. (If you do not see the descriptive information about drive A at the left of the window, pull down the **Tools menu**, click the **Folder Options command**, and click the option button to **Enable Web content in folders**.)

➤ You should see a total of six files in the Drive A window. Five of these are the practice files on the data disk. The sixth file is the original file that you downloaded earlier. This file is no longer necessary, since it has been already been expanded.

➤ Select (click) the **Win2000data file**. Pull down the **File menu** and click the **Delete command**, or click the **Delete button** on the toolbar. Pause for a moment to be sure you want to delete this file, then click **Yes** when asked to confirm the deletion as shown in Figure 9e.

➤ The Win2000Data file is permanently deleted from drive A. (Items deleted from a floppy disk or network drive are not sent to the Recycle Bin, and cannot be recovered.)

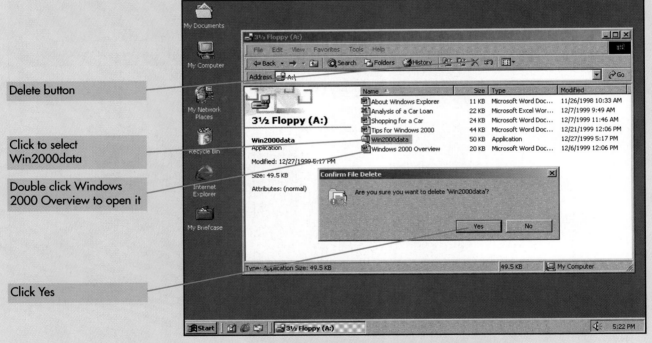

(e) Delete the Compressed File (step 5)

FIGURE 9 *Hands-on Exercise 2 (continued)*

SORT BY NAME, DATE, FILE TYPE, OR SIZE

Files can be displayed in ascending or descending sequence by name, date modified, file type, or size by clicking the appropriate column heading. Click Size, for example, to display files in the order of their size. Click the column heading a second time to reverse the sequence; that is, to switch from ascending to descending, and vice versa.

Step 6: **Modify a Document**

➤ Double click the **Windows 2000 Overview** document from within My Computer to open the document as shown in Figure 9f. (The document will open in the WordPad accessory if Microsoft Word is not installed on your machine.) If necessary, maximize the window for Microsoft Word.

➤ If necessary, click inside the document window, then press **Ctrl+End** to move to the end of the document. Add the sentence shown in Figure 9h followed by your name.

➤ Pull down the **File menu**, click **Print**, then click **OK** to print the document and prove to your instructor that you did the exercise.

➤ Pull down the **File menu** and click **Exit** to close the application. Click **Yes** when prompted to save the file.

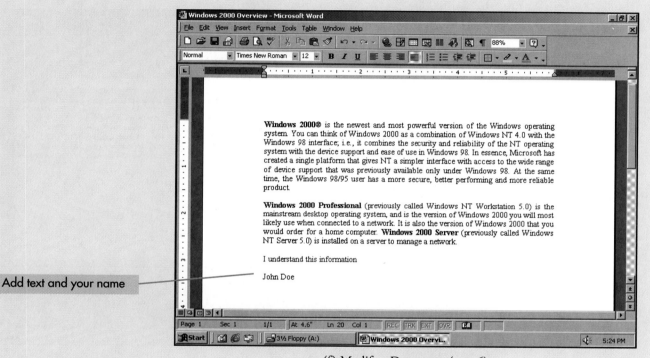

Add text and your name

(f) Modify a Document (step 6)

FIGURE 9   *Hands-on Exercise 2 (continued)*

THE DOCUMENT, NOT THE APPLICATION

All versions of Windows are document oriented, meaning that you are able to think in terms of the document rather than the application that created it. You can still open a document in traditional fashion by starting the application that created the document, then using the File Open command in that program to retrieve the document. It's often easier, however, to open the document from within My Computer (or Windows Explorer) by double clicking its icon. Windows then starts the application and opens the data file. In other words, you can open a document without explicitly starting the application.

Step 7: **Check Your Work**

➤ You should be back in the My Computer window as shown in Figure 9g. If necessary, click the **Views button** to change to the Details view.

➤ Look closely at the date and time that is displayed next to the Windows 2000 Overview document. It should show today's date and the current time (give or take a minute) since that is when the document was last modified.

➤ Look closely and see that Figure 9g also contains a sixth document, called "Backup of Windows 2000 Overview". This is a backup copy of the original document that will be created automatically by Microsoft Word if the appropriate options are in effect. (See the boxed tip below.)

➤ Exit Windows or, alternatively, continue with steps 8 and 9 to return to our Web site and explore additional resources.

Views button

Backup of original document

Date and time change to indicate date/time of last modification

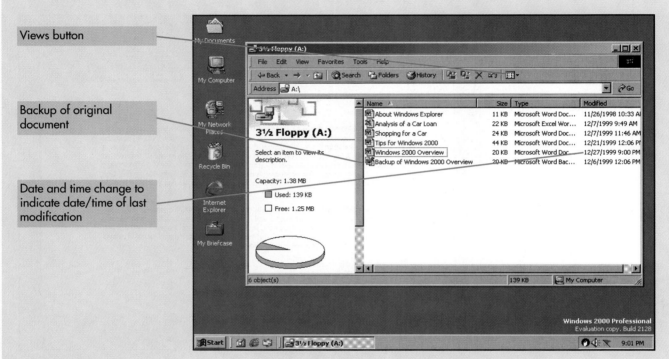

(g) Check Your Work (step 7)

FIGURE 9 *Hands-on Exercise 2 (continued)*

USE WORD TO CREATE A BACKUP COPY

Microsoft Word enables you to automatically create a backup copy of a document in conjunction with the Save command. The next time you are in Microsoft Word, pull down the Tools menu, click the Options command, click the Save tab, then check the box to always create a backup copy. Every time you save a file from this point on, the previously saved version is renamed "Backup of document," and the document in memory is saved as the current version. The disk will contain the two most recent versions of the document, enabling you to retrieve the previous version if necessary.

Step 8: **Download the PowerPoint Lecture**

➤ Restart Internet Explorer and connect to **www.prenhall.com/grauer**. Click the book for **Office XP**, click the link to **Student Resources**, then choose **PowerPoint Lectures** to display the screen in Figure 9h.

➤ Click the down arrow until you can click the link to the PowerPoint slides for **Essentials of Windows 2000**. The File Download dialog box will appear. Click **Save**.

➤ Click the **drop-down arrow** on the Save in list box, and select **drive A**. Be sure that the floppy disk is still in drive A, then click **Save** to begin downloading the file. Click **OK** when you see the dialog box indicating that the download is complete.

➤ Click the taskbar button to return to the **My Computer window** for drive A. You should see all of the files that were previously on the floppy disk plus the file you just downloaded.

➤ Double click the **Win2000ppt file**, then follow the onscreen instructions to unzip the file to drive A.

Click the Student Resources tab

Click the link to PowerPoint Lectures

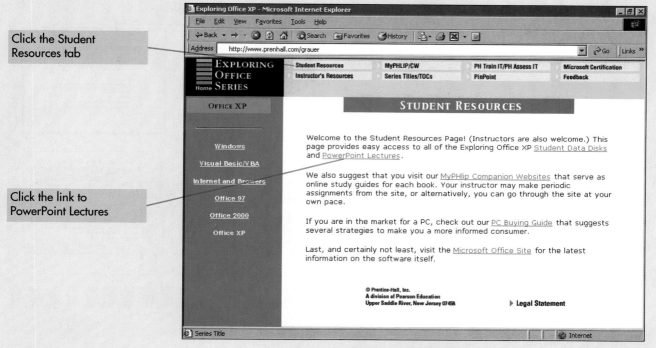

(h) Download the PowerPoint Lecture (step 8)

FIGURE 9 *Hands-on Exercise 2 (continued)*

THE MyPHLIP WEB SITE

The MyPHLIP (Prentice Hall Learning on the Internet Partnership) Web site is another resource that is available for the Exploring Office series. Click the MyPHLIP tab at the top of the screen, which takes you to www.prenhall.com/myphlip, where you will register and select the text you are using. See exercise 3 at the end of the chapter.

Step 9: **Show Time**

➤ Drive A should now contain a PowerPoint file in addition to the self-extracting file. (Pull down the **View menu** and click the **Refresh command** if you do not see the PowerPoint file.)

➤ Double click the PowerPoint file to open the presentation, then click the button to Enable Macros (if prompted). You should see the PowerPoint presentation in Figure 9i. (You must have PowerPoint installed on your computer in order to view the presentation.)

➤ Pull down the **View menu** and click **Slide Show** to begin the presentation, which is intended to review the material in this supplement. Click the left mouse button (or press the **PgDn key**) to move to the next slide.

➤ Click the left mouse button continually to move from one slide to the next. Close PowerPoint at the end of the presentation.

➤ Exit Windows if you do not want to continue with the next exercise at this time.

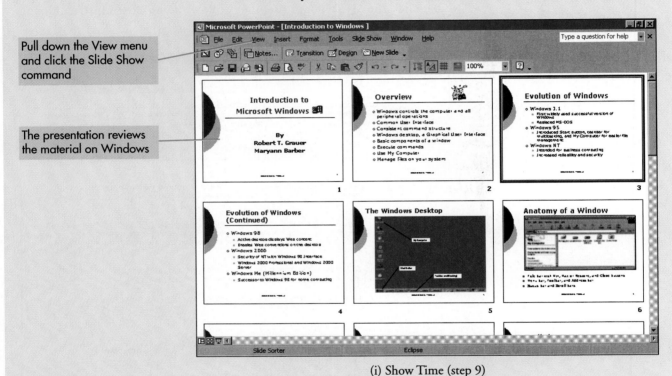

Pull down the View menu and click the Slide Show command

The presentation reviews the material on Windows

(i) Show Time (step 9)

FIGURE 9   *Hands-on Exercise 2 (continued)*

MISSING POWERPOINT—WHICH VERSION OF OFFICE DO YOU HAVE?

You may have installed Microsoft Office on your computer, but you may not have PowerPoint. That is because Microsoft has created several different versions of Microsoft Office, each with a different set of applications. Unfortunately, PowerPoint is not included in every configuration and may be missing from the suite that is shipped most frequently with new computers.

Windows has two different programs to manage the files and folders on a system, My Computer and Windows Explorer. My Computer is intuitive, but less efficient, as you have to open each folder in succession. Windows Explorer is more sophisticated, as it provides a hierarchical view of the entire system in a single window. A beginner might prefer My Computer, whereas a more experienced user will most likely opt for Windows Explorer.

Assume, for example, that you are taking four classes this semester, and that you are using the computer in each course. You've created a separate folder to hold the work for each class and have stored the contents of all four folders on a single floppy disk. Assume further that you need to retrieve your third English assignment so that you can modify the assignment, then submit the revised version to your instructor. Figure 10 illustrates how Windows Explorer could be used to locate your assignment.

The Explorer window in Figure 10a is divided into two panes. The left pane contains a tree diagram (or hierarchical view) of the entire system showing all drives and, optionally, the folders in each drive. The right pane shows the contents of the active drive or folder. Only one object (a drive or folder) can be active in the left pane, and its contents are displayed automatically in the right pane.

Look carefully at the icon for the English folder in the left pane of Figure 10a. The folder is open, whereas the icon for every other folder is closed. The open folder indicates that the English folder is the active folder. (The name of the active folder also appears in the title bar of Windows Explorer and in the Address bar.) The contents of the active folder (three Word documents in this example) are displayed in the right pane. The right pane is displayed in Details view, but could just as easily have been displayed in another view (e.g., Large Icons).

As indicated, only one folder can be open (active) at a time in the left pane. Thus, to see the contents of a different folder such as Accounting, you would open (click on) the Accounting folder, which automatically closes the English folder. The contents of the Accounting folder would then appear in the right pane. You should organize your folders in ways that make sense to you, such as a separate folder for every class you are taking. You can also create folders within folders; for example, a correspondence folder may contain two folders of its own, one for business correspondence and one for personal letters.

Windows Explorer can also be used to display a Web page, as shown in Figure 10b. All you do is click the icon for Internet Explorer in the left pane to start the program and display its default home page. Alternatively, you can click in the Address bar and enter the address of any Web page directly; for example, click in the Address bar and type www.microsoft.com to display the home page for Microsoft. Once you are browsing pages on the Web, it's convenient to close the left pane so that the page takes the complete window. You can reopen the Folders window by pulling down the View menu, clicking the Explorer Bar command, and toggling Folders on.

THE SMART TOOLBAR

The toolbar in Windows Explorer recognizes whether you are viewing a Web page or a set of files and folders, and changes accordingly. The icons that are displayed when viewing a Web page are identical to those in Internet Explorer and include the Search, Favorites, and History buttons. The buttons that are displayed when viewing a file or folder include the Undo, Delete, and Views buttons that are used in file management.

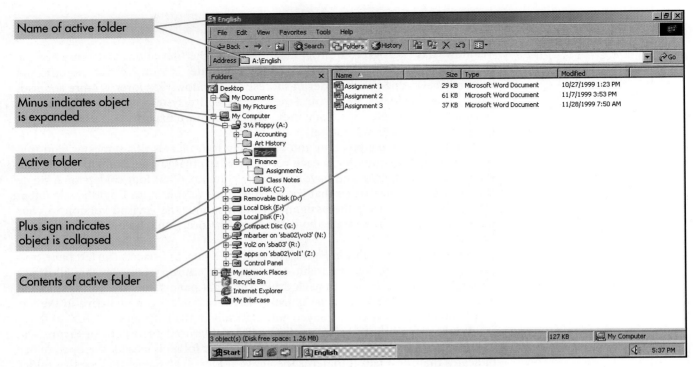

Name of active folder

Minus indicates object is expanded

Active folder

Plus sign indicates object is collapsed

Contents of active folder

(a) Drive A

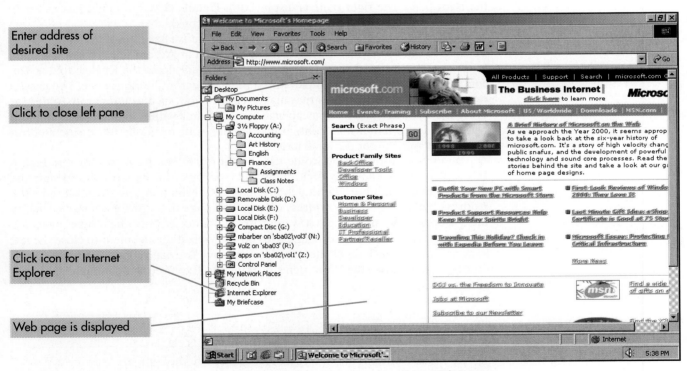

Enter address of desired site

Click to close left pane

Click icon for Internet Explorer

Web page is displayed

(b) A Web Page

FIGURE 10 *Windows Explorer*

Expanding and Collapsing a Drive or Folder

The tree diagram in Windows Explorer displays the devices on your system in hierarchical fashion. The desktop is always at the top of the hierarchy, and it contains icons such as My Computer, the Recycle Bin, Internet Explorer, and My Network Places. My Computer in turn contains the various drives that are accessible from your system, each of which contains folders, which in turn contain documents and/or additional folders. Each object may be expanded or collapsed by clicking the plus or minus sign, respectively. Click either sign to toggle to the other. Clicking a plus sign, for example, expands the drive, then displays a minus sign next to the drive to indicate that its subordinates are visible.

Look closely at the icon next to My Computer in either Figure 10a or 10b. It is a minus sign (as opposed to a plus sign) and it indicates that My Computer has been expanded to show the devices on the system. There is also a minus sign next to the icon for drive A to indicate that it too has been expanded to show the folders on the disk. Note, however, the plus sign next to drives C and D, indicating that these parts of the tree are currently collapsed and thus their subordinates (in this case, folders) are not visible.

Any folder may contain additional folders, and thus individual folders may also be expanded or collapsed. The minus sign next to the Finance folder, for example, indicates that the folder has been expanded and contains two additional folders, for Assignments and Class Notes, respectively. The plus sign next to the Accounting folder, however, indicates the opposite; that is, the folder is collapsed and its subordinate folders are not currently visible. A folder with neither a plus nor a minus sign, such as Art History, does not contain additional folders and cannot be expanded or collapsed.

The hierarchical view within Windows Explorer, and the ability to expand and collapse the various folders on a system, enables you to quickly locate a specific file or folder. If, for example, you want to see the contents of the Art History folder, you click its icon in the left pane, which automatically changes the display in the right pane to show the documents in that folder. Thus, Windows Explorer is ideal for moving or copying files from one folder or drive to another. You simply select (open) the folder that contains the files, use the scroll bar in the left pane (if necessary) so that the destination folder is visible, then click and drag the files from the right pane to the destination folder.

The Folder Options command functions identically in Windows Explorer and in My Computer. You can decide whether you want to single or double click the icons and/or whether to display Web content within a folder. You can also use the View menu to select the most appropriate view. Our preferences are to double click the icons, to omit Web content, and to use the Details view.

CONVERGENCE OF THE EXPLORERS

Windows Explorer and Internet Explorer are separate programs, but each includes some functionality of the other. You can use Windows Explorer to display a Web page by clicking the Internet Explorer icon within the tree structure in the left pane. Conversely, you can use Internet Explorer to display a local drive, document, or folder. Start Internet Explorer in the usual fashion, click in the Address bar, then enter the appropriate address, such as C:\ to display the contents of drive C.

THE PRACTICE FILES VIA A LOCAL AREA NETWORK

Objective   To use Windows Explorer to copy the practice files from a network drive to a floppy disk. The exercise requires a formatted floppy disk and access to a local area network. Use Figure 11 as a guide in the exercise.

Step 1:   **Start Windows Explorer**

> ➤ Click the **Start Button**, click **Programs**, click **Accessories**, then click **Windows Explorer**. Click the **maximize button** so that Windows Explorer takes the entire desktop as shown in Figure 11a. Do not be concerned if your desktop is different from ours.
> ➤ Make or verify the following selections using the **View menu**. You have to pull down the View menu each time you choose a different command.
>   • The **Standard buttons** and **Address bar** toolbars should be selected.
>   • The **Status Bar command** should be checked.
>   • The **Details view** should be selected.
> ➤ Click (select) the **Desktop icon** in the left pane to display the contents of the desktop in the right pane. Your desktop may have different icons from ours, but your screen should almost match Figure 11a. We set additional options in the next step.

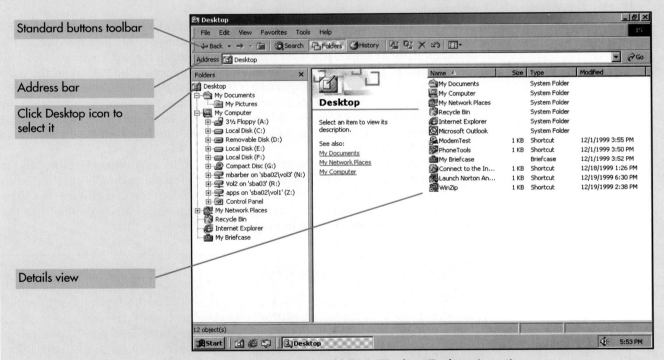

Standard buttons toolbar

Address bar

Click Desktop icon to select it

Details view

(a) Start Windows Explorer (step 1)

FIGURE 11   *Hands-on Exercise 3*

Step 2: **Change the Folder Options**

➤ Click the **minus** (or the **plus**) **sign** next to My Computer to collapse (or expand) My Computer and hide (or display) the objects it contains. Toggle the signs back and forth a few times for practice. End with a minus sign next to My Computer as shown in Figure 11b.

➤ Place a newly formatted floppy disk in drive A. Click the drive icon next to drive A to select the drive and display its contents in the right pane. The disk does not contain any files since zero bytes are used.

➤ Displaying Web content at the left of a folder (as is done in Figure 11b) is fine when a drive or folder does not contain a large number of files. It is generally a waste of space, however, and so we want to change the folder options.

➤ Pull down the **Tools menu** and click the **Folder Options command** to display the Folder Options dialog box in Figure 11a. Click the option to **Use Windows classic folders**. Click **OK**.

Select Use Windows classic folders

Click minus and plus to practice; end with minus sign

Click to select drive A

Click plus sign next to network drive containing files to be copied

Floppy disk is empty

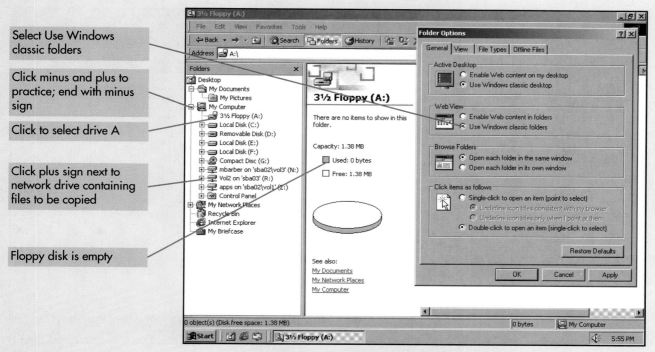

(b) Change the Folder Options (step 2)

FIGURE 11 *Hands-on Exercise 3 (continued)*

THE PLUS AND MINUS SIGN

Any drive, be it local or on the network, may be expanded or collapsed to display or hide its folders. A minus sign indicates that the drive has been expanded and that its folders are visible. A plus sign indicates the reverse; that is, the device is collapsed and its folders are not visible. Click either sign to toggle to the other. Clicking a plus sign, for example, expands the drive, then displays a minus sign next to the drive to indicate that the folders are visible. Clicking a minus sign has the reverse effect.

Step 3: **Select the Network Drive**

➤ Click the **plus sign** for the network drive that contains the files you are to copy (e.g., drive **R** in Figure 11c). Select (click) the **Exploring Windows 2000 folder** to open this folder.

➤ You may need to expand other folders on the network drive (such as the Datadisk folder on our network) as per instructions from your professor. Note the following:
  • The Exploring Windows 2000 folder is highlighted in the left pane, its icon is an open folder, and its contents are displayed in the right pane.
  • The status bar indicates that the folder contains five objects and the total file size is 119KB.

➤ Click the icon next to any other folder to select the folder, which in turn deselects the Exploring Windows 2000 folder. (Only one folder in the left pane is active at a time.) Reselect (click) the **Exploring Windows 2000 folder**.

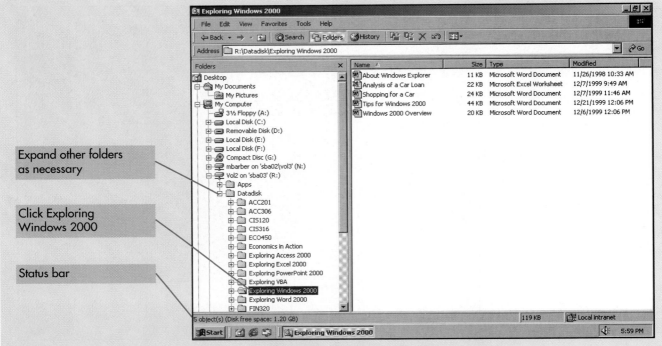

(c) Select the Network Drive (step 3)

FIGURE 11 *Hands-on Exercise 3 (continued)*

CUSTOMIZE WINDOWS EXPLORER

Increase or decrease the size of the left pane within Windows Explorer by dragging the vertical line separating the left and right panes in the appropriate direction. You can also drag the right border of the various column headings (Name, Size, Type, and Modified) in the right pane to increase or decrease the width of the column. And best of all, you can click any column heading to display the contents of the selected folder in sequence by that column. Click the heading a second time and the sequence changes from ascending to descending and vice versa.

Step 4: **Copy the Individual Files**

➤ Select (click) the file called **About Windows Explorer**, which highlights the file as shown in Figure 11d. Click and drag the selected file in the right pane to the **drive A icon** in the left pane:

• You will see the ⊘ symbol as you drag the file until you reach a suitable destination (e.g., until you point to the icon for drive A). The ⊘ symbol will change to a plus sign when the icon for drive A is highlighted, indicating that the file can be copied successfully.

• Release the mouse to complete the copy operation. You will see a pop-up window, which indicates the status of the copy operation.

➤ Select (click) the file **Tips for Windows 2000** after the pop-up window disappears. Copy the selected file to drive A by dragging its icon from the right pane to the drive A icon in the left pane.

➤ Copy the three remaining files to drive A as well. Select (click) drive **A** in the left pane, which in turn displays the contents of the floppy disk in the right pane. You should see the five files you have copied to drive A.

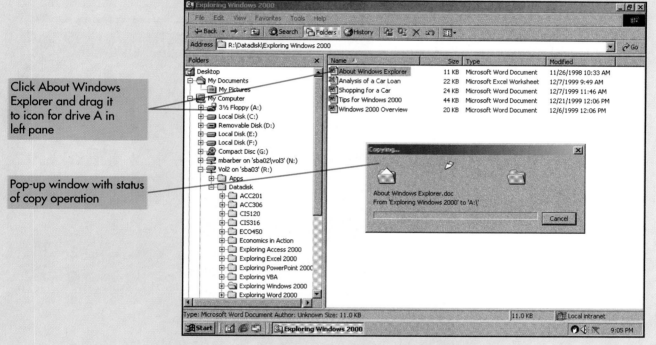

Click About Windows Explorer and drag it to icon for drive A in left pane

Pop-up window with status of copy operation

(d) Copy the Individual Files (step 4)

FIGURE 11 *Hands-on Exercise 3 (continued)*

SELECT MULTIPLE FILES

Selecting one file automatically deselects the previously selected file. You can, however, select multiple files by clicking the first file, then pressing and holding the Ctrl key as you click each additional file. Use the Shift key to select multiple files that are adjacent to one another by clicking the first file, then pressing and holding the Shift key as you click the last file.

Step 5: **Display a Web Page**

➤ This step requires an Internet connection. Click the **minus sign** next to the network drive to collapse that drive. Click the **minus sign** next to any other expanded drive so that the left pane is similar to Figure 11e.

➤ Double click the **Internet Explorer icon** to start Internet Explorer and display the starting page for your configuration. The page you see will be different from ours, but you can click in the Address bar near the top of the window to enter the address of any Web site.

➤ Look closely at the icons on the toolbar, which have changed to reflect the tools associated with viewing a Web page. Click the **Back button** to return to drive A, the previously displayed item in Windows Explorer. The icons on the toolbar return to those associated with a folder.

➤ Close Windows Explorer. Shut down the computer if you do not want to continue with the next exercise at this time.

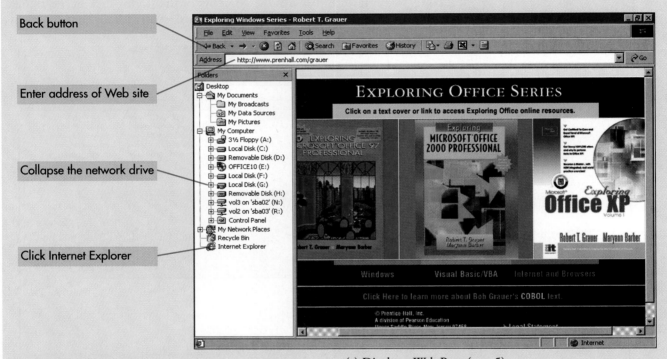

(e) Display a Web Page (step 5)

FIGURE 11 *Hands-on Exercise 3 (continued)*

SERVER NOT RESPONDING

Two things have to occur in order for Internet Explorer to display the requested document—it must locate the server on which the document is stored, and it must be able to connect to that computer. If you see a message similar to "Server too busy or not responding", it implies that Internet Explorer has located the server but was unable to connect because the site is busy or is temporarily down. Try to connect again, in a minute or so, or later in the day.

As you grow to depend on the computer, you will create a variety of files using applications such as Microsoft Word or Excel. Learning how to manage those files is one of the most important skills you can acquire. The previous hands-on exercises provided you with a set of files with which to practice. That way, when you have your own files you will be comfortable executing the various file management commands you will need on a daily basis. This section describes the basic file operations you will need, then presents another hands-on exercise in which you apply those commands.

Moving and Copying a File

The essence of file management is to move and copy a file or folder from one location to another. This can be done in different ways, most easily by clicking and dragging the file icon from the source drive or folder to the destination drive or folder, within Windows Explorer. There is one subtlety, however, in that the result of dragging a file (i.e., whether the file is moved or copied) depends on whether the source and destination are on the same or different drives. Dragging a file from one folder to another folder on the same drive moves the file. Dragging a file to a folder on a different drive copies the file. The same rules apply to dragging a folder, where the folder and every file in it are moved or copied as per the rules for an individual file.

This process is not as arbitrary as it may seem. Windows assumes that if you drag an object (a file or folder) to a different drive (e.g., from drive C to drive A), you want the object to appear in both places. Hence, the default action when you click and drag an object to a different drive is to copy the object. You can, however, override the default and move the object by pressing and holding the Shift key as you drag.

Windows also assumes that you do not want two copies of an object on the same drive, as that would result in wasted disk space. Thus, the default action when you click and drag an object to a different folder on the same drive is to move the object. You can override the default and copy the object by pressing and holding the Ctrl key as you drag. It's not as complicated as it sounds, and you get a chance to practice in the hands-on exercise, which follows shortly.

Deleting a File

The **Delete command** deletes (erases) a file from a disk. The command can be executed in different ways, most easily by selecting a file, then pressing the Del key. It's also comforting to know that you can usually recover a deleted file, because the file is not (initially) removed from the disk, but moved instead to the Recycle Bin, from where it can be restored to its original location. Unfortunately, files deleted from a floppy disk are not put in the Recycle Bin and hence cannot be recovered.

The **Recycle Bin** is a special folder that contains all files that were previously deleted from any hard disk on your system. Think of the Recycle Bin as similar to the wastebasket in your room. You throw out (delete) a report by tossing it into a wastebasket. The report is gone (deleted) from your desk, but you can still get it back by taking it out of the wastebasket as long as the basket wasn't emptied. The Recycle Bin works the same way. Files are not deleted from the hard disk per se, but moved instead to the Recycle Bin from where they can be restored to their original location.

The Recycle Bin will eventually run out of space, in which case the files that have been in the Recycle Bin the longest are permanently deleted to make room for additional files. Accordingly, once a file is removed from the Recycle Bin it can no longer be restored, as it has been physically deleted from the hard disk. Note, too, that the protection afforded by the Recycle Bin does not extend to files deleted from a floppy disk. Such files can be recovered, but only through utility programs outside of Windows 2000.

Renaming a File

Every file or folder is assigned a name at the time it is created, but you may want to change that name at some point in the future. Point to a file or a folder, click the right mouse button to display a menu with commands pertaining to the object, then click the **Rename command**. The name of the file or folder will be highlighted with the insertion point (a flashing vertical line) positioned at the end of the name. Enter a new name to replace the selected name, or click anywhere within the name to change the insertion point and edit the name.

Backup

It's not a question of if it will happen, but when—hard disks die, files are lost, or viruses may infect a system. It has happened to us and it will happen to you, but you can prepare for the inevitable by creating adequate backup *before* the problem occurs. The essence of a **backup strategy** is to decide which files to back up, how often to do the backup, and where to keep the backup. Once you decide on a strategy, follow it, and follow it faithfully!

Our strategy is very simple—back up what you can't afford to lose, do so on a daily basis, and store the backup away from your computer. You need not copy every file, every day. Instead, copy just the files that changed during the current session. Realize, too, that it is much more important to back up your data files than your program files. You can always reinstall the application from the original disks or CD, or if necessary, go to the vendor for another copy of an application. You, however, are the only one who has a copy of your term paper.

Write Protection

A floppy disk is normally **write-enabled** (the square hole is covered with the movable tab) so that you can change the contents of the disk. Thus, you can create (save) new files to a write-enabled disk and/or edit or delete existing files. Occasionally, however, you may want to **write-protect** a floppy disk (by sliding the tab to expose the square hole) so that its contents cannot be modified. This is typically done with a backup disk where you want to prevent the accidental deletion of a file and/or the threat of virus infection.

Our Next Exercise

Our next exercise begins with the floppy disk containing the five practice files in drive A. We ask you to create two folders on drive A (step 1) and to move the various files into these folders (step 2). Next, you copy a folder from drive A to the My Documents folder (step 3), modify one of the files in the My Documents folder (step 4), then copy the modified file back to drive A (step 5). We ask you to delete a file in step 6, then recover it from the Recycle Bin in step 7. We also show you how to write-protect a floppy disk in step 8. Let's get started.

FILE MANAGEMENT

Objective Use Windows Explorer to move, copy, and delete a file; recover a deleted file from the Recycle Bin; write-protect a floppy disk. Use Figure 12 as a guide in the exercise.

Step 1: **Create a New Folder**

> ➤ Start Windows Explorer, maximize its window, and if necessary, change to **Details view**. Place the floppy disk from Exercise 2 or 3 in drive A.
> ➤ Select (click) the icon for **drive A** in the left pane of the Explorer window. Drive A should contain the files shown in Figure 12a.
> ➤ You will create two folders on drive A, using two different techniques:
> > • Point to a blank area anywhere in the **right pane**, click the **right mouse button** to display a context-sensitive menu, click (or point to) the **New command**, then click **Folder** as the type of object to create.
> > • The icon for a new folder will appear with the name of the folder (New Folder) highlighted. Type **John Doe's Documents** (use your own name) to change the name of the folder. Press **Enter**.
> > • Click the icon for **drive A** in the left pane. Pull down the **File menu**, click (or point to) the **New command**, and click **Folder** as the type of object to create. Type **Automobile** to change the name of the folder. Press **Enter**. The right pane should now contain five documents and two folders.
> ➤ Pull down the **View menu**. Click the **Arrange icons command**, then click the **By Name command** to display the folders in alphabetical order.

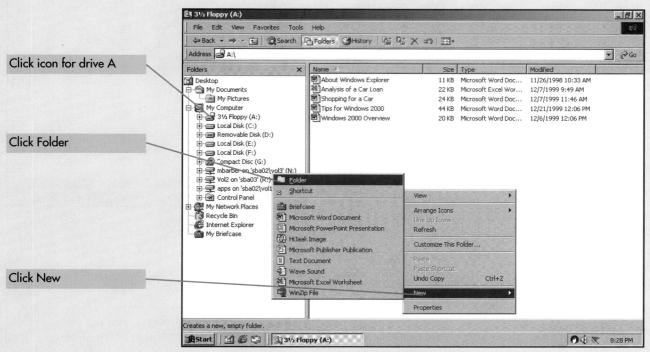

(a) Create a New Folder (step 1)

FIGURE 12 *Hands-on Exercise 4*

Step 2:   **Move a File**

➤ Click the **plus sign** next to drive A to expand the drive as shown in Figure 12b. Note the following:
  • The left pane shows that drive A is selected. The right pane displays the contents of drive A (the selected object in the left pane).
  • There is a minus sign next to the icon for drive A in the left pane, indicating that it has been expanded and that its folders are visible. Thus, the folder names also appear under drive A in the left pane.
➤ Click and drag the icon for the file **About Windows Explorer** from the right pane, to the **John Doe's Documents folder** in the left pane, to move the file into that folder.
➤ Click and drag the **Tips for Windows 2000** and **Windows 2000 Overview** documents to the **John Doe's Documents folder** in similar fashion.
➤ Click the **John Doe's Documents folder** in the left pane to select the folder and display its contents in the right pane. You should see the three files that were just moved.
➤ Click the icon for **Drive A** in the left pane, then click and drag the remaining files, **Analysis of a Car** and **Shopping for a Car**, to the **Automobile folder**.

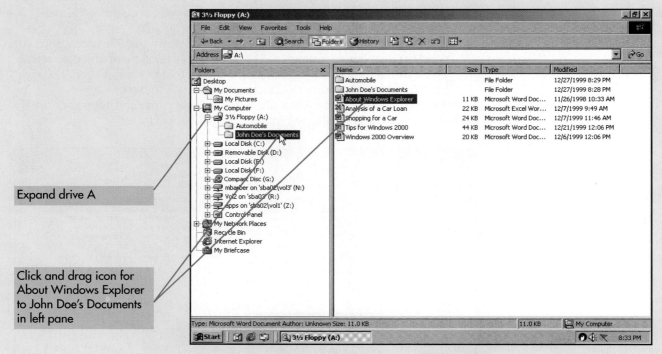

Expand drive A

Click and drag icon for About Windows Explorer to John Doe's Documents in left pane

(b) Move a File (step 2)

FIGURE 12   *Hands-on Exercise 4*

RIGHT CLICK AND DRAG

Click and drag with the right mouse button to display a shortcut menu asking whether you want to copy or move the file. This simple tip can save you from making a careless (and potentially serious) error. Use it!

Step 3:   **Copy a Folder**

➤ Point to **John Doe's Documents folder** in either pane, click the **right mouse button**, and drag the folder to the **My Documents folder** in the left pane, then release the mouse to display a shortcut menu. Click the **Copy Here command**.
- You may see a Copy files message box as the individual files within John Doe's folder are copied to the My Documents folder.
- If you see the Confirm Folder Replace dialog box, it means that you already copied the files or a previous student used the same folder when he or she did this exercise. Click the **Yes to All button** so that your files replace the previous versions in the My Documents folder.

➤ Click the **My Documents folder** in the left pane. Pull down the **View menu** and click the **Refresh command** (or press the **F5 key**) so that the tree structure shows the newly copied folder. (Please remember to delete John Doe's Documents folder at the end of the exercise.)

Click Copy Here

Right click and drag the file to My Documents folder

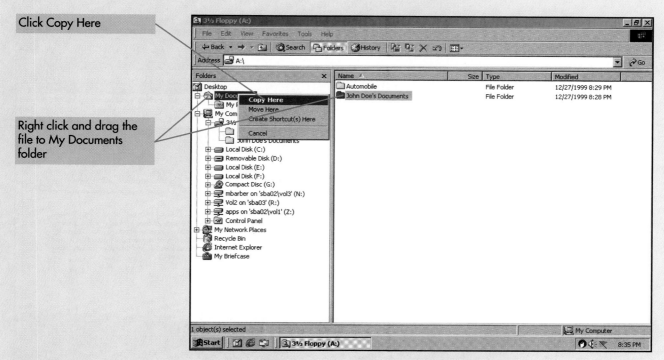

(c) Copy a Folder (step 3)

FIGURE 12   *Hands-on Exercise 4 (continued)*

THE MY DOCUMENTS FOLDER

The My Documents folder is created by default with the installation of Microsoft Windows. There is no requirement that you store your documents in this folder, but it is convenient, especially for beginners who may lack the confidence to create their own folders. The My Documents folder is also helpful in a laboratory environment where the network administrator may prevent you from modifying the desktop and/or from creating your own folders on drive C, in which case you will have to use the My Documents folder.

Step 4:   **Modify a Document**

➤ Click **John Doe's Documents folder** within the My Documents folder to make it the active folder and to display its contents in the right pane. Change to the **Details view**.

➤ Double click the **About Windows Explorer** document to start Word and open the document. Do not be concerned if the size and/or position of the Microsoft Word window are different from ours.

➤ If necessary, click inside the document window, then press **Ctrl+End** to move to the end of the document. Add the sentence shown in Figure 12d.

➤ Pull down the **File menu** and click **Save** to save the modified file (or click the **Save button** on the Standard toolbar). Pull down the **File menu** and click **Exit**.

➤ Pull down the **View menu** in Windows Explorer and click **Refresh** (or press the **F5 key**) to update the contents of the right pane. The date and time associated with the About Windows Explorer file has been changed to indicate that the file has just been modified.

Double click About
Windows Explorer to
open it

Click John Doe's
Documents folder within
My Documents folder

Add text and your name

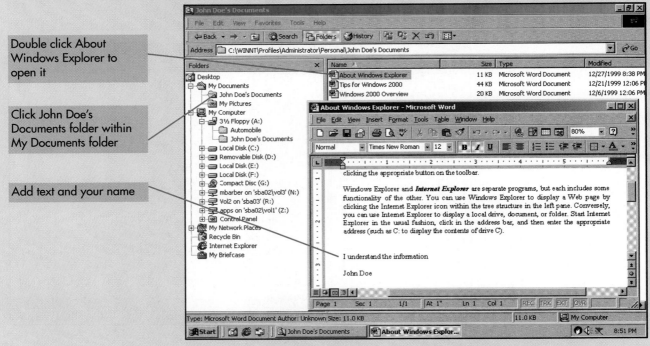

(d) Modify a Document (step 4)

FIGURE 12   *Hands-on Exercise 4 (continued)*

KEYBOARD SHORTCUTS

Ctrl+B, Ctrl+I, and Ctrl+U are shortcuts to boldface, italicize, and underline, respectively. Ctrl+X (the X is supposed to remind you of a pair of scissors), Ctrl+C, and Ctrl+V correspond to Cut, Copy, and Paste, respectively. Ctrl+Home and Ctrl+End move to the beginning or end of a document. These shortcuts are not unique to Microsoft Word, but are recognized in virtually every Windows application. See practice exercise 11 at the end of the chapter.

Step 5: **Copy (Back Up) a File**

➤ Verify that **John Doe's folder** within My Documents is the active folder, as denoted by the open folder icon. Click and drag the icon for the **About Windows Explorer** file from the right pane to John Doe's Documents folder on **Drive A** in the left pane.

➤ You will see the message in Figure 12e, indicating that the folder (on drive A) already contains a file called About Windows Explorer and asking whether you want to replace the existing file. Click **Yes** because you want to replace the previous version of the file on drive A with the updated version from the My Documents folder.

➤ You have just backed up the file; in other words, you have created a copy of the file on the disk in drive A. Thus, you can use the floppy disk to restore the file in the My Documents folder should anything happen to it.

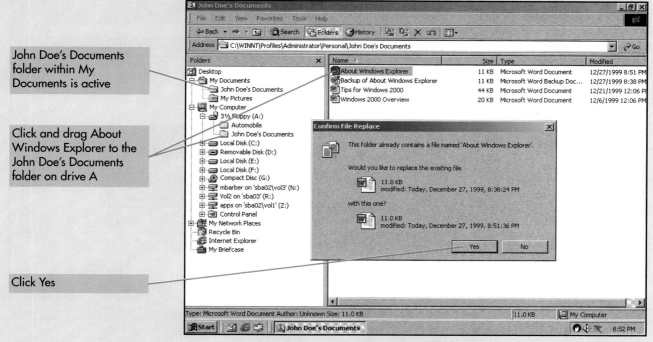

(e) Copy (Back Up) a File (step 5)

FIGURE 12 *Hands-on Exercise 4 (continued)*

FILE EXTENSIONS

Long-time DOS users remember a three-character extension at the end of a file name to indicate the file type; for example, DOC or XLS to indicate a Word document or Excel workbook, respectively. The extensions are displayed or hidden according to a setting in the Folder Options command. Pull down the Tools menu, click the Folder Options command to display the Folder Options dialog box, click the View tab, then check (or clear) the box to hide (or show) file extensions for known file types. Click OK to accept the setting and exit the dialog box.

Step 6:   **Delete a Folder**

➤ Select (click) **John Doe's Documents folder** within the My Documents folder in the left pane. Pull down the **File menu** and click **Delete** (or press the **Del key**).

➤ You will see the dialog box in Figure 12f asking whether you are sure you want to delete the folder (i.e., send the folder and its contents to the Recycle Bin). Note the recycle logo within the box, which implies that you will be able to restore the file.

➤ Click **Yes** to delete the folder. The folder disappears from drive C. Pull down the **Edit menu**. Click **Undo Delete**. The deletion is cancelled and the folder reappears in the left pane. If you don't see the folder, pull down the **View menu** and click the **Refresh command**.

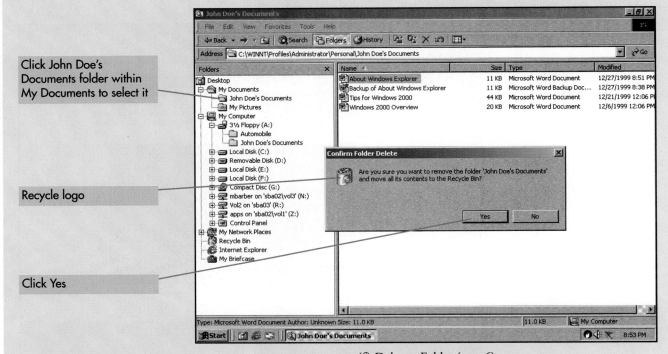

Click John Doe's
Documents folder within
My Documents to select it

Recycle logo

Click Yes

(f) Delete a Folder (step 6)

FIGURE 12   *Hands-on Exercise 4 (continued)*

THE UNDO COMMAND

The Undo command is present not only in application programs such as Word or Excel, but in Windows Explorer as well. You can use the Undo command to undelete a file provided you execute the command immediately (within a few commands) after the Delete command. To execute the Undo command, right-click anywhere in the right pane to display a shortcut menu, then select the Undo action. You can also pull down the Edit menu and click Undo to reverse (undo) the last command. Some operations cannot be undone (in which case the command will be dimmed), but Undo is always worth a try.

Step 7:   **The Recycle Bin**

➤ Select John Doe's Documents folder within the My Documents folder in the left pane. Select (click) the **About Windows Explorer** file in the right pane. Press the **Del key**, then click **Yes**.

➤ Click the **Down arrow** in the vertical scroll bar in the left pane until you see the icon for the **Recycle Bin**. Click the icon to make the Recycle Bin the active folder and display its contents in the right pane.

➤ You will see a different set of files from those displayed in Figure 12g. Pull down the **View menu**, click (or point to) **Arrange icons**, then click **By Delete Date** to display the files in this sequence.

➤ Click in the **right pane**. Press **Ctrl+End** or scroll to the bottom of the window. Point to the **About Windows Explorer** file, click the **right mouse button** to display the shortcut menu in Figure 12g, then click **Restore**.

➤ The file disappears from the Recycle bin because it has been returned to John Doe's Documents folder.

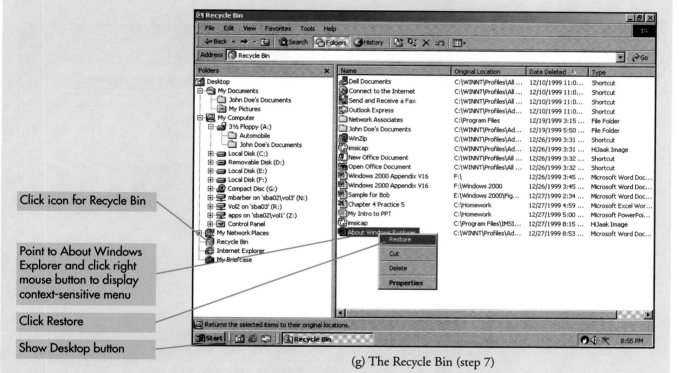

Click icon for Recycle Bin

Point to About Windows Explorer and click right mouse button to display context-sensitive menu

Click Restore

Show Desktop button

(g) The Recycle Bin (step 7)

FIGURE 12   *Hands-on Exercise 4 (continued)*

THE SHOW DESKTOP BUTTON

The Show Desktop button on the taskbar enables you to minimize all open windows with a single click. The button functions as a toggle switch. Click it once and all windows are minimized. Click it a second time and the open windows are restored to their positions on the desktop. If you do not see the Show Desktop button, right click a blank area of the taskbar to display a context-sensitive menu, click Toolbars, then check the Quick Launch toolbar.

Step 8: **Write-Protect a Floppy Disk**

➤ Remove the floppy disk from drive A, then move the built-in tab on the disk so that the square hole on the disk is open. Return the disk to the drive.

➤ If necessary, expand drive A in the left pane, select the **Automobile folder**, select the **Analysis of a Car Loan document** in the right pane, then press the **Del key**. Click **Yes** when asked whether to delete the file.

➤ You will see the message in Figure 12h indicating that the file cannot be deleted because the disk has been write-protected. Click **OK**. Remove the write-protection by moving the built-in tab to cover the square hole.

➤ Repeat the procedure to delete the **Analysis of a Car Loan document**. Click **Yes** in response to the confirmation message asking whether you want to delete the file.

➤ The file disappears from the right pane, indicating it has been deleted. The **Automobile folder** on drive A should contain only one file.

➤ Delete **John Doe's Documents folder** from My Documents as a courtesy to the next student. Exit Windows Explorer. Shut down the computer.

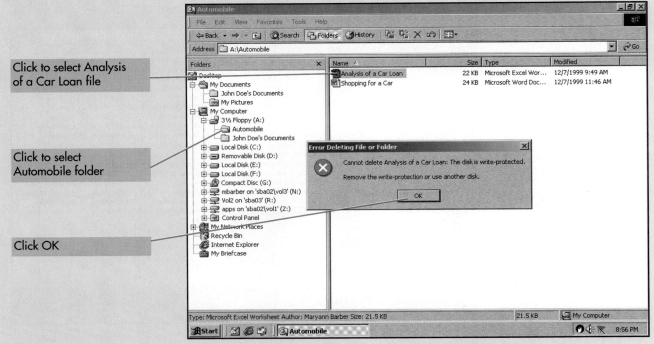

(h) Write-Protect a Floppy Disk (step 8)

FIGURE 12   *Hands-on Exercise 4 (continued)*

BACK UP IMPORTANT FILES

We cannot overemphasize the importance of adequate backup and urge you to copy your data files to floppy disks and store those disks away from your computer. You might also want to write-protect your backup disks so that you cannot accidentally erase a file. It takes only a few minutes, but you will thank us, when (not if) you lose an important file and don't have to wish you had another copy.

Microsoft Windows controls the operation of a computer and its peripherals. Windows 98 and its successor, Windows Me, are geared for the home user and provide extensive support for games and peripheral devices. Windows NT and its successor, Windows 2000, are aimed at the business user and provide increased security and reliability. Windows XP replaces all current versions of Windows. All versions of Windows follow the same conventions and have the same basic interface.

All Windows operations take place on the desktop. Every window on the desktop contains the same basic elements, which include a title bar, a control-menu box, a minimize button, a maximize or restore button, and a close button. Other elements that may be present include a menu bar, vertical and/or horizontal scroll bars, a status bar, and various toolbars. All windows may be moved and sized. The Help command in the Start menu provides access to detailed information.

Multitasking is a major benefit of the Windows environment as it enables you to run several programs at the same time. The taskbar contains a button for each open program and enables you to switch back and forth between those programs by clicking the appropriate button.

A dialog box supplies information needed to execute a command. Option buttons indicate mutually exclusive choices, one of which must be chosen. Check boxes are used if the choices are not mutually exclusive or if an option is not required. A text box supplies descriptive information. A (drop-down or open) list box displays multiple choices, any of which may be selected. A tabbed dialog box provides access to multiple sets of options.

A floppy disk must be formatted before it can store data. Formatting is accomplished through the Format command within the My Computer window. My Computer enables you to browse the disk drives and other devices attached to your system. The contents of My Computer depend on the specific configuration.

A file is a set of data or set of instructions that has been given a name and stored on disk. There are two basic types of files, program files and data files. A program file is an executable file, whereas a data file can be used only in conjunction with a specific program. Every file has a file name and a file type. The file name can be up to 255 characters in length and may include spaces.

Files are stored in folders to better organize the hundreds (or thousands) of files on a disk. A folder may contain program files, data files, and/or other folders. There are two basic ways to search through the folders on your system, My Computer and Windows Explorer. My Computer is intuitive but less efficient than Windows Explorer, as you have to open each folder in succession. Windows Explorer is more sophisticated, as it provides a hierarchical view of the entire system.

Windows Explorer is divided into two panes. The left pane displays all of the devices and, optionally, the folders on each device. The right pane shows the contents of the active (open) drive or folder. Only one drive or folder can be active in the left pane. Any device, be it local or on the network, may be expanded or collapsed to display or hide its folders. A minus sign indicates that the drive has been expanded and that its folders are visible. A plus sign indicates that the device is collapsed and its folders are not visible.

The result of dragging a file (or folder) from one location to another depends on whether the source and destination folders are on the same or different drives. Dragging the file to a folder on the same drive moves the file. Dragging the file to a folder on a different drive copies the file. It's easier, therefore, to click and drag with the right mouse button to display a context-sensitive menu from which you can select the desired operation.

The Delete command deletes (removes) a file from a disk. If, however, the file was deleted from a local (fixed or hard) disk, it is not really gone, but moved instead to the Recycle Bin from where it can be subsequently recovered.

MULTIPLE CHOICE

1. Which versions of the Windows operating system were intended for the home computer?
   (a) Windows NT and Windows 98
   (b) Windows NT and Windows XP
   (c) Windows NT and Windows 2000
   (d) Windows 98 and Windows Me

2. What happens if you click and drag a file from drive C to drive A?
   (a) The file is copied to drive A
   (b) The file is moved to drive A
   (c) A menu appears that allows you to choose between moving and copying
   (d) The file is sent to the recycle bin

3. Which of the following is *not* controlled by the Folder Options command?
   (a) Single or double clicking to open a desktop icon
   (b) The presence or absence of Web content within a folder
   (c) The view (e.g., using large or small icons) within My Computer
   (d) Using one or many windows when browsing My Computer

4. What is the significance of a faded (dimmed) command in a pull-down menu?
   (a) The command is not currently accessible
   (b) A dialog box will appear if the command is selected
   (c) A Help window will appear if the command is selected
   (d) There are no equivalent keystrokes for the particular command

5. Which of the following is true regarding a dialog box?
   (a) Option buttons indicate mutually exclusive choices
   (b) Check boxes imply that multiple options may be selected
   (c) Both (a) and (b)
   (d) Neither (a) nor (b)

6. Which of the following is the first step in sizing a window?
   (a) Point to the title bar
   (b) Pull down the View menu to display the toolbar
   (c) Point to any corner or border
   (d) Pull down the View menu and change to large icons

7. Which of the following is the first step in moving a window?
   (a) Point to the title bar
   (b) Pull down the View menu to display the toolbar
   (c) Point to any corner or border
   (d) Pull down the View menu and change to large icons

8. How do you exit from Windows?
   (a) Click the Start button, then click the Shut Down command
   (b) Right click the Start button, then click the Shut Down command
   (c) Click the End button, then click the Shut Down command
   (d) Right click the End button, then click the Shut Down command

9. Which button appears immediately after a window has been maximized?
   (a) The close button
   (b) The minimize button
   (c) The maximize button
   (d) The restore button

10. What happens to a window that has been minimized?
    (a) The window is still visible but it no longer has a minimize button
    (b) The window shrinks to a button on the taskbar
    (c) The window is closed and the application is removed from memory
    (d) The window is still open but the application is gone from memory

11. What is the significance of three dots next to a command in a pull-down menu?
    (a) The command is not currently accessible
    (b) A dialog box will appear if the command is selected
    (c) A Help window will appear if the command is selected
    (d) There are no equivalent keystrokes for the particular command

12. The Recycle Bin enables you to restore a file that was deleted from:
    (a) Drive A
    (b) Drive C
    (c) Both (a) and (b)
    (d) Neither (a) nor (b)

13. The left pane of Windows Explorer may contain:
    (a) One or more folders with a plus sign
    (b) One or more folders with a minus sign
    (c) Both (a) and (b)
    (d) Neither (a) nor (b)

14. Which of the following was suggested as essential to a backup strategy?
    (a) Back up all program files at the end of every session
    (b) Store backup files at another location
    (c) Both (a) and (b)
    (d) Neither (a) nor (b)

ANSWERS

1. d	5. c	9. d	13. c
2. a	6. c	10. b	14. b
3. c	7. a	11. b	
4. a	8. a	12. b	

1. My Computer: The document in Figure 13 is an effective way to show your instructor that you understand the My Computer window, and further that you have basic proficiency in Microsoft Word.

a. Open My Computer to display the contents of your configuration. Pull down the View menu and switch to the Details view. Size the window as necessary. Press Alt + Print Screen to capture the copy of the My Computer window to the Windows clipboard. (The Print Screen key captures the entire screen. Using the Alt key, however, copies just the current window.)

b. Click the Start menu, click Programs, then click Microsoft Word.

c. Pull down the Edit menu. Click the Paste command to copy the contents of the clipboard to the document you are about to create. The My Computer window should be pasted into your document.

d. Press Ctrl+End to move to the end of your document. Press Enter two or three times to leave blank lines as appropriate. Type a modified form of the memo in Figure 13 so that it conforms to your configuration.

e. Finish the memo and sign your name. Pull down the File menu, click the Print command, then click OK in the dialog box to print the document.

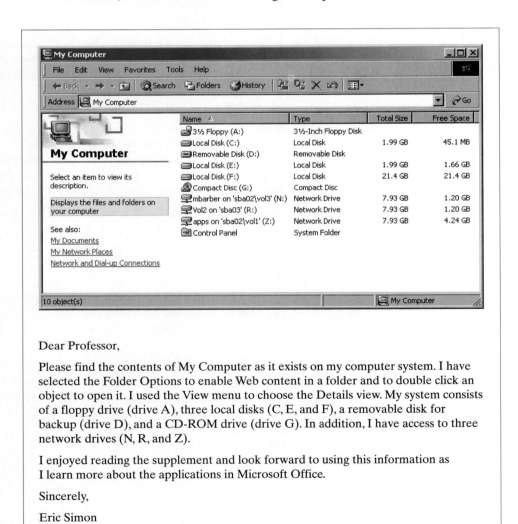

Dear Professor,

Please find the contents of My Computer as it exists on my computer system. I have selected the Folder Options to enable Web content in a folder and to double click an object to open it. I used the View menu to choose the Details view. My system consists of a floppy drive (drive A), three local disks (C, E, and F), a removable disk for backup (drive D), and a CD-ROM drive (drive G). In addition, I have access to three network drives (N, R, and Z).

I enjoyed reading the supplement and look forward to using this information as I learn more about the applications in Microsoft Office.

Sincerely,

Eric Simon

FIGURE 13   *My Computer (exercise 1)*

2. Windows Explorer: Prove to your instructor that you have completed the fourth hands-on exercise by creating a document similar to the one in Figure 14. Use the technique described in the previous problem to capture the screen and paste it into a Word document.

Compare the documents in Figures 13 and 14 that show My Computer and Windows Explorer, respectively. My Computer is intuitive and preferred by beginners, but it is very limited when compared to Windows Explorer. The latter displays a hierarchical view of your system, showing the selected object in the left pane and the contents of the selected object in the right pane. We urge you, therefore, to become comfortable with Windows Explorer, as that will make you more productive.

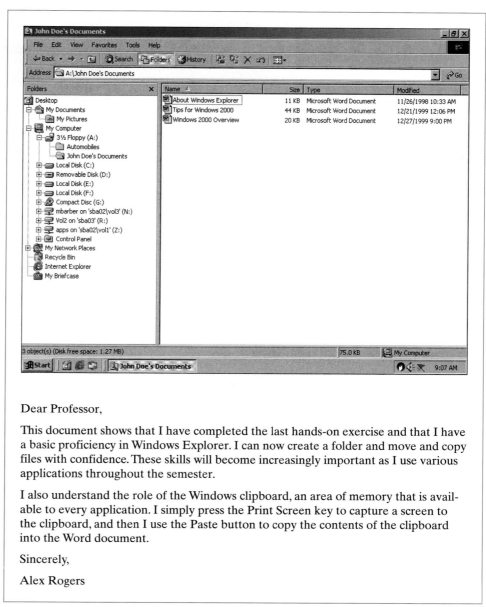

Dear Professor,

This document shows that I have completed the last hands-on exercise and that I have a basic proficiency in Windows Explorer. I can now create a folder and move and copy files with confidence. These skills will become increasingly important as I use various applications throughout the semester.

I also understand the role of the Windows clipboard, an area of memory that is available to every application. I simply press the Print Screen key to capture a screen to the clipboard, and then I use the Paste button to copy the contents of the clipboard into the Word document.

Sincerely,

Alex Rogers

FIGURE 14   *Windows Explorer (exercise 2)*

3. MyPHLIP Web Site: Every text in the *Exploring Office XP* series has a corresponding MyPHLIP (Prentice Hall Learning on the Internet Partnership) Web site, where you will find a variety of student resources as well as online review questions for each chapter. Go to www.prenhall.com/myphlip and follow the instructions. The first time at the site you will be prompted to register by supplying your e-mail address and choosing a password. Next, you choose the discipline (CIS/MIS) and a book (e.g., *Exploring Microsoft Office XP, Volume I*), which in turn will take you to a page similar to Figure 15.

Your professor will tell you whether he or she has created an online syllabus, in which case you should click the link to find your professor after adding the book. Either way, the next time you return to the site, you will be taken directly to your text. Select any chapter, click "Go", then use the review questions as directed.

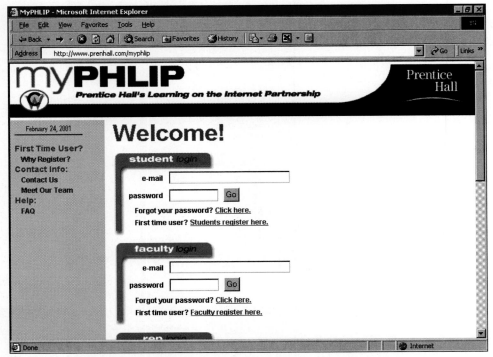

FIGURE 15   *MyPHLIP Web Site (Windows module) (exercise 3)*

4. Organize Your Work: A folder may contain documents, programs, or other folders. The My Classes folder in Figure 16, for example, contains five folders, one folder for each class you are taking this semester. Folders help you to organize your files, and you should become proficient in their use. The best way to practice with folders is on a floppy disk, as was done in Figure 16. Accordingly:
   a. Format a floppy disk or use the floppy disk you have been using throughout the chapter.
   b. Create a Correspondence folder. Create a Business and a Personal folder within the Correspondence folder.
   c. Create a My Courses folder. Within the My Courses folder create a separate folder for each course you are taking.
   d. Use the technique described in problems 1 and 2 to capture the screen in Figure 16 and incorporate it into a document. Add a short paragraph that describes the folders you have created, then submit the document.

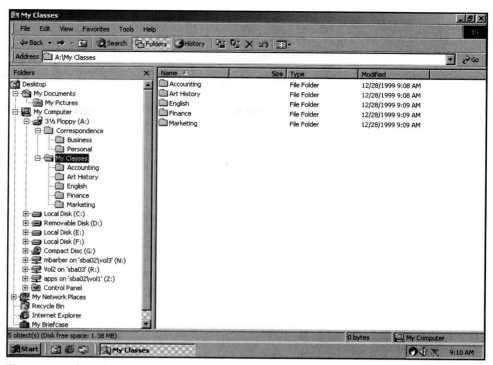

FIGURE 16 *Organize Your Work (exercise 4)*

5. The Windows Web Site: The Web is the best source for information on any application. Go to the Windows home page (www.microsoft.com/windows) as shown in Figure 17, then write a short note to your instructor summarizing the contents of that page and the associated links. Similar pages exist for all Microsoft applications such as www.microsoft.com/office for Microsoft Office.

6. Implement a Screen Saver: A screen saver is a delightful way to personalize your computer and a good way to practice with Microsoft Windows. This is typically not something you can do in a laboratory setting, but it is well worth doing on your own machine. Point to a blank area of the desktop, click the right mouse button to display a context-sensitive menu, then click the Properties command to open the Display Properties dialog box in Figure 18. Click the Screen Saver tab, click the Down arrow in the Screen Saver list box, and select Marquee Display. Click the Settings command button, enter the text and other options for your message, then click OK to close the Options dialog box. Click OK a second time to close the Display Properties dialog box.

7. The Active Desktop: The Active Desktop displays Web content directly on the desktop, then updates the information automatically according to a predefined schedule. You can, for example, display a stock ticker or scoreboard similar to what you see on television. You will need your own machine and an Internet connection to do this exercise, as it is unlikely that the network administrator will let you modify the desktop:
   a. Right click the Windows desktop, click Properties to show the Display Properties dialog box, then click the Web tab. Check the box to show Web content on the Active desktop.
   b. Click the New button, then click the Visit Gallery command button to go to the Active Desktop Gallery in Figure 19 on page 59. Choose any category, then follow the onscreen instructions to display the item on your desktop. We suggest you start with the stock ticker or sports scoreboard.
   c. Summarize your opinion of the active desktop in a short note to your instructor. Did the feature work as advertised? Is the information useful to you?

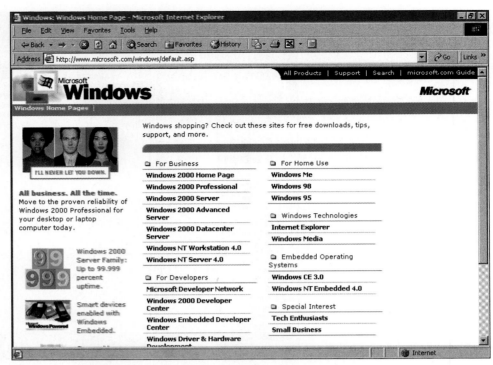

FIGURE 17 *The Windows Web Site (exercise 5)*

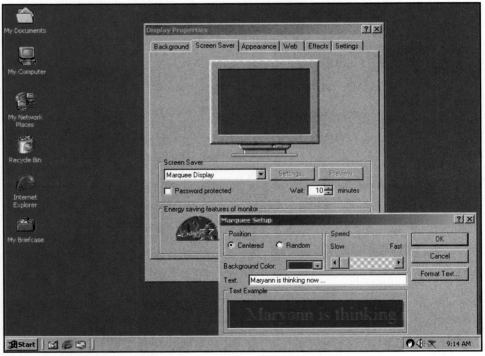

FIGURE 18 *Implement a Screen Saver (exercise 6)*

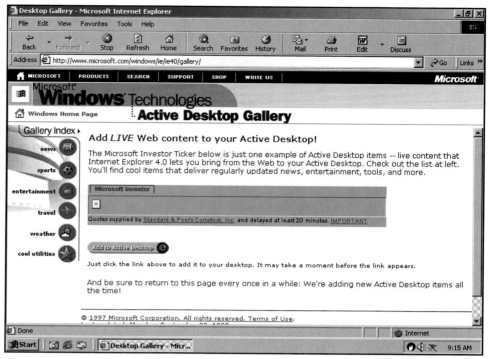

FIGURE 19 *The Active Desktop (exercise 7)*

8. The Control Panel: The Control Panel enables you to change the hardware or software settings on your system. You will not have access to the Control Panel in a lab environment, but you will need it at home if you change your configuration, perhaps by installing a new program. Click the Start button, click Settings, then select Control Panel to display the Control Panel window. Click the down arrow on the Views button to change to the Details view as shown in Figure 20. (The Control Panel can also be opened from My Computer.)

    Write a short report (two or three paragraphs is sufficient) that describes some of the capabilities within Control Panel. *Be careful about making changes, however, and be sure you understand the nature of the new settings before you accept any of the changes.*

9. Users and Passwords: Windows 2000 enables multiple users to log onto the same machine, each with his or her own user name and password. The desktop settings for each user are stored individually, so that all users have their own desktop. The administrator and default user is created when Windows 2000 is first installed, but new users can be added or removed at any time. Once again you will need your own machine:

    a. Click the Start button, click Settings, then click Control Panel to open the Control Panel window as shown in Figure 21. The Control Panel is a special folder that allows you to modify the hardware and/or software settings on your computer.

    b. Double click the Users and Passwords icon to display the dialog box in Figure 20. *Be very careful about removing a user or changing a password, because you might inadvertently deny yourself access to your computer.*

    c. Summarize the capabilities within the users and passwords dialog box in a short note to your instructor. Can you see how these principles apply to the network you use at school or work?

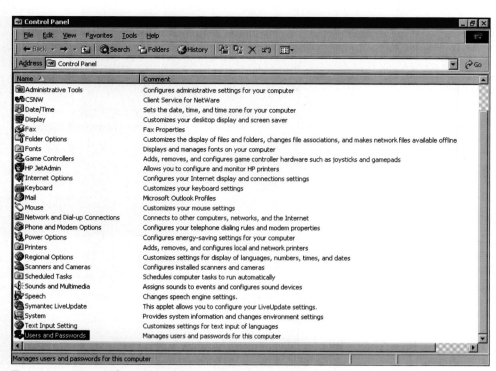

FIGURE 20 *The Control Panel (exercise 8)*

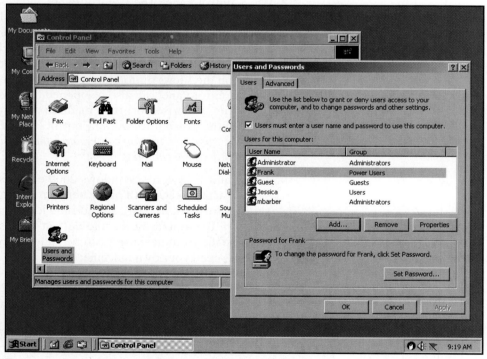

FIGURE 21 *Users and Passwords (exercise 9)*

10. The Fonts Folder: The Fonts folder within the Control Panel displays the names of the fonts available on a system and enables you to obtain a printed sample of any specific font. Click the Start button, click (or point to) the Settings command, click (or point to) Control Panel, then double click the Fonts icon to open the Fonts folder and display the fonts on your system.

    a. Double click any font to open a Fonts window as shown in Figure 22, then click the Print button to print a sample of the selected font.

    b. Open a different font. Print a sample page of this font as well.

    c. Locate the Wingdings font and print this page. Do you see any symbols you recognize? How do you insert these symbols into a document?

    d. How many fonts are there in your fonts Folder? Do some fonts appear to be redundant with others? How much storage space does a typical font require? Write the answers to these questions in a short paragraph.

    e. Start Word. Create a title page containing your name, class, date, and the title of this assignment (My Favorite Fonts). Center the title. Use boldface or italics as you see fit. Be sure to use a suitable type size.

    f. Staple the various pages together (the title page, the three font samples, and the answers to the questions in part d). Submit the assignment to your instructor.

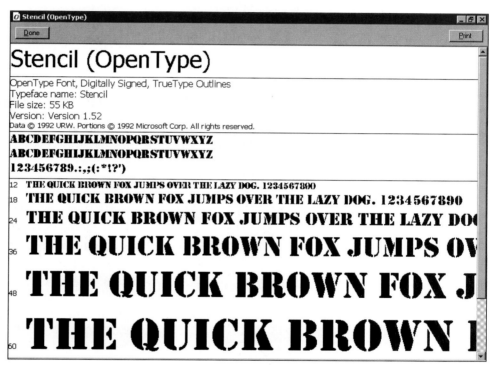

FIGURE 22   *The Fonts Folder (exercise 10)*

11. Keyboard Shortcuts: Microsoft Windows is a graphical user interface in which users "point and click" to execute commands. As you gain proficiency, however, you will find yourself gravitating toward various keyboard shortcuts as shown in Figures 23a and 23b. There is absolutely no need to memorize these shortcuts, nor should you even try. A few, however, have special appeal and everyone has his or her favorite. Use the Help menu to display this information, pick your three favorite shortcuts, and submit them to your instructor. Compare your selections with those of your classmates.

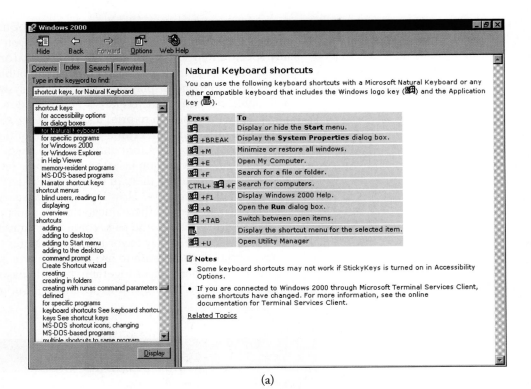

(a)

(b)

FIGURE 23   *Shortcut Keys for Natural Keyboard (Exercise 11)*

Planning for Disaster

Do you have a backup strategy? Do you even know what a backup strategy is? You had better learn, because sooner or later you will wish you had one. You will erase a file, be unable to read from a floppy disk, or worse yet suffer a hardware failure in which you are unable to access the hard drive. The problem always seems to occur the night before an assignment is due. The ultimate disaster is the disappearance of your computer, by theft or natural disaster. Describe, in 250 words or less, the backup strategy you plan to implement in conjunction with your work in this class.

Your First Consultant's Job

Go to a real installation such as a doctor's or attorney's office, the company where you work, or the computer lab at school. Determine the backup procedures that are in effect, then write a one-page report indicating whether the policy is adequate and, if necessary, offering suggestions for improvement. Your report should be addressed to the individual in charge of the business, and it should cover all aspects of the backup strategy; that is, which files are backed up and how often, and what software is used for the backup operation. Use appropriate emphasis (for example, bold italics) to identify any potential problems. This is a professional document (it is your first consultant's job), and its appearance should be perfect in every way.

File Compression

You've learned your lesson and have come to appreciate the importance of backing up all of your data files. The problem is that you work with large documents that exceed the 1.44MB capacity of a floppy disk. Accordingly, you might want to consider the acquisition of a file compression program to facilitate copying large documents to a floppy disk in order to transport your documents to and from school, home, or work. (A Zip file is different from a Zip drive. The latter is a hardware device, similar in concept to a large floppy disk, with a capacity of 100MB or 250MB.)

You can download an evaluation copy of the popular WinZip program at www.winzip.com. Investigate the subject of file compression and submit a summary of your findings to your instructor.

The Threat of Virus Infection

A computer virus is an actively infectious program that attaches itself to other programs and alters the way a computer works. Some viruses do nothing more than display an annoying message at an inopportune time. Most, however, are more harmful, and in the worst case, erase all files on the disk. Use your favorite search engine to research the subject of computer viruses in order to answer the following questions. When is a computer subject to infection by a virus? What precautions does your school or university take against the threat of virus infection in its computer lab? What precautions, if any, do you take at home? Can you feel confident that your machine will not be infected if you faithfully use a state-of-the-art antivirus program that was purchased in January 2001?

The Briefcase

It is becoming increasingly common for people to work on more than one machine. Students, for example, may alternate between machines at school and home. In similar fashion, an office worker may use a desktop and a laptop, or have a machine at work and at home. In every instance, you need to transfer files back and forth between the two machines. This can be done using the Copy command from within Windows Explorer. It can also be done via the Briefcase folder. Your instructor has asked you to look into the latter capability and to prepare a brief report describing its use. Do you recommend the Briefcase over a simple Copy command?

Cut, Copy, and Paste

The Cut, Copy, and Paste commands are used in conjunction with one another to move and copy data within a document, or from one Windows document to another. The commands can also be executed from within My Computer or Windows Explorer to move and copy files. You can use the standard Windows shortcuts of Ctrl+X, Ctrl+C, and Ctrl+V to cut, copy, and paste, respectively. You can also click the corresponding icons on the Standard Buttons toolbar within Windows Explorer or My Computer.

Experiment with this technique, then write a short note to your instructor that summarizes the various ways in which files can be moved or copied within Windows 2000.

Register Now

It is good practice to register every program you purchase, so that the vendor can notify you of new releases and/or other pertinent information. Windows provides an online capability whereby you can register via modem. To register your copy of Windows, click the Start button, click Programs, click Accessories, click Welcome to Windows, then click the Registration Wizard. Follow the directions that are displayed on the screen. (Registering a program does carry the risk of having unwanted sales messages sent to you by e-mail. At the Web site, look for a check box in which you choose whether to receive unsolicited e-mail.) You can do this exercise only if you are working on your own computer.

INDEX